THE END OF SOCIAL WORK

THE END OF SOCIAL WORK

A DEFENSE OF THE SOCIAL WORKER IN TIMES OF TRANSFORMATION

STEVE BURGHARDT

Hunter College
Silberman School of Social Work

SAN DIEGO

Bassim Hamadeh, CEO and Publisher
Amy Smith, Senior Project Editor
Celeste Paed, Associate Production Editor
Emely Villavicencio, Senior Graphic Designer
Stephanie Kohl, Licensing Coordinator
Natalie Piccotti, Director of Marketing
Kassie Graves, Senior Vice President of Editorial
Jamie Giganti, Director of Academic Publishing

cognella® | ACADEMIC PUBLISHING

3970 Sorrento Valley Blvd., Ste. 500, San Diego, CA 92121

Dedicated with love to
Patricia Beresford, my wife,
hospital candy striper, camp counselor, therapist with teens,
policy analyst, leader on adolescent pregnancy prevention,
executive in a foster care/youth development agency,
New York State assistant commissioner for child welfare,
consultant, and mentor.
Whose career path always embraced social justice and social work as
one and the same

BRIEF CONTENTS

DETAILED CONTENTS

FOREWORD

I AM WRITING THIS piece while sitting on the front porch of my quintessential Philadelphia row home that shelters my daughter, a slew of rescue cats, and me. It is a beautiful late summer day. The gardens are bursting, having survived the horrid heat and humidity. Bees are buzzing. Birds are chirping. One hears the laughter of children as they cram as much playtime in before the start of school as they can. People are out walking their dogs. My neighbors on either side of my house touch base about gathering for cocktails later in the day. In my little bubble, one would think that all was right with the world.

But it is the year 2020, and no matter when you are reading this, you would have to remember that for weeks, really months, on end, this year has been nothing short of an epic disaster. As of this writing, the COVID-19 pandemic has killed nearly 200,000 Americans. The economy is crashing. Unemployment rates are staggering. Individuals and families are going hungry. Thanks to a stunning absence of national leadership, coupled with an anti-science movement that defies logic and the wearing of protective masks, we are likely to remain in virus purgatory for quite some time. As if this isn't enough, the spike in police violence against Black communities and individuals has inflicted and reinforced deep racial trauma. In many cities, people have galvanized; protests, mostly organized by Black Lives Matter, valiantly attempt to focus this country's attention on the historic and contemporary manifestations of White supremacy. These demonstrations for racial justice have been countered with heightened police aggression, White vigilantes gunning down protesters, cities being invaded by federal "marshals" who scoop protesters off the streets and take them to unknown destinations, and a president, along with his supporters, who feels no obligation to understand the pain or concerns of Black citizens and instead threatens to eliminate programs that support diversity and inclusion. Then there is the most recent disaster—the wildfires that are burning out of control in the western part of this country. The massive destruction, which has charred millions of acres, killed humans and wildlife, and (as if from a sci-fi movie) turned the skies orange, is the latest extreme example of climate change running amok. Yet again, leadership fails us and turns away from offering any assistance to those impacted by the infernos. The year 2020 is very cruel.

If ever there was a moment in time for social work to step up, this is it. And many social workers have. They serve with first responders, check on vulnerable individuals and families isolated by the virus, engage clients through telehealth, organize food distribution sites, push forth equity proposals, and march in the streets. But as a whole, I have found the response by social work as a *collective entity* that espouses social justice to be tepid at best. We wring our hands, issue statements, and bemoan current events. But innovative and bold initiatives seem few and far between. Why? Why are we mostly reactive and so "in the system" that we can't enact strategies that address the root causes of these challenges? Why, in far too many instances, are we more part of the problem than the solution? Why can't we move beyond good intentions and "woke" rhetoric to lead courageous, systemic, and meaningful change?

In *The End of Social Work*, Steve Burghardt seeks to answer these questions (and more) with an insightful and impassioned analysis that accounts for what he calls the "diminished" quality and status of social work. This is an angry book, and rightfully so. Once one pulls back the curtains, as Steve has done, on the missteps, the denial, the skewed priorities of the profession, one should be angry on behalf of social workers and the people we serve. This is also a timely book because what the pandemic, and policy brutality, and climate crises have laid bare are the extreme inequities in our society. Our economic, educational, and political systems are killing us with the fatality rates being so much higher for members of oppressed and disenfranchised groups. Yet, as Burghardt shows, these conditions and repercussions shouldn't surprise anyone who has been paying attention for the last several decades. The real problem, he argues, is that too many of us didn't pay attention, and in the process, we became cogs in this death machine. What is so seductive about the American "way of life" is the mythology that anyone, with hard work and a bit of spunk, can make it. So individually and collectively, we cede ground through silence or inaction to score a coveted invite to the success table. We commodify ourselves and, ultimately, lose our way. Very, very few achieve real "success."

Those readers familiar with Burghardt's earlier works will recognize some cross-cutting themes in this book. As he laid out in *The Other Side of Organizing*, he continues to center social work practice on the nurturing of authentic relationships. This is not the perfunctory working interaction between practitioner and client. Rather, Steve has long called for rich, engaging, and reflective relationships in which racism, classism, sexism, and other "isms" are called out and addressed (also discussed in *A Guide for Sustaining Conversations on Racism, Identity, and Our Mutual Humanity*, coauthored with Kalima DeSuze, Linda Bryant, and Mohan Vinjamuri) so that practitioners see themselves in their clients (rather than impose themselves on their clients) and partner with them. In turn, organizations promote and expand learning cultures that support member growth and development in which rich support networks make mobilization possible. All this takes commitment and time, two elements that are badly damaged or in many cases rendered nonexistent by current working conditions. As Burghardt notes, you can't engage in meaningful practice, nor can you find fulfillment in that practice, when you have a ridiculously large caseload or a treatment session of 15 minutes with a high-need client. Nor, I would add, can you help mobilize a community when members of that community don't have even the most basic needs met at even a subsistence level. Extreme hunger and homelessness, lack of health care, and schools that are pipelines to prisons generate a level of collective despair that shreds the social fabric.

While much of this book focuses on the working conditions in which social workers toil (and these conditions aren't pretty), Steve situates this discussion in a broader look at the historical and contemporary trends inside and outside of social work that got us to this rather dismal point. This framing expands the analyses that he and his colleague, Mike Fabricant, developed in *The Welfare State Crisis and the Transformation of Social Service Work*, in which they articulated the push-pull of agency work because practitioners are caught in the contradictory functions of the advanced capitalist welfare state. As in that prior work, in this book, Burghardt is careful, and I want to emphasize this, that his argument is not with the social workers in the trenches for whom he has great admiration. Rather, he takes aim at the decisions, prioritizations, and actions (or inactions) of social work leadership in professional organizations and academic institutions. At critical moments in social work's history, poor choices were made, and even if well-intentioned, these determinations set into motion dynamics and conditions that undermine the craft of social work.

Upon reading *The End of Social Work*, I felt inspired to articulate what I see as the problematic trends and priorities of social work, many of which are amplified in Burghardt's analysis. First and foremost, we are a stunningly atheoretical discipline. I know that academics assign various intervention theories (many of which really aren't theories but instead prescriptive guides) for students to digest. However, we shy away from the more rigorous and challenging theoretical frameworks that illuminate the world for reasons that I've never really understood, although I suspect it has something to do with a lack of concrete application to specific practice modalities. Social workers should be well versed in, for example, critical race theory, feminist theory, queer theory, Marxist/neo-Marxist theory—but they aren't. Maybe we get summaries through textbooks, which don't begin to do these theories justice, but I know of very few educational programs or even courses that encourage students to do deep dives into any or all of these frameworks (apparently that's what independent studies are for).

As a consequence, social workers do not have a critical understanding of their working conditions and the factors that create and maintain them. They know that these conditions are onerous and unhealthy. They know that they are exhausted. They know they have been charged with nearly impossible tasks. But without a solid analytical grounding, social workers don't know why, and without the why, one can't successfully push back. Instead, overworked practitioners are admonished to manage their time better, take up yoga, eat healthier meals, or take up some other self-care regimen (there's nothing inherently wrong with any of these suggestions, but they don't solve structural issues). If, however, social workers read their Karl Marx, they would understand that burnout is actually alienation from self and others, which is manufactured by the economic and political structures and processes in which they labor. Further, individual responses and adjustments to what are structural issues of exploitation turn us into participants in our own subordination. We tacitly consent to these arrangements, believing that if we just recommit or do more, then everything will work out fine. And besides, there's always someone who needs our help.

In dismissing theory, we sabotage intellectual curiosity and lean into standardized outcomes. Social work has reduced itself to a list of competencies that on the surface sound wonderful. Of course, we need to know how to assess, engage, implement, and evaluate. Yes, we should demonstrate ethical behavior (hint—just follow the code of ethics). Who wouldn't want to engage in research-informed practice? The problem, however, is that the field wants everything definable and measurable. Did a client's self-esteem improve and if so by how many points on the Likert scale? Did you reunify five families this month, and if not, what did you do wrong? Did your agency deliver food baskets to 100 needy households and were they, in turn, appropriately thankful? Check, check, check. What these outcome measures, and the competencies that align with them, don't tell you is whether that client now feels capable of undertaking new adventures, those reunified families have a newfound appreciation for their members, or that those needy households actually want to engage in a distribution process that builds their communities rather than always being passive recipients. Measurable outcomes narrow our vision and scope. Risk and innovation are not encouraged, as that could threaten a "successful" (read: predictable) outcome. Clients or communities are labeled as resistant or unworkable because what they need is not what is prescribed as the "correct" outcome. We do not capture how we interact with others, the quality of our relationships, the emotional arcs of our work, the messiness of life. But isn't that what social work is about?

This atheoretical, competency, and outcomes orientation of ours is bolstered by the empiricism that has infiltrated social work, especially its educational arenas. I do believe that research is necessary and that quality research can illuminate conditions in ways that can lead to change. I have used research methodologies in my organizing work as a way of engaging communities and constituents; indeed, participatory action research is designed for that. But I've also witnessed far too many times the prioritizing of doing tricks with data at the expense of telling the actual story. I've talked with too many doctoral students who can tell me myriad ways to do structural equation modeling but cannot articulate how their work informs or is informed by theory. And as many of us in the academy know, far too much emphasis is placed on getting grant dollars for doable research at the expense of exploring the messy world that most of us live, work, and play in. Indeed, we are a discipline that, in an effort to gain academic credibility (meaning funded research), more and more seeks non-social workers as our deans and senior colleagues. While rationalized as being interdisciplinary (it really isn't), these decisions to name non-social workers in key leadership positions is really a vote of no confidence in social work and a confirmation that money talks. I can think of no other discipline that does this.

Truthfully, I doubt we need yet another study on racial disparities in health care. Instead, those funds should be going to creating a nonracist system of health care. And this isn't the only example. Millions of dollars from the government and foundations go to support investigations on poverty, illiteracy, housing scarcity, mass incarceration, and other "societal ills." But what percentage of these funds gets into the communities that are most in need? We need to rethink this funding game that too many of us are playing because careers are being built on the lives of those on the margins. And yes, I realize that there is some high-quality, meaningful research that has been produced. But if we are really honest with ourselves, I think we can acknowledge that there's a lot of self-aggrandizing, talking within topical silos, and appropriating of grassroots knowledge and experiences.

Perhaps part of the problem is a dissemination issue. Social workers have not done a particularly good job of advocating for themselves and their issues or promoting their work outside of their own confines. During this time of racial uprisings, I've been impressed by the number of sociologists who have put on their "public intellectual" hats and hit every media outlet possible to discuss everything from the history of racist police practices, to generational racial trauma and its effect on Black and Brown communities, to the boycotts by athletes in support of Black Lives Matter, to the school-to-prison pipeline as an intentional strategy to subjugate people of color, and so forth. These individuals are passionate and well versed in their fields, and they are on the right side of justice. Or consider how public health leaders have been key players in addressing the pandemic. In many states (at least those who have governors who actually believe in science), public health practitioners have demonstrated the interpretation and use of data to advise on quarantine measures, designed reopening plans, and consulted with local officials on various health and safety measures. Doctors and nurses have been collectively vocal on the conditions with which they are dealing, the need for more supplies and equipment, and the sheer exhaustion they face, with many taking to social media and more traditional outlets to get their stories to the public. Teacher unions are demanding a role in school reopening plans, and some union locals have gone so far as to have "obituary write-ins," in which teachers compose their death notices and send them to politicians in states and municipalities who are not taking the virus threat seriously. In all these cases, and countless others, academics and practitioners are shaping and engaging in public discourse, often using research data to address systemic problems and search for comprehensive solutions. They embody excellence.

Social work needs to move from competency, which I think is a flat and uninspiring term, to excellence. We need to reorient ourselves to collectively advocate for the issues that really matter so that we can do our jobs to the best of our abilities. This means, for example, less focus on licensure and much more focus on working environments. This means being aggressively involved in the policy arena to stop harmful measures from being put into place and promote those that uplift clients, constitutes, and practitioners. This means that we must refuse to constantly martyr ourselves in the name of serving others and shining a very bright light in an unflinching way on the conditions that make it impossible to live, let alone thrive.

Embracing these strategies would necessitate a fundamental rethinking of what is means to be a social work "professional." Personally, I'm not a fan of this term, nor do I like it as a vocational aspiration, as I think it is embedded with classist notions that reward particular expertise and then use it to gain authority over others. But I'm willing to concede that, for some, being professional signifies the quality of and commitment to a given field. Nonetheless, the long trek to being accepted as a profession has, I think, derailed the core mission of social work. While we rhetorically promote social justice, we don't necessarily practice it. Instead, too many social workers have become agents of control and surveillance. In the name of "helping" families, they monitor and report, reinforcing dominant society's behavioral norms and expectations that are disconnected from the environments and cultures of these families. We convince ourselves that by working within various human service institutions that we are improving lives while keeping society safe when we are really handmaidens for a punitive regime that sees people who are poor as expendable. Somehow, professional has come to mean, for many, rule follower and enforcer.

For others, to be a professional social worker is to be in private practice. I understand that desire: autonomy from bureaucratic rules and regulations, determining your own hours, and working with the clients who are "preferable." This vision, however, is a gross misreading of the realities of advanced capitalism and its encroachment on all aspects of one's work. It also signals an abdication of responsibility for working with disenfranchised groups because we all know that it costs money to run a private practice. Yet the solo-flying therapist is often held up as the gold standard for the profession. Those agency workers are biding time and building a client base so that they can make the jump. By not questioning the merits of this career development trajectory, social work has abdicated considerable responsibility regarding systemic change.

More specifically, social work has turned its back on macro, specifically organizing and mobilization, practice. We love to tout the work of Jane Addams and maybe some know about Frances Perkins. But macro practitioners, educators, and researchers have had to continuously fight for recognition and inclusion in organizational, community, and policy foci in professional associations and educational institutions. It often feels like a version of Sisyphus's challenge to have to constantly remind folks that macro social work is social work. I have been engaged in some form of macro social work for 40-plus years, and, frankly, I'm tired of having to browbeat colleagues into acknowledging that macro matters, to include this content in the curriculum, and to have it reflected (not in a token way) in conferences and initiatives. By not taking macro social work seriously, we deny students and practitioners, indeed the field overall, with system-level explanations of and solutions to the challenges that confront us.

The End of Social Work is a tough-love book and as such can be a difficult, challenging read. My guess is that some will become defensive over its content and claim that social work has accomplished much, so why is Burghardt being so mean. Others might assert that Steve has "thrown the baby out with the bathwater" and that yes, there are challenges, but he has gone too far with his analysis and solutions. I suspect that Steve wouldn't deny either claim, although he probably would add that he is well aware of the important contributions of social workers and that sometimes one needs to be provocative to, in his words, "force a conversation." For some of us, this book will provide needed sustenance, affirm much of what we have been thinking, and urge us to continue. Reading this book should not be viewed as something to check off one's social change list. Rather, it is a starting point. We need to debate the ideas and analyses that Burghardt has set forth, and then we need to collectively act in ways that address the conditions he documents.

Social work, I believe, is at a crossroads. If we continue to go down our current paths, I don't think we will survive, or if we do, we will be a shell of our original selves. We need to gain clarity as to which side we are on, because there are sides, and we ought to be standing firm with those we serve. We need to collectively advocate for more humane and better-resourced settings for our clients and ourselves. We need to make partnering with communities to promote their capacities and well-being a priority, not an afterthought. We need to be at the policy table, and if we're not invited, we need to barge our way in. We need to place relationships, along with justice, back at the center of our craft. So, I need to get off my porch, out of my bubble, and recommit myself to the struggle. I hope others will join.

Cheryl A. Hyde
Temple University
School of Social Work

ACKNOWLEDGMENTS

AFTER ALMOST 50 years in the profession, there are more than a few folks to thank. So let's start with all the students who passed through my classrooms and every frontline social worker, supervisor, and executive I ever met. I didn't love them all, and I'm pretty sure a lot of them don't even remember me. That aside, so many have enriched my life, deepened my understanding, forced me to grow, and honored me by their presence that I know how fortunate I am to still love the work that I do—because of them.

A few folks must be mentioned. Over the last 5 years, Darlene Bailey, Mark Homan, my long-time colleague and friend Terry Mizrahi, and Tracy Soska inspired me by their servant leadership within the Special Commission to Advance Macro Practice and their lifelong commitment to both macro practice and social justice. They showed me how to press on toward the commission's goals to expand macro offerings in our programs regardless of opposition or the inertia of others. Closer to home, Dean Mary Cavanaugh and Associate Dean Caroline Gelman at the Silberman School of Social Work have done much to foster an environment of academic inquiry and to support faculty in whatever academic path we choose to walk, including my own. Meg Bausman, Carol Bennett-Speight, Robyn Brown-Manning, Julie Cadenhead, Michelle Desir, Kalima DeSuze, SJ Dodd, Geetha Gopalan, Nancy Giunta, Colleen Henry, Michael Lewis, Rob Lorey, Jim Mandiberg, Abby Miller, Anna Ortega-Williams, Joanne Rizzi, Marit Sadaka, Jama Shelton, Andy Silver, Willie Tolliver, Tony Young, and Rong Zhao have each, in their distinct ways, proven to be insightful and supportive colleagues for me over the years as well. School staff members Jim Agoli, Rich Caruso, Matt caron, Leslie Casanova, Mike Dunham, Jacob Gutter, Wilma James, Juliana Lopez-Rendon, Ana Rendon, Johnny Sanchez, Irene Stater, Anne Thompson, and Irene Vargas have helped me out in ways large and small for so many years that they deserve gold medals for their skills, patience, and kindness.

As with almost everything I've thought about—let alone written—over most of my career, Mike Fabricant has been a cherished friend, fierce comrade in struggle, and bracingly honest reviewer of my work. He, along with my great friend Eric Zachary, have been models for me as to what a community organizer is supposed to be. A special shout-out goes to Bob Fisher over at UConn School of Social Work as well.

A few others have lightened the journey and enriched my life: family members Josh, Lila, Jenny, Lisa, Eric, and Matt; and those beloved grandchildren Desmond, Sara, and Simone; friends Betsy Fabricant, Liz Laboy, Susannah Laskaris, Bill McKeithan, and Evelyn Pedersen.

Cheryl Hyde, a woman of great humor, sterling intelligence, and a willingness to speak truth to power no matter the cost, was kind enough to write the foreword to this book. I remain indebted to her on many levels, which I am sure she never will make me repay—but I'll try! At Cognella, Amy Smith, Celeste Paed, and Emely Villavicencio have shepherded this book with intelligence and tact, which had to have been a challenge at times. Melissa Brown Levine is a copy editor extraordinaire as well. Finally, how lucky I am to have Kassie Graves as a publisher and dear friend. She is a wonderful example that a person can provide honest feedback and affection at the same time.

INTRODUCTION

THE END OF *Social Work*. What a ludicrous title; maybe even offensive. After all, the field is projected to grow by 16% over the coming decade—some of the best job growth in the nation. There are social workers still toiling where others fear to tread: with the urine-stained homeless man others cross the street to avoid, the frightened child cowering in a corner as her mother rages at the protective child welfare professional, and the frail 88-year-old whose taken to hoarding now that she sees no one else all week. Social work is far from ending!

Except there's another much less discussed social work at play in all of the afore-mentioned examples. The bachelor of social work outreach practitioner trying his best to coax that huddled figure into his van to get a shower and a safe place to sleep? He is also working 20 hours a week part time as a barista. Why? In order to pay off his student loans because his $35,000 annual salary barely covers rent and food—and since the pandemic, that barista job is gone. That child welfare worker suffering from hypertension caused by the 50+ hours she puts in every week, along with the untended secondary trauma from so many removals of crying children? She had to cancel her own doctor's appointment because this removal would require work until at least 7 p.m. The loving masters of social work practitioner who just spent an extra hour with their client? They leave the cramped apartment with a slight fear nestled in the back of their mind. Like their client, they, too, have no pension beyond social security. Will they one day be just as afraid?

Now, guess who these professionals also are: First responders. They are the brave and courageous folks who, even during the pandemic of 2020, continued to show up for work because potentially abused children need to be seen, elder folk are even more isolated and afraid, and there are more homeless people needing outreach for services. Was there any mention anywhere, outside our own news-letters, of the Herculean role social workers have played during the pandemic? Doctors, nurses, postal carriers, grocery store clerks, pharmacists, UPS and FedEx drivers, delivery workers—they all deservedly received accolades, 7 p.m. community applause, and end-of-the nightly news hosannas. Social workers, so many of them also first responders throughout the pandemic, have been all but invisible until the post-George Floyd calls for defunding the police mentioned "social services." Such invisibility is not an accident—as these pages will explore, it's been 40 years in the making.

This short book is a polemic. It is not a measured, balanced assessment of the state of the field, complete with reams of data-driven evidence. It is arguing for a larger truth not found in reams of evidence alone. While mindful of neither over-stating the comparison nor assuming equivalent heft, this work is based on the tradition of Jonathan Swift's *An Immodest Proposal* and Tom Paine's *Common Sense*. One written at the time of the Irish famine, the other immediately before the American Revolutionary War, their mutual purpose was a furious appeal to attend to conditions no longer tolerable yet all too often overlooked by those with power and prestige. Your frontline social worker isn't starving, but there's a definite chance she's on food stamps and clips coupons to get through the week. As for revolution, that may not be in the offing, but a radical transformation of what social workers deserve and how to go about getting it surely is. The 2020 Black Lives Matter's call to defund the police has at times carried a call for refund-ing social services. That such a demand has been raised creates a potential for transformative possibilities—as long as social work embraces it fully and not just as a momentary opportunity for more of the downtrodden same. It's time to end the idea that a commitment to social work values and social justice means a worklife of exhaustion and a home life of unending financial strain. If social work is ever again to matter in the larger public discourse and not as an add-on, *social workers must matter as much as the clients they serve and the communities in which they work.*

There are many reasons for the forlorn conditions under which most social workers now toil; later chapters will analyze them in more detail. At the outset, I want to make clear that there is no conspiracy or cabal of mendacious social work leaders who have plotted such conditions at the behest of greedy capitalist over-lords and their political minions. Such a paranoid mindset, were it accurate, would ironically be easier to correct than what lies ahead: one could change the leadership and then all would be right with the profession. As Specht and Courtney (1995) made evident 25 years ago in their trenchant, prescient yet immediately ignored analysis of social work's drift into private practice, it has been a confluence of forces, both academic and professional, that have led to the decline both in the profession's status and workers' financial and emotional well-being.

The actual causes of the present malaise have been incremental, operating in tandem more by a mix of happenstance and short-term opportunity over many years rather than by design of a few. There are, however, obvious shifts in how the context of social work practice has been framed, interpreted, and researched.

The result has been a paradigm shift that all too often externally emphasizes client and community well-being while ignoring the conditions of the social worker charged with improving that well-being. Instead of rightly combining client, community, and social worker interests within the same framework for change, the actual labor of social workers who toil in the public and nonprofit sectors is at best an afterthought. This is especially obvious when funding beyond resource-rich demonstration projects are replaced by financially watered-down alternatives, even though the required outcomes remain the same. The implicit imperative then focuses on preparing students and frontline professionals for private practice. When professional push comes to practical shove, the profession has long opted for fighting for licensure, not working conditions (Specht & Courtney, 1995, p. 128). Such an investment in those opting for private practice and its emphasis on individuated treatment necessarily has meant that those who labor in actual social work agencies and programs (who are disproportionately people of color) confront degraded, demoralizing, and diminished conditions. In today's 21st-century social work, "inequality" is not just a buzzword for an election cycle or a slogan for militant demonstrations but a lived experience for those who care about working directly with the poor, disenfranchised, and oppressed.

What reasons are there for this draconian shift? To begin, the larger political-economic context once mattered in a very different, more dynamic way within the profession than it does today. From the origins of the field at the turn of the 20th century up through the early 1970s, newly minted social workers were exposed to the dynamics of capitalism and the ensuing push-pull such dynamics played within the welfare state and upon the field itself. While the radicalism of Jane Addams, the Rank-and-File Movement of the 1930s, and the National Welfare Rights Organization of the late 1960s and early '70s were never the dominant actors across the profession, their vibrant presence was impossible to ignore (Fisher, 1994; Wenocur & Reisch, 2001). The ensuing discourse—whether on charitable impulses versus public goods, the need for collective unionism versus professionalism, or entitlement rights versus social service needs—had a consistent reckoning over the role of the social worker herself that made one an active subject in the larger world. Today, that larger worldview, complete with attention to globalization, change in the structure of capitalism, and shifts in population need and welfare state functioning, has all but disappeared from our own present-day discourse. Such analytical atrophy has left social work on the furthest margins of dominant political debate. Likewise, while there is at present long-overdue attention to systemic racism, such awareness all too often focuses more on cultural symbols and microaggressions than on the structural, economic causes of racial inequality. As with these other economic factors, such focus requires a far deeper analysis of power and wealth that cannot sidestep a more sustained and contentious strategic approach that our professional leadership has long avoided.

It is thus no accident that while there are countless social workers still doing admirable and even Herculean work on behalf of the marginalized and dispossessed, there are no nationally recognized social worker heroes anymore, no matter what type of practice they champion. Jane Addams, Mary Richmond, Ida B. Wells, Mary Van Kleeck, Frances Perkins, Harry Hopkins, Bertha Reynolds, Antonia Pentoja, Whitney Young, and Dorothy Height easily come to mind—often for work as much outside the profession as within—and, with the exception of Pentoja and Height, their work has the cobwebs of half a century or more clinging to it (Banks, 2011; Gronberg, 2001; Lipsky & Smith, 1989; Simpson & Murr, 2015; Ryan, 1999). The heroic mix of courage, tenacity, and willingness to sacrifice personal gain for the greater good, writ large on the public stage and demanding a place upon it, has all but disappeared within the profession.

With such disappearance has come a loss of professional stature. Where once social work ranked equally alongside the "sister professions" of nursing and teaching, today's ranking finds nurses the most admired of 25 professions, with teachers third. *Social workers did not even make the list.* There are of course well-known social workers-turned politicians, such as Ronald Dellums and Barbara Mikulski, the longest serving female senator in U.S. history. Dellums made his significant mark through foreign affairs, with an emphasis on anti-apartheid work. Mikulski, head of the powerful Appropriations Committee for a brief period, successfully pushed through legislation on child care and pay equity for women. Their important contributions were obviously influenced by their social work background—which is the point. It was in the background. Part of this lack of national stature outside the profession arises from the simple reason that *the work of social work* has become exhausting and, for some, fearful. As we will detail later, today's social worker spends so much time on forms, inputting data for measurable outcomes, and fulfilling compliance regulations that the actual attention to relationship building, responding to community need, or helping a troubled teen almost becomes an add-on. The only way they can find meaning in their work is to add on a few extra hours to each workday, staying late to input that data or taking it home to complete once their kids are in bed. (As will be discussed later, a social worker's interest in private practice perhaps emerges far more from proletarianized agency working conditions than either selfishness or disinterest in the poor. All people want to do interesting work that pays them a living wage. Social workers are people too.)

The fear in the work is another matter. It's not just the frontline worker afraid for a suicidal teen client; it's the executive who's fearful of their funders. As will be documented, many agencies live under the constant financial threat of funders' late payments. There are of course those rare, old-line agencies established a century ago by Jane Addams's and Mary Richmond's wealthy friends and other Progressive Era benefactors, who now have endowments that can be drawn upon in an emergency. However, today's average social service agency limps along from contract payment to contract payment, using funds from one part of a pot to pay all their workers one month and making up the difference from another the following month. Over time, such constant financial strain creates a starvation mentality among these agency executives. Such a mentality is not unlike that identified long ago as a mindset that seemingly separates the identified short-term thinking of working and lower classes from the longer-range thinking of the middle and upper classes. For executives under the constant strain of budgetary shortfalls, "living in the present" has little to do with mindfulness and everything to do with paying the next overdue bill.

Executives and managers, coming to experience such short-term mindsets as normal, justify their trepidations about engaging with longer range, more systemic issues as "being professionally pragmatic" and thus avoidant of even the mildest advocacy. For example, a New York City settlement house working with older residents refused to join 30 other cosponsors in a "Rally for Age Justice" out of fear of offending city funders, even though the rally was focusing on the prevalence of ageism in society, not an attack on politicians or city agencies. Likewise, an urban social work school refused to challenge an agency's unwillingness to take a DACA intern because the agency only hires U.S. citizens for employment based on their federal grant requirements. To have challenged the agency decision meant jeopardizing the other placements at the agency—an outcome that the stretched-thin fieldwork staff could ill afford. Rationalizing their fears as sensible professionalism based on established contractual norms, the leaders responsible for such decisions would be aghast not to be seen as deeply committed to social justice. Of course, social justice is always easier to support when one champions a courageous fighter of the past, such as Bertha Reynolds (who died penniless), or if the issue doesn't affect one's own standing, such as the aforementioned settlement house director who was despondent over the separation of migrant families 1,500 miles away from her agency door. Real courage begins with the awareness that your actions on behalf of a cause or principle might personally hurt your professional status or personal well-being and that it's worth making a stand, nevertheless. Starved long enough, one might forget such a mindset entirely.

For courage to reappear as a present-day norm and not an antiquated, albeit deeply honored, ideal, social work professional and academic leadership would have to redevelop the more activist-centered role they once played on behalf of the worker. At one time, different schools of social work, reflecting the dynamic temper of the times, were identified with various contested theories of practice: Addams challenged Richmond, of course; likewise, the functionalist school at Penn versus the diagnostic schools at Columbia and Chicago debated practice terms throughout the 1930s and '40s (Fisher, 1994; Specht & Courtney, 1995). Activist academics in the early 1960s played significant roles in the organizational incubator of later federal efforts to end poverty, Mobilization for Youth (MFY) also simultaneously challenged traditional modes of service delivery taught within most schools of social work. Today, schools are known (and inevitably ranked) not for their contested practice frameworks or committed activism but for the level of their funded research—no matter the focus of the research itself. Furthermore, up through the 1970s, there were robust academic analyses of the welfare state and its effect on the profession, the contradictory yet vital roles of social workers caused by these conflicting welfare state demands, and the ensuing dynamics between professional and client (Gough, 1979; O'Conner, 1973). The almost complete disappearance of such analyses over the last 30 years has necessarily narrowed the type of research undertaken so that it is either posed inside an agency's doors or tied to further investigation solely of the clients and communities themselves (Abramovitz & Zelnick, 2018).

"Evidence" is thus all too often to be found within a manageable research design of individuals' and families' histories or, at a macrolevel, seemingly self-contained communities of identity where history is of selves, not a wider ranging social collectivity. While of great value in the collection of scoops of publishable data, its reliability and validity for the larger world, given how untethered it is to larger social and political dynamics, is another matter. Yes, some of this research shines a valuable light on important topics, from overlooked populations (e.g., homeless, trans, youth of color), to emerging issues (food justice applied to communities of color), and strengths-based participatory research with urban youth on systemic trauma. However, lacking an integrated framework that connects each of these topics to broader systemic arguments now at play in America, these valuable contributions remain on the national sidelines, with their authors more likely to talk among themselves at conferences than to join larger currents of change now underway in our society. To cite a few that affect social workers and the profession itself: wealth concentration and growing racial and social inequality; the spread of the authoritarian state with its implicit support for White supremacy; the effect of climate change on immigration patterns across the world; the surprisingly robust growth of widespread interest in socialism among Millennials and Generation Zers; and the untreated effect of historic racial trauma on Black, Brown, and Indigenous families and their children. Besides, such committed advocacy on such issues, as leaders of Black Lives Matter understandably call for, with its inevitable expectation of long-term effort, will eat into time needed for developing one's research pipeline to procure the Holy Grail of research funding: a federal grant. As of this writing, such a grant has never been tendered (nor will it ever be) for an investigation of itself.

The organization of this book is thus straightforward. But before turning to a brief synopsis of the chapters ahead, there are two other summary points to guide you: First, woven throughout each chapter will be the stories of *social workers* deeply admired and whose careers have followed a path of remarkable commitment and tenacity to social justice and the well-being of the dispossessed and destitute. They are, indeed, the unknown champions of this field who deserve our admiration. Second (borrowing from civil rights icon Fannie Lou Hamer), they are, nevertheless, sick and tired of how sick and tired so many social workers are today—tired of having to work part-time gigs on top of their 50-hour social work job; sick from over-researched but untreated secondary trauma given the stress of working in child welfare or homelessness or antiviolence projects for lesbian, gay, bisexual, transgender, or queer or questioning youth; sick and tired of retiring to live at the margins solely off their $1,800 monthly Social Security check. Be forewarned: alongside the stories of love and care and purpose that every reader can aspire to is a theme of anger at the injustice as to how so many fine people's well-being could have been ignored for so long. It's this kind of social work that must end. (One stylistic point with social meaning as well: this text will proportionately intersperse the individual pronouns "he," "she," and "they" throughout.)

Chapter 1 examines why there is so little healthy intellectual conflict and debate today within social work compared to the past. By reviewing not only well-known examples of the past but seeing how such arguments fit within other major social currents in society, the chapter explores an unseen cause of today's theoretical languor—topical insularity bred by leaders unwilling to connect their analyses of professional tensions and dilemmas of the present-day currents rippling throughout our society (such as systemic racism, immigration, environmentalism, and income inequality). Chapter 2 explores this decontextualizing of practice from the larger world by the unwillingness to offer interpretations of globalization and its effect on the welfare state. By highlighting still valuable contributions of welfare state analysis written decades ago but more relevant today than ever, the chapter spells out ways for the profession to enter such discourse, especially as a way to connect to systemic racism. Such discourse, by placing social work as a more modest yet relevant player within these societal debates, would have the paradoxical effect of ending the otherwise implicit and explicit blaming of social workers for inadequate responses to poverty, homelessness, and child removal.

Chapter 3 moves from the discussion of the welfare state and the profession to agency work life—from the beleaguered executive forced to deal with permanent cash shortfalls to the exhausted worker expected to handle the stress of overwork and secondary trauma solely through their self-care regimen. Modest data will be provided to show the extent of the exhaustion, as well as the diminished professional quality of the work itself. Chapter 4 provides a unique take on why clinical social work has emerged as so powerful a choice for so many social workers—not because of greed or disinterest in working with the poor but because of the proletarianized working conditions and diminished income of most agency life. Because of agency starvation and a diminished welfare state, too many social workers are shut out of managerial advancement, substituting lateral movement from agency to agency before coming to the conclusion that they must strike out on their own through the wonders of their clinical license and establish a private practice. They begin such practice initially unaware that present-day market conditions promise little in the secure advancement of their material and professional well-being. They, too, will end up more like 21st century part-time gig workers than well-paid professionals forced to combine exhausted agency life with part-time hours at the end of their workday.

Chapter 5 moves on to academia, both inside schools and its accrediting body, the Council on Social Work Education. The chapter begins with a brief review of the pedagogical research on how one develops critical reflection and a capacity for theory among adult learners. Such reflection has long been recognized as central to professional skill development. Based on this review, the chapter offers a critique on the continuing expansion of core competencies as a fractured measure of reflective thought. An exclusively competency-based educational model places an over-reliance on evidence, which necessarily focuses on measures of behavior and short-term results that belie the nature of personal and collective change. Such narrowness underscores why it is thus no accident that more and more schools develop professional degree-granting programs based on speed and timeliness—as if actual professional skill can be learned, practiced, and habituated in 12 to 16 months!

Chapter 6 examines the corresponding diminishment of pedagogic rigor through the lens of how social work schools are handling "cultural competency." While correctly championed as a central dimension to effective practice and made even more salient since the murder of George Floyd and countless other African Americans, the actual long-term engagement in such issues within social work programs is another matter. As more and more schools both rely on adjuncts and recruit students who must work full time in the globalized economy, the inevitable shortcuts to "competency" are resulting in something far less than cross-cultural efficacy and far more like a mix of fear, frustration, defensiveness, and, for those "othered" all over again, anger. Such outcomes do little to project the deserved station of the field within larger social currents of our society.

Chapter 7 provides fragments of hope by developing the outline of a long-term campaign to recenter social work as a profession uniquely capable of effective work with the poor, disenfranchised, and oppressed. Such a campaign replaces the illusion of quick fixes with the needed development of new groups of social workers who believe that collective well-being for themselves is as worthy as it is for their clients and communities. This organizing approach begins with a long-term strategic focus on reimagining what professional life and work can be in the 21st century. Such an approach combines ways of developing new professional leaders, old-time organizing models of resistance and strategic resilience learned from the civil rights and labor movements of the past, the use of present-day social media tools for mobilization, and a revitalized academic activist group whose members use their skill set for a needed critique of both the welfare state and the shortfalls of 21st-century social work agency life. By embracing the new tools of social media without discarding the best and well-tested organizing approaches of the old, activists can carve out a way forward that is centered on the worker and client alike. Through such an amalgam, may social workers and the people with whom they work foster a new beginning for social work itself.

CHAPTER 1

NICE IS NOT ENOUGH

The Erosion of Necessary Professional Debate

Fragments for Reflection

Social Work Leadership Responds to the Special Commission (SC) to Advance Macro Practice Versus the Entire World of Social Work

Please read the following leadership statements in response to social work faculty organizing around the need for a greater emphasis on macro practice in the profession, paying attention to the underlining:

MEMO FROM SOCIETY OF SOCIAL WORK RESEARCH (SSWR)—MAY 2018
PRESIDENT RUTH DUNKLE

"The SSWR supports the Special Commission agenda and has been moving in a similar direction on many of the issues identified by the Special Commission ... . The entire Board is open to engaging in further dialogue, but we particularly encourage your group to reach out for an initial deeper, developmental conversation with those current members of the Board with identified macro-level interests and expertise."

STATEMENT FROM THE NASW BOARD—FEBRUARY 2018
PRESIDENT KATHY WEHRMANN

"The NASW Board supports the Special Commission's goals and objectives and will work to collaborate with the Special Commission."

STATEMENT IN THE COUNCIL ON SOCIAL WORK EDUCATION'S (CSWE) "FULL CIRCLE" ONLINE PUBLICATION
SEPTEMBER 2017

"CSWE Affirms the Need to Advance Macro Practice"

"At its June 2017 meeting, the CSWE Board of Directors affirmed the need to ensure that the preparation of social workers be rooted in the professions' historic mission to promote social justice through social change. One of the goals of the Special Commission to Advance Macro Practice is to have 20% of MSW students concentrating their studies in macro practice by the year 2020. CSWE commends the focus and leadership of the Special Commission on advancing macro practice. CSWE and the Special Commission will continue to work together to identify activities and devote resources to furthering macro practice in social work education."

BACKGROUND TO THE ORGANIZING EFFORTS OF THE SPECIAL COMMISSION TO ADVANCE MACRO PRACTICE

In 2012, Jack Rothman, emeritus professor of social work at UCLA, and Tracy Soska, professor of community practice at the University of Pittsburgh, worked together to produce a report that documented that less than 8% of social work schools offered "macro" practice as a distinct option for their students. Even by categorizing "macro" as broadly as possible—community organizing, policy practice, leadership or management, social planning—that 8% was a shocking number for a field purportedly dedicated to social justice. The report's results galvanized a cross-section of dedicated academic leaders and activists within the profession, leading to the creation of the Special Commission to Advance Macro Practice.

Imagining itself to be a 3-year campaign with a long-term goal of "20% by 2020," the commission was fortunate to be chaired by two tenacious and strategically savvy luminaries: then–Bryn Mawr dean (now dean emeritus) and Kellogg fellow Darlyne Bailey and Silberman School of Social Work professor and former National Association of Social Workers (NASW) president Terry Mizrahi. Assisted by such equally able activists and scholars as Mimi Abramovitz, Linda Blitt Donaldson, Bruce Friedman, Sunny Harris Rome, Mark Homan, and Soska, their work over what is now the last 6 years has achieved a number of extraordinary accomplishments: they have worked with more than 90 schools or programs that have provided financial and voluntary staff resources; they produced the CSWE-sponsored *Guide for Macro Practice*; they strengthened CSWE Educational and Policy Accreditation (EPA) standards to better integrate macro content; they presented more than 50 macro-based papers at annual meetings over the ensuing years; they have lobbied the U.S. Department of Labor to broaden its occupational categories of "social work" to include macro job titles; and they are now in the process of creating the *Encyclopedia of Macro Social Work Practice* to be published by 2021 (I was on the Commission as well).

And yet, the list of accomplishments speaks only to the group's extraordinarily hard and accomplished work, not fundamental change within the field. As experienced strategists, the Commission's leadership knew that winning the active support of established leaders in the profession would be vital to long-term success. Bailey and Mizrahi set out to do just that, holding meetings with leaders of NASW and CSWE, and as soon as possible, they gained their endorsements for change. As the previous quotations make clear, those endorsements were eventually forthcoming, but please pay attention to what the commitments meant concretely:

Hmm ... SSWR is "open to engage in further dialogue ... but ... reach out (first) to members ... identified ... with macro interests." You mean "talk among ourselves"? NASW leaders support "the goals and objectives and will work to collaborate with the Special Commission." Huh? What does "work to collaborate" actually mean? Why not just collaborate? And CSWE "commends the focus and leadership of the SC on advancing macro practice"? Drs. Bailey and Mizrahi are not the kind of leaders looking for pats on the back! As for "working together to identify activities and devote resources to further macro practice," since the SC already stated what that was—demand schools integrate more macro curriculum and placements— what exactly was such work on the part of CSWE going to be? While unyielding efforts by the commission's leadership have resulted in CSWE-sponsored webinars in 2019 and publication of the *Macro Guide*, movement to embrace macro practice in ways that require programs to better integrate such material is another matter. Perhaps the extraordinary efforts underway wrought by the post–George Floyd Black Lives Matter (BLM) demand for systemic change will force leaders to do more than "commend" the Special Commission for their efforts again.

Future activists need to see such statements for what they are: lofty in tone, proudly in agreement on far-off goals, and way short on anything concrete beyond what the SC itself created. The pronouncements fit nicely on the lower to middle rungs of Shelley Arnsterin's classic "ladder of citizen participation," where one locates the degree of actual power being brokered between the haves and have-nots (Arnstein, 1969). Each testimony places the SC at rungs four and five: "consultation," with agreements to provide surveys and information and share ideas, but no commitment on decision making or power sharing, and "placation," which allows for advice yet those in power retain the right to judge the feasibility of that advice. A webinar is okay, but not an enforced standard that guarantees programs create more macro (or racial) content like they must on, say, human behavior and the social environment.

To locate the SC's efforts in the middle of the participation ladder with a voice but no decision-making power is, in fact, a real accomplishment of the SC—after all, with an 8% standing in the polls of schools' "opinion," they did better than one could expect a politician running for office with such numbers to have done. Indeed, progress was made as CSWE suggested SC leaders create the *Guide for Macro Practice* to help programs develop curricula. However, what's at stake here is something that transcends either rungs on a ladder or macro percentages in a school and is far more problematic for the profession itself. Throughout all the time and effort by the SC and its members—brokered meetings, special sessions at conferences, leaflets at their plenaries, research and policy papers, chats on the internet—*nobody seemed to substantively disagree with the need for more macro work*. Instead, they did something far more insidious by doing one of two things. Most voted to support the CSWE "macro" resolution and then ignored the subject entirely (thus putting the topic at the bottom of Arnstein's ladder). Others reduced their opposition to a tautology: We can't offer more macro subjects because students don't ask for them, thus accepting as pedagogical rigor that students "don't know what they don't know" is justification for never letting them know it at all.

Such narrowness of thought is a bitter irony, for no profession cloaks itself in the *macro words of social justice* as much as social work does—from the ethics of empowerment to the value of self-determination and educational standards that stand tall against oppression and affirm the rights of marginalized groups across the land. The NASW Code of Ethics and CSWE's EPAs read almost like primers for mass mobilization! It should be a no-brainer to advance macro alongside other forms of direct practice, and yet most of the profession doesn't care enough to even find reasons to substantively disagree. Commission members and their allies have done extraordinary work—whether the field is more focused on macro practice is another matter.

As this book will explore, there are many reasons why a profession could come to talk so tall and yet walk with such a crooked gait. As the previous case example suggests, one of them is the lack of present-day substantive intellectual debate over different points of view within the profession itself. The SC has done remarkable work in spite of wider institutional indifference, but such indifference is a symptom of the narrowness of thought that would have been unacceptable in the halcyon days of the profession's past. While there has been a modest albeit short-lived dustup at the turn of this century over strengths-based frameworks (McMillen, Morris, & Sherraden, 2004), such ferment is rare. (Indeed, as we shall see, that disagreement was notable as much for its tongue-in-cheek, condescending sexist language as its actual substance.) Today's social work debates are the mirror opposite of the legal profession, where internal debates on such topics as abortion, gun control, states' rights, and citizenship correspond to the social ferment within the larger society. Developing the analytical rigor required for its own conceptual understanding, the legal profession's arguments enter the mainstream with deserved influence (both among conservatives and progressives). By 2020, such rich controversy within our own field hardly exists.[1] Replacing intellectual rigor with the dried-up empathy of bland support for another's efforts can do little to elevate social work's future

---

1   Whether the powerful conversations underway in the summer of 2020 on systemic racism within our society and its institutions (including social work) will move to structural change alongside newly fervid commitments to improve language and expand curricular offerings

standing as a profession. That today's social media–fueled rage across the political spectrum exists is no reason to step back from debate; indeed, it is part of the reason to engage in it. For only by engaging in vibrant and challenging controversy can one develop the intellectual sinew capable of standing up to false, albeit sophisticated, arguments on, for example, poverty, immigration, and the welfare state.

A brief look in this chapter at how past leaders approached the development of the profession through spirited debates over ideas and interests that corresponded to those within the larger polity will show how far we have wandered away from such a path today. That the debates to modern ears may sound dated and incomplete will be obvious and yet beside the point. What matters here is that these debates happened among spirited professional actors as a way to advance the profession *as well as* to position themselves within the larger American discourse of their times. For our field and its members to walk away from the same challenges among our own is to diminish our legitimacy as actors within the larger society. After all, if we don't sharpen our skills over how disparate macro and micro work may or may not be, who would bother listening to a profession's ideas on a larger stage dealing with historical and present-day forms of racism and inequality?

ADDAMS VERSUS RICHMOND AND THE ORIGINS OF THE SOCIAL WORK PROFESSION

Jane Addams and Mary Richmond—are there any two names more linked together in social work? Richmond, doubly orphaned of parents and all her siblings by the age of 7, was raised by a devoted grandmother and aunts, arriving at adulthood near poverty but skilled and educated through early, rigorous homeschooling by her suffragette grandmother. Addams, who also lost her mother at the age of 2, as well as four of her seven siblings before she turned 10, was doted on by her wealthy father. While suffering from a severe spinal condition, she completed college and inherited a sum equal today to $1.6 million. With so many similarities, save their social class, Addams and Richmond were destined to frame the early debates of what social work could be (Wenocur & Reisch, 1989).

While Addams is consistently identified as the more radical of the two, Richmond was also very much a woman of her times, and those times were the Progressive Era—a time animated by very different ideologies, programs, and beliefs yet united by one: Through rational effort and systematic research, *progress*—over political corruption, economic centralization, and unhealthy living conditions of urban life—could be achieved. Richmond, seen as the more conservative of the two icons, was in her own way a progressive reformer seeking to limit the moralism

---

remains to be seen. Activists would be wise to study Arnstein's "ladder of participation" closely as proposed reforms are offered and debated.

of friendly visitors, attempting to create a collective body of social workers rather than disparate groupings of friendly visitors, and lobbying for legislation to protect widows, mothers, and children abandoned by their husbands, as well as orphans (Gonzalez & Gelman, 2015). Richmond, forever seen as the conservative diagnostician of the two, was far more liberal than were many of the rich board members and frontline workers of the community organization societies that she headed throughout her career.

Addams, a lesbian, was the only social worker to win the 1931 Nobel Peace Prize. She was a courageous pacifist who went to prison for her beliefs during World War I and was the founder of Hull House. Embraced as a radical heroine for generations and dedicated to the "cause" tradition of our field, Addams also wrote for years as a eugenicist. "Our generation ... may at last have the courage to insist upon a child's right to be well born and to start in life with its tiny body free from disease. Certainly allied to this understanding is the new science of eugenics ... . When this new science makes clear to the public that those diseases which are a direct outcome of the social evil are clearly responsible for race deterioration, effective indignation may at last be aroused, both against the preventable infant mortality for which these diseases are responsible, and against the ghastly fact that the survivors among these affected children infect their contemporaries and hand on the evil heritage to another generation" (Elshtain, 2002). Addams also, while opposing the lynching of Black men in the South, initially wrote with the *a priori* assumption of their guilt rather than an awareness of how such violence served not the law but the upholding of Black servitude and a people's systemic disenfranchisement. In support of, if not an active proponent of Prohibition, the profession's most famous radical reformer was a woman of her times too.

In short, these were two brilliant women, founders of our profession, whose well-shod, high-top shoes of the day supported the same feet of clay as the rest of us. That they always are joined together in our history books is not because of their similarities or political inconsistencies but because of their differing intellectual debates over the contours of what it meant to do social work practice—cause versus function, social reform versus social service (Fisher, 1994; Jansson, 2018). Both supported the value of research and the systematic collection of data as a replacement for the moralism of those starched visitors to the immigrant families of their cities—but in profoundly different ways. To Addams, Richmond saw the social worker as the essential, requisite arbiter of necessary guidelines for client improvement. Such cool elitism, Addams argued, undermined the desired "friendship" and more egalitarian relationship required if true acculturation to the democratic American mainstream was to happen. Richmond, *in direct response to Addams*, powerfully responded by citing their clients' inherent improvement through "organized charity" as opposed to the far more disorganized, relational approach of the settlement house movement.

The settlement house worker focused on closer social relationships with community members as fundamental to civic, as well as interpersonal, improvement; the charity worker used the systematic push for organizational efficiency and the boundaries of professional expertise as the guarantor of forward progress for the client and profession alike. As their personal correspondence makes clear, they directly confronted each other on their ideas, uses of research, and philosophies of how reform needed to occur if the democratic character of community life in America was to be advanced. Furthermore, as women of their times, their ideas rested within the larger discourse of the day, whether Progressive Bull Moosers of Teddy Roosevelt in 1912, with their platform for social insurance and women's suffrage, or the overarching Progressive Era belief that government could be cleansed through the work of more scientific and rational means—and actors. Who those actors should include—the mass of workers, farmers, Black people, and other groups of citizens inspired by the likes of Eugene V. Debs, Ida B. Wells, W.E.B. Du Bois, and Sinclair Lewis or elevated elites, such as Roosevelt, Woodrow Wilson, and Frederick Taylor—was part of that debate.

What a time it must have been! Looked at closely, it was as messy as any other period—combining reformers' zeal for social welfare with more than a touch of eugenics' desire for family cleansing; militant women's suffragettes marched alongside fervent teetotalers, and many of these leaders were one and the same. Right inside this glorious mess of remarkable possibility and embarrassing elitism and racism strode social workers whose arguments forced even deeper thought and more refinement on either side. Such thinking was resonant of the era itself. Richmond came to deplore elitists unable to see the mutual humanity of those with whom they worked; Addams saw the value of reliably collected data to inform future social welfare efforts. Their philosophical fights and practical disagreements fit within the temper of the times, not outside them; together, they formed the contours of what social work has become (Fisher, 1994; Gonzalez & Gelman, 2015). Both their differences and similarities, as well as their unflinching willingness to push against the other's ideas, allowed them to build the bridge between micro and macro long before the terms existed. Today, no one pushes against other ideas and practice approaches much at all, preferring the security of their own research agenda to speak for itself. In 2020 and beyond, can a hundred blooming flowers, each in their separate tidy gardens, withstand the gale-force winds blowing across our land?

1930S CLASS STRUGGLE AND THE SHIFTING PERSPECTIVES ON AGENCY-BASED PRACTICE

Strong winds blew throughout the 1930s, and social work leaders were an active, dynamic part of the forces of change sweeping American society. Mary Van Kleeck, Jacob Fisher, and Bertha Reynolds were among the radical firebrands; Virginia

Robinson, Grace Coyle, Jessie Taft, and Paul Kellogg were some of the noted, more traditional leaders (Jansson, 2019). Notably, their arguments within the profession corresponded with those raging across America: The radicals saw the working conditions of social workers as necessitating trade unionism, just as the Congress of Industrial Workers (CIO) sought to unionize their counterparts inside the growing industries of auto, rubber, and steel. As could be found throughout American society, intellectual debate was so intense that the two most prominent social work journals, *Social Work Today* and *Survey*, consistently engaged in debate on workers' rights versus professionalization, the types of authority to be used by social workers and their agencies, and what "equality" meant within the client-worker relationship (Fisher, 1936; Hunter, 1999; Lloyd, 2008; Reynolds, 1975).

The radical wing focused on the idea of a "just practice" in the "Casework Notebook" section of *Social Work Today*. Their practice focus emphasized how the worker both respected the effect that social conditions had on clients and likewise sought others outside the agency who could be of help: "Earnest, thoughtful practitioners ... have shown that they are aware of the importance of realities and have directed their energies toward the fostering of a 'therapeutic' life situation for their clients. They consult with teachers, principals, group-leaders, to encourage better understanding of a particular child, to foster a 'therapeutic approach' for him" (Alexander & Lichtenberg, 1978; Hunter, 1999).

Such an approach was in direct opposition to other models of practice. For example, Taft argued for a much more autonomous level of authority for the social worker: "The worker sets up the conditions as found in his agency function and procedure; the client ... tries to accept, to reject, to attempt to control, or to modify that function until he finally comes to terms with it enough to define or discover what he wants, if anything, from this situation" (Taft, 1933).

There have been volumes written about the differences between the rank and file, functionalist and diagnostic schools, and the ensuing battles that took place within the profession (Alexander & Lichtenberg, 1978; Fisher, 1994; Wenocur & Reisch, 2001). The complexities and nuances within these debates are not the focus of this chapter. What matters here is that the debates occurred as a fundamental element of the profession's discourse, *thus replicating similar arguments coursing through society at the same time.* Issues of authority and the locus of power were at play *everywhere*—the vertical, socially conservative craft unions of the American Federation of Labor versus the far more horizontal and socially progressive unions of the CIO battled over who could best represent the American worker; the benign patriarchy of the Franklin D. Roosevelt (FDR) New Deal versus the widespread currents of socialist- and communist-influenced social movements within the labor, tenant, consumer, and farmers' movements of the day (Fisher, 1994; Wenocur & Reisch, 2001). Social workers of all political stripes were well aware that their arguments on working conditions and worker autonomy corresponded to—and were a part of—the wider arguments of the day. Today's discourse on working conditions has been supplanted by the profession's focus on licensure and the professional's responsibility for self-care as the primary ways to respond to worker burnout and work-induced stress. The idea of the collective self-interest of the social worker that animates the environmental, food justice, and immigrant struggles of today is literally not imagined, let alone acted upon. (At the 2018 CSWE Annual Public Meeting, there were 16 papers on variations of self-care; there was one indirectly focused on work life [Council on Social Work Education, 2018).

It may be difficult for most of today's readers to feel emotional resonance with such experiences of the Progressive Era or the 1930s, for they have not occurred with *sustained interconnectedness* since perhaps the mid-1970s, when the civil rights movement began to wane and the student and anti-war movements fell apart after the end of the Vietnam War. While the more recent Occupy Wall Street and early BLM movements have had a short burst of genuine impact in the last 10 years (as did the lesbian, gay, bisexual, and transgender–led fight against AIDS in the 1980s), they are magnificent exemplars of solitary struggles, not interconnected ones. Whether such debates underway in 2020 on racial justice will be a welcome shift back to earlier times of sustained debate remains to be seen. The Depression Era debates over authority in social work practice *and* the fight for tenants' housing rights to have authority within their housing leases *and* workers' rights to have authority in collective bargaining were experienced by each group of activists as *one and the same.* One thus felt less separate from people of other walks of life, even in the momentary loneliness of an agency office or shop floor. Such connectedness had the cascading effect of making "solidarity" mean something in their lived experiences and was not just an abstraction. In the 1930s, social workers' struggles over authority, power, equality, and service were as much a part of the American discourse as any other. Such connection, personal and intellectual, further emboldened all parties to act with a sense of agency and purpose.

It is thus no accident that historians consistently highlight the rank-and-file's versus traditional association members' battles over working conditions and professionalism, followed by a later 1930s focus on functionalist versus diagnostic schools (Lloyd, 2008). Indeed, I would argue that Robinson's and Taft's focus in the late 1930s on a client's responsiveness to agency context was enriched by the earlier debates over working conditions and the degree of autonomy and authority granted to clients. The functionalist emphasis on "helping" within the client-agency context rather than solely clinically diagnosing corresponds with the earlier rank-and-file claims of joint (social) worker-to-worker (client) relationships as the focus of casework. Such richness did not occur without struggle, debate, and refinement. Our heroines and heroes of the 1930s leaned into debate, not away from it. Controversy, if handled with a mix of respect for your adversaries, openness to debate, and a willingness to *state your own point of view directly and openly*, will enrich a profession, not diminish it. Never has that been truer—and more needed—than it is today.

1960S RACE-FUELED MILITANCY AND GRASSROOTS MOBILIZATION MEETS THE WELFARE STATE BUREAUCRACY

Not surprisingly, the 1960s saw the reemergence of fierce debate, at first within a cross-section of agencies addressing both juvenile delinquency and poverty and later that decade among groups that in many ways replicated the battle between the rank and file and the traditionalist professionals in the 1930s. A number of historical works have addressed these struggles over professional turf and practice frameworks, notably Fisher's *Let the People Decide*, Reisch and Andrews's *The Road Not Taken*, and Brager and Purcell's *Community Action Against Poverty: The Mobilization Experience* provide thorough assessments of these tumultuous times and their effect on the field (Brager & Purcell, 1967; Fisher, 1994; Reisch & Andrews, 2002). Like the times themselves, the debates and their lead actors were reflective of the underlying dynamics of the period itself. First, in the late 1950s and early 1960s was the contestation between old-line New York City settlement house leaders, such as the esteemed Helen Hall, now firmly established with the political elites in the mayor's and governor's offices, and, to her left, young academics such as Richard Cloward and Frances Fox Piven. Hall pursued an uplift approach to juvenile delinquency, seeing settlement houses as incubators of new civic engagement for wayward youth; the academics saw delinquency as a symptom of poverty requiring not uplift but a willingness to let poor people's righteously angry voices into the room. "We were not prepared to be enablers of contentious protest ... Miss Hall ... brought neighbors to City Hall under the protective arm of the settlement house ... . (She) was not prepared for the neighbors to go by themselves" (Cazenave, 2007).

Other conflicts were at play throughout this earlier period as well. The federal government sought control over Mobilization For Youth through two means: first, by demanding established relations with the school system, as well as other public entities, as a way to diminish settlement houses' historic independence from oversight. Such mechanisms of oversight, as will be seen in Chapter 3, have only grown, thus marking a significant turning point in governmental nonprofit funding relationships. Second, they required a social research component with an affiliated university so that "applied social science" tools would be used throughout the life of the project. While the first demand was achieved and expanded upon, the second, because of the temper of the times and the personnel selected to lead the project, proved to be another matter entirely. Columbia University's Lloyd Ohlin and his younger colleague Richard Cloward, while established academics in juvenile delinquency prevention research, were paying close attention to the new forms of neighborhood mobilization inspired by the civil rights movement that were emerging in the North.

This Lower East Side ferment over differences in elite-controlled versus grassroots-inspired forms of mobilization of poor people stood alongside the equivalent strategic fights between Roy Wilkins's National Association for the Advancement of Color People (NAACP), with its focus on legal means for reform, and Martin Luther King's Southern Christian Leadership Conference's (SCLC) emphasis on widespread community activism. As the 1950s ended and the even more tumultuous 1960s began, the ensuing battles within social work corresponded to the militancy of the period as well, with a lasting effect on the profession itself.

While much of the 1960s is bookended in remembrance by the historic 1963 March on Washington, the ensuing passage of the Civil Rights Act of 1964 (both championing fundamental civil rights for all citizens, including Black and Brown people in the South) and, in the late 1960s by the heartbreaking mix of militancy in the anti-war and Black Power movements next to the assassinations of Martin Luther King Jr. and Robert F. Kennedy, the actual on-the-ground social work focus was on poverty. Made aware of its pervasiveness across the nation by Michael Harrington's groundbreaking *The Other America: Poverty in the United States* and fueled by the TV images of Mississippi shacks with outdoor plumbing, Chicago slums infested with vermin, and Appalachian children with the swollen bellies of severe malnutrition, community organizing exploded in urban cities and rural hamlets in a way not seen since the 1930s (Harrington, 1962/1997). (To show how different these times were from today, President Richard Nixon, a staunch Republican, responded to the income demands of the day, emanating from a variety of poor people's campaigns and affiliated movements, with the Family Assistance Plan: a modest yet nevertheless real guaranteed annual income. Influenced by the National Welfare Rights Organization, NASW leaders lobbied against it as inadequate to the needs of the poor.)

Reisch and Andrews (2002) nicely detailed these tumultuous times and their ensuing effect on the profession. As hard as it might be, imagine today's CSWE's Annual Public Meeting or SSWR's annual conference being taken over by large numbers of poor, militant, mostly African American women and men, allied by significant sectors of progressive social workers. Then imagine them bolting closed the plenary session's doors with a demand for $35,000 to support their organization, the National Welfare Rights Organization (NWRO). Leaving aside the strategic effectiveness of the action—its long-term effect was nil at best—such actions were reflective of a time where sit-ins, protests, and the term "question authority" was less a slogan and more a fact of everyday life. Such intense militancy would, of course, enter the agencies, schools, and the profession itself.

Not unlike the 1930s, radical social work groups developed alongside the NWRO, especially the Social Welfare Workers Movement. Like their 1930s rank-and-file counterparts, they pushed for trade union representation over professionalization and advocated for nonprofessionals to be allowed into social service jobs. "Social action" again became a legitimate method of practice, and the number of schools offering "community practice" as a method choice expanded exponentially. Like the times themselves, activism became an integral part of the field.

"Integral" did not mean primary, of course. Historians seem to agree that the effect on the profession itself was limited to the growth of bachelor of social work (BSW) programs, further enrollment of more people of color in social work schools, and inclusion of language espousing support for the values of self-determination, empowerment, and human dignity (Reisch & Andrews, 1989). Significant changes, to be sure, but hardly transformative. How could it have been otherwise? The '60s hardly eradicated poverty, ended racism, or put to rest the misuse of authority. Sandals and sneakers may have replaced high-top shoes but not the amount of clay activists stood on. Responding to and reflecting the times of ferment, possibility, and tragedy, the profession grew accordingly—activism alongside diagnostic tradition and Black and Brown professionals a growing minority of membership instead of a mere speck. As social work historian Robert Fisher once said, "History moved," and the profession did so as well.

THE 21ST-CENTURY DISAPPEARANCE OF DEBATE: CUTENESS REPLACES THE CUTTING EDGE

Decades have elapsed, so how has history moved? As Specht and Courtney (1995) made clear in their prescient work from 25 years ago, the previous push-pull between progressive and more conservative forces that are aligned with other larger social movements for change has all but disappeared. The result, they argued, is a rise in private practitioners and a diminishment of the profession (Specht & Courtney, 1995). In 1968, there were twice as many social workers as psychologists engaged in psychotherapy; in 2020, there are also data to bolster this claim: there are more social workers doing private clinical work than all other mental health professionals combined (Goleman, 1985). However, as mentioned in the Introduction, regarding the profession's status, where in the 1960s it ranked equally alongside the "sister professions" of teaching and nursing, today, nurses are ranked first in a national survey and teachers third (behind military officers). Social workers did not even make the list (McCarty, 2018).

It is quite possible that responses to BLM underway in 2020 may augur a return to previous robust, societal-wide discussions inside and outside the profession. However, the debates that have taken place over the last 20 years, as modest as they are, have the flavor of both isolation from larger social movements and a degree of trivialization of the arguments themselves. Perhaps the best example of this was the dustup regarding debates between "the problem-solving" versus "strengths-based" proponents of these two practice frameworks at the turn of the 21st century. The arguments themselves had historic roots, as the authors rightly claimed: The problem solvers invested more in the Richmond traditional camp espousing the central role of the professional; the strengths proponents emphasized the Addams-like emphasis on a more equal role of the client in decision making. In earlier periods of history, these arguments aligned within the tenor of their progressive times, with one more "scientific" and rational and the other more egalitarian and within the community.

However, the summary of the modern debate synthesizing these two sides decidedly placed these debates in an ahistorical frame unrelated to the temper of the post-9/11 times in which it appeared. As the authors wrote, "In one corner, in black spandex, we can find the social worker therapist with a keen focus on his client's psychopathology, waving above him a copy of the [APA's] *Diagnostic and Statistical Manual.* In the other corner, with her white flowing robes, open arms, and olive branch in her teeth, stands the social work partner ready to work as an equal with her disempowered neighbors to create sustainable change" (McMillan, et al., 2004). Black spandex versus white flowing robes—what delightful images they conjure! Despite the disingenuous use of the male pronoun, everyone knows spandex has been primarily marketed to women—ironically, either as sexualized workout clothing or for women perceived as overweight (O'Connor, 2008). As for the lady in the flowing robes (complete with an olive branch in her mouth!), where does she live? On a faded hippie commune listening to Joni Mitchell and Tori Amos? Ms. Spandex is waving her DSM manual, all toned eagerness to intervene; the Stevie Nicks practitioner, probably getting her tongue cut, her arms stretching out to work with her clients. The images are less about a serious debate and seem more like a tryout for *GLOW*, the Netflix show on women's wrestling. (That the journal in which this article appeared highlighted the previous quote is all the more disconcerting.)

The discourse between the proponents of these two practice frameworks has had modest merit, although the leading strengths proponent, Dennis Saleebey, responded in a later commentary that to his mind, a strengths-based practitioner had to consider the problems challenging the client and that a few "problem solvers" seemed to ignore working with clients (Saleebey, 2004). Years later, few remember the debate much at all, suggesting its actual resonance. During that time, Occupy Wall Street, the immigration crisis, BLM, the environmental movement, and conservative populism shifted the nation's focus in new and challenging ways. Little of those movements' ideas, insights, and causes of ferment have entered the profession's discourse about *itself.* When professional discourse remains unattended to larger societal discourse, debate, and discussion, the inevitable insularity can breed vigorous exchange but little analytical growth. Look at the classical Freudian psychoanalytical societies of today—much smaller numbers, less credibility, perceived as musty and out of date. (Who besides Woody Allen can afford therapy four times a week? And he is hardly a role model of client well-being.) They may argue intensely among themselves, but no one's really listening (Bornstein, 2001).

The disconnect between our own practice frameworks of how we interpret and act in the world alongside other societal actors need not occur, for there are theories of interpretation and action worthy of active consideration that correspond to today's wide-ranging social dynamics. For the sake of jump-starting a discussion and debate, I will cite two. First, queer theory has a rich and challenging analysis that explores (among many other issues) the centrality of gender fluidity and the emerging, less hierarchical and restrictive, norms on gender expression that would have an enormous effect on child rearing (Butler, 2006). You and I might hope for validation of those expanded norms, but hope is not particularly empirical—just ask old-time settlement house workers. Why not embrace the study of this question alongside traditional notions of child rearing? Queer theory, central to today's societal debates on family, marriage, gender identification, and human development, can stand up to whatever the data might reveal, and all children would benefit.

As for practice models, the liberation health model (LHM) for clinical practice, developed by Dawn Belkin-Martinez and her allies, is an exciting and potentially transformative model of clinical intervention that combines Freirian steps of reflection and action between the client and worker, mutual aid support groups among clients with similar life situations, and an ongoing integration of personal, institutional, and cultural factors (Belkin-Martinez, 2014). Embracing a blend of micro, mezzo, and macro elements throughout the intervention, its mix of genuine empowerment strategies and concrete actions may be a compelling direction for agency-based practice that situates such work within present-day immigration, income inequality, BLM, and youth-led environmental struggles. It's also a direct challenge to today's traditional, more eclectic models of agency-based practice. Where are the researchers willing to test out comparisons? Clients and workers alike have much to gain from the results—as would the profession itself.

THE CONCLUDING POLEMIC: DON'T DENY OR DEFLECT, DEBATE!

Queer theory and Liberation Health are but two brief examples of where rich and exciting work, one based on theory and the other on practice, are crying out not simply for acceptance but also for testing, challenging, and intellectual fermenting and, eventually, either acceptance, modification, or rejection. To avoid their inherent challenge by allowing them simply to exist alongside multiple theories and forms of practice is to relegate both to tiny, isolated pockets of support and sustenance by those already committed to them. *To create challenge leading to refinement of theory and practice would mean the entire profession needs to embrace them.* Queer theory on child development is not just for lesbian, gay, bisexual, transgender, and queer or questioning (LGBTQ) folks—it might just be for everybody, standing tall alongside disciples of the heavily skewed group of straight white men, such as Erikson, Freud, Maslow, Bowlby, and Piaget. Likewise, LHM deserves to be studied for its effect on client well-being alongside the plethora of psychotherapeutic interventions now used by social workers—classic psychotherapy, dialectical behavioral therapy (DBT), cognitive behavioral therapy (CBT), object relations, Rogerian, existential, transactional, rational emotive, and, well, whatever (Specht & Courtney, 1995). Instead of letting the lure of "eclecticism" serve as a cover for the fatuous embrace of just about anything, LHM just might serve as a foundation capable of elevating the profession's stature because it stands for something of provable worth to client and worker alike.

Embracing any and all theories of development and any form of practice intervention is a fool's errand; it may provide short-term benefit for a beleaguered worker trying to get through the day or the junior faculty member needing a theoretical or practice hat to hang their tenure prospects on, but the profession, by being all things to all disciplines, theories, and practice frameworks, has diminished both its rigor and standing along the way. The end result of these forms of "eclectic practice" is not nuanced flexibility but a hodgepodge lodge without shared framework or purpose. Rather than wresting with the discomfort of rigorous debate leading to a *narrowing and strengthening of the approach in working with the poor and marginalized*, it is better to blandly accept a touch of everything! In a world where entrenched and expanding inequality is systemically rooted and where expressions of racism, homophobia, and xenophobia are now worldwide movements, such insular indifference to actual rigor is a sign of intellectual torpor that removes social work from the world stage. Contesting and willingly examining the merits of queer theory as opposed to Eriksonian models of development, or whether liberation health models as opposed to other forms of clinical intervention are more efficacious in work with poor and marginalized clients would be exciting intellectual enterprises. Likewise, measuring whether macro and micro can exist alongside each other as equal practice partners in the sustained improvement of clients' and communities' 21st century conditions is another type of intellectual debate that would strengthen the profession, not diminish it. Why avoid them?

Such insulated apathy toward substantive debate on critical issues that resonate with the larger world extends to the ongoing inattention to the structural foundations in which social workers actually toil: the welfare state itself. Such inattention to the dynamics between global capitalism and the size and strength of the welfare state leaves the worker on their own to interpret and act on the world, leading to burnout, cynicism, exhaustion, or retreat. As the next chapter will explore, understanding the dynamics of the welfare state within 21st century global capitalism can have a paradoxically liberating effect on social workers: *If social workers recognize their more modest roles in today's political economy, they can be far more effective practitioners.* For that to happen, however, one must examine how the present-day welfare state functions under global capital—not avoid the subject.

CHAPTER 2

SHAME ON YOU!

The "Invisible" Decline of the Welfare State at the Expense of the Social Worker

---

Fragments for Reflection

A few years into the 21st century, leading social work academics created the Academy of Social Work and Science, modeled after the long-standing Academy of Arts and Sciences. They took as their first significant project the "12 Grand Challenges," whereby leading analysts and researchers would lay out a framework and policy agenda for action on issues such as child welfare, homelessness, and mental health. Coming from such a distinguished group, the expectation was that their work would serve as a road map for the social work profession over the coming years. Included in their work was how social workers could work to "[r]educe extreme poverty and inequality" (American Academy of Social Work and Social Welfare, 2008). However, an examination of the 12 Grand Challenges framework and focus reveals inattention to the dynamics of the political economy that have diminished welfare state resources for generations, thus greatly affecting the state's capacity to perform the economic redistributive functions that had defined its history between the mid-1930s through the 1970s.

For example, in addressing how "to achieve equal opportunity and justice," one challenge focuses on stigma: "The ... forms of stigma are ... illustrative of populations to which social scientists may have unique access in addressing the problem of social stigma" (Goldbach et al., 2018). While discussing a variety of social groups suffering from stigma, the framework fails to address how the expansion of inequality over the last 50 years has intensified specific experiences of stigma in relation to these social factors (such as race and gender). Only by joining the political, economic context with questions addressing intensified stigma can people affected by both be well served. The absence of a political-economic frame in part explains the academy's narrow focus for future research. Most of their proposals emphasize small-group empowerment models whose solutions lie primarily within the subjective intergroup realm rather than the larger polity, thus leaving social work professionals and stigmatized community members alike without answers or direction when inequality and thus stigma intensifies (Piketty, 2014).

A more supple "grand challenge" is a direct focus on extreme economic inequality and intense poverty. The academy's work group policy recommendations include improving labor standards, job creation, and childcare tax credits. However, this essay, again, ignores the larger global dynamics at play in our society that would situate social work within a modest yet significant role. Instead, the authors suggest, "[The] contract elements proposed here include innovations to increase income and assets at the bottom of society and to reduce inequality in income and wealth. The social work profession is uniquely positioned to confront political opposition to activist social policies and lead this important challenge" (Elliot et al., 2018). "Uniquely"? Not likely. "Lead"? Even chutzpah has its limits. Such an analysis continues to ignore active forms of economic and political discrimination that *cannot be overcome by the social work profession itself*. Only by purposely ignoring the larger economic and political forces at play that, in fact, challenge the autonomy of the social work profession could one pose such independent—and for the worker, inevitably dispiriting and disappointing—actions.

INTRODUCTION

By ignoring dynamics of globalization and the ensuing contraction of the welfare state over the last 40 years—and thus the diminished effect of the profession itself—the above Grand Challenge analyses by Goldbach, Elliot, and their coauthors have the unintended consequence of unmooring the social worker from an understanding of the actual effectiveness that both they and the profession itself can have, *if left unsupported by other political and social forces*, on the eradication of poverty, stigma, and economic marginalization. In its place, as Gibson (2016) reported in a meta-review of 1,600 social work articles assessing causes for social worker shame, are professionals who are all too often embarrassed by the noble work they do because poverty and its attendant dysfunctions have not been eliminated.

Embarrassment and shame are hardly the ingredients needed for a sense of agency, drive, and transformative purpose. This chapter lays out a different framework of analysis of what the profession and its members can do to be active, vibrant actors in 21st-century struggles for social change. To do so, of course, means to live within the liberating, albeit paradoxical, understanding of the modest, *interdependent*, and vital roles we can play in the fight for social justice. Social workers are neither the overly empathic minions of the ruling capitalist class derided by some radical writers (Kivel, 2000, 2018) nor independent operators of broad-scale systemic change who *through their sustained efforts alone* eradicate inequality or any other systemic oppression. With a grounded understanding of the political, economic context, social workers can find themselves being valued contributors to the critique of the unparalleled social violence and economic unfairness wrought by present economic and political arrangements abetted by historical racial conditions revealed (again) by BML and their supporters. To do that, however, the social work profession and its academic partners must rediscover how present-day dynamics of our global economy affect the welfare state—and both the people it purports to serve and those who toil within.

A BRIEF PRIMER ON GLOBAL CAPITAL: THE POLITICAL ECONOMY OF MUFFINS

I remember vividly when I first taught a course on the political economy of social work. Arriving with the latest writing on the welfare state crisis from Gough (1979) and O'Connor (1973, 1984), Fabricant's work on the industrialization of social work (1985), and Fisher's history of community organizing (1994) as a response to capitalism's growing forms of inequality, I was unprepared for the students' response: *total, paralyzing fear.* (Regardless of race, gender, sexuality, age, disability, or class, students were bonded together tightly by their mutual terror of all things economic and most things political. As more than one remarked, part of their attraction to social work was their lack of love for or understanding of math—whether finance or algebra.) That they had taken the course to challenge themselves—they stated a need for an analysis that didn't make them agents of social control—didn't diminish their dry-mouthed terror. Trying to explain shifts in welfare state functioning and capitalist dynamics through the jargon-filled language of neo-Marxism was clearly a nonstarter. By the second class, it was clear that I was doomed if I didn't find a better approach.

Luckily, the next day, I stopped by a local bodega for a cup of coffee and decided to purchase a muffin—a big, tasty cappuccino muffin, complete with cinnamon swirls. Taking my first bite back in my office, it all clicked: If I wanted to explain global capital, all I had to do was explain the political economic history of muffins! While in 2020 many first- and second-generation immigrant families might not have lived this history, there are enough old movies and TV shows that illustrate the story of these baked goods. In America, throughout most of the 20th century, the almost exclusive time you ate a muffin was at a special holiday or family event. The muffins were small, either bran or corn, and they were produced at home, almost always by a female family member. Soon after being produced, they were consumed with others around the festive dinner table.

By 1990, things had drastically changed—there were 20 different combinations of muffins down at the local coffee shop, not just bran or corn. They were no longer produced by Aunt Kaye, as she was now working full time outside the home. No longer knowing the producer and consuming it alone at your desk or work station, at least now you had the compensation that the raisin, blueberry, and sunflower-seeded muffin was twice as big as those homemade ones. Of course, in 2020, if you are really busy at work or get hungry late in the day when the coffee shop is closed, you can order a chia seed muffin via Grubhub or some other food-service delivery app and have it delivered to your door, probably by either an undocumented immigrant or that tired-looking man or woman working their second gig job of the day. He or she used to work full time at the local bakery, but that closed 6 months ago.

These three muffins—family-made bran, bodega-purchased cappuccino, or Grubhub chia seed—and how they were produced, delivered, and consumed correspond to the contours of the dominant economic system and ensuing social relations of that period: what was made and who and how they made it. The first reflects the dynamics wrought by the U.S. manufacturing economy of the 20th century through the 1970s—produced in a concrete, recognizable place and developed as a collective social experience (people ate together and worked together too), reflecting gendered dynamics (men at work, women at home [although women of color rarely had such a gendered experience regarding work *outside* the home]) produced, delivered, and consumed near each other). While, of course, profitable, the modest levels of profit in the '50s compared to today correspond to those differences in the size of muffins as well (Giovannoni, 2014). So does the level of inequality.

By 1990, that larger muffin purchased at the café corresponded to the dominance of the service-based economy and its social relations—how people were organized to do work *and* eat muffins. Production was now dispersed and could occur throughout the day or night. Like services themselves, the muffins could be consumed individually any day of the week, not just on holidays or special occasions. No longer needing a large, concrete location like a manufacturing plant, services could happen in a variety of settings—as many places as your choice of muffins. Of course, it was less relational—you knew and loved Aunt Kaye but have no idea who the producer is beyond the new label—Millie's, or Mrs. Brown, or Choco-Lite. Likewise, you have many more choices, but you're eating that muffin alone. It's great that Aunt Kaye has more job options, but you rarely see her anymore. As Karl Marx wrote so presciently about the fundamental dilemma of a capitalist economy: "The great contradiction of capitalism is that as material life improves, spiritual life declines" (Woods, 2013). That modern muffin may be larger, but it isn't more filling.

The use of Grubhub at 2 a.m. for that late-night muffin corresponds to the information-driven economy of today—dispersed even more globally, emphasizing the sharing of data for purchase and delivery, using lower paid workers exhausted through the gig economy to get you what you want. Where you once loved Aunt Kaye and in 1995 knew the bodega owner by name, now all you know is whether a person delivered your muffin on time so you could decide on the size of the tip. A muffin can come at midnight, but who produced it and delivered it is another matter. They don't know you either, except that the next day, two ads showed up in your email to purchase a weekly shipment of baked goods.

This tale of three muffins has its limits, of course: It doesn't explain the racism embedded in the manufacturing economy and the state's support of White industrial workers, or how the service economy both hired more women and paid them less, or how the information economy as its globally organized increases levels of economic inequality. There are books that do that (Davis, 1999; Piketty, 2014; Sales, 1975). Our muffins simply alert the reader that the social relations between people and what we do and how we do it—including what, how, and when we eat—correspond to larger economic dynamics at play that need to be understood so that we respond to them actively, not passively. If those economic relations affect what and how we eat, they have to affect how we work too. To understand that, let's take a comparative look at capitalism, the welfare state, and social relations in society in the 1930s and today.

FROM THE NEW DEAL TO THE DECLINE OF THE WELFARE STATE: THE RISE OF ECONOMIC INEQUALITY AFFECTS SOCIAL WORKERS TOO

An All-Too Brief Economic History of the United States and the Equally Brief Rise of the Welfare State

Every history book on social work has the seemingly different stories of Mary Richmond and Jane Addams, the Rank-and-File Movement, Mary Van Kleeck, and the diagnostic/functionalist schools of social work in the 1930s and '40s, the 1960s militancy of the NWRO, and the ensuing institutionalized separation of entitlements from services (Fisher, 1994; Jansson, 2019). As different as they were, they all shared a striking commonality: Even allowing for the Great Depression, they spanned a unique period of history when our national economy grew in production and profitability—and with it, the welfare state itself. The 1930s—that period of history spanning the Great Depression, the New Deal, and preparations for entry into World War II—was, of course, the dawn of the modern welfare state in the United States. Everyone in social work knows that. From a political economic point of view, however, there are two different questions that need to be answered as they relate to the political impact on the profession and those who work within it. *First, why did the American economy need a welfare state when there had been none before?*

Second, why did the welfare state operate in ways that were part of the overall economic improvement in most American lives when that is less true today?

The answers to the first question were filled with tumult at the time but in hindsight were straightforward: Capitalism as an economic system, if it were to survive, needed the state to intervene more systematically to save it. The crisis of 1930s capitalism was one of overproduction and underconsumption—companies had produced too much stuff for too few consumers able to purchase it all. Pictures of desperate farmers pouring out excess milk and factories closed with huge, idle inventories of cars, steel, and rubber were almost as common as breadlines (Jansson, 2019).

Think about it: How do you get consumers to buy things? Well, before consumers can buy anything, they need money, and there are two ways to get that: through their own work or somebody giving it to them. As every good social welfare history book informs us, the New Deal did something the federal government had never done in large numbers before: create jobs. The numbers seem staggering today.

> The Public Works Administration (PWA) put hundreds of thousands of people to work on a variety of heavy construction projects that gave a face-lift to the nation's crumbling infrastructure. Then, in April 1935, Congress inaugurated the Works Progress Administration (WPA), which put nearly three million people to work, including semi-skilled and unskilled, on projects as diverse as building athletic stadiums, making books for the blind, stuffing rare birds and improving airplane landing fields and army camps. In its first six years, the WPA spent $11 billion, three-fourths of it on construction and conservation projects and the remainder on community service programs. In those six years, WPA employed about 8,000,000 workers. Monthly earnings for all types of workers averaged $41.50 in 1935 and $50 in 1939 (Kelbe, 2014).

This unprecedented job creation through these programs, when combined with relief efforts through welfare benefits and social security for retirees, meant that more than 20 million Americans (one out of six!) were receiving "public assistance" from the "welfare state." The New Deal, while not ending the economic crisis, laid the foundation for a national welfare state that, over time and definitely through fits and starts, functioned in ways that lessened economic inequality.

What matters here is that these numbers spoke to a new set of dynamics as to how capitalism would henceforth work in North America. Instead of seeming to operate independently of the state, capitalism's survival depended on active state support. However, given the enormous militancy, working-class anger, and ensuing pressure on the state to help working and poor people out of their desperate conditions during the Great Depression, the state would also have to provide a new safety net. It accomplished this by establishing permanent economic assistance and regulating the worst excesses of factories' and banks' approaches to profit making. Please pause and reflect: Where there had been little regulation of commerce and banking, now there was some; where public job creation had been all but nonexistent, now the government was creating jobs; where once only states and cities provided relief to widows, orphans, and laid-off workers, now the federal government would do so. Knowing this history is important as BLM activists and their allies seek reparations for historic racism in 2020 and beyond and the subsequent trauma and economic disenfranchisement within Black and Brown communities. What once was fiscally impossible is tomorrow's new normal as the authority within political and economic relationships shifted toward greater equality.

Importantly, given these competing interests—to support capitalism's profitability *and* at some level the well-being of the people who labored within it—the state thus came to be seen as an arena in which political and social struggle would occur. That battle would be over how much capitalist subsidy and degree of regulation, as well as how much relief would be provided—not only in factories between owners and workers but also through massive political activity at the federal level. The term "political economy" was shorthand for the mix of activities between capitalism's growth, working people's response, and the state's mediation between the two.[1] This dynamic debate is exactly what is at play in North America today, with the racialized overtones this debate deserves.

---

1   This extended explanatory footnote explicates in more analytical terms common to the political economy than used here in the bulk of the chapter. All theories of capitalism begin within a basic theoretical understanding that the primary *mode of production* (the economic system most capable of generating profit and expanding markets for growth) creates *the relations of production* (how people are organized to work within that system). *The dynamic tension between the mode of production as it seeks growth and the relations of production as people respond to the impact that such growth has on their own lives reveals the broad contours of a society's functioning*: manufacturers and the working class, the service industries and service workers, finance capital, and globalized part-time labor. The ensuing struggles between these primary groups lead to variations within the welfare state itself: under a manufacturing economy, a new welfare state; under a service economy, a diminishing welfare state; and under today's global economy, clashes as yet unresolved over further contraction (Trump and others demanding further deregulation and "freedom" for the free market versus BLM activists, pro-Keynesian political economists, and progressive politicians demanding a more economically redistributive tax system and greater investment in health care, infrastructure, and reparations through education and housing in communities of color).

Embedded within each historical struggle between owners of the mode of production and those who worked within it were implicit questions about the welfare state itself. As Claus Offe (1984) argued, there were two primary questions: "First, what is the *desirable form of organization of society and state* and how can we demonstrate that it is workable, i.e., consistent with our basic normative and factual assumptions about social life? This is the problem of defining a consistent model ... of transformation (e.g., what type of work force will we have in 2020 [*italics-by author*]). Second, *how do we get there?* This is the problem of identifying forces

As discussed in the first chapter, social workers played vital roles throughout this earlier painful and exciting period of American social welfare history. Whether Harry Hopkins and Frances Perkins inside the FDR administration, communist-leaning social workers like Mary van Kleeck and a young Bertha Reynolds, or mainstream social work leaders like Virginia Robinson and Grace Coyle, all of them saw their work within the larger social and political dynamics of the day, not independent of it. The social contract then established between the state and the capitalist economy henceforth would, in fits and starts, regulate the worst excesses of the economy while also providing for its workforce. This contract would remain an integral backdrop to the struggles for social reform that played out for the next 40 years. Post–World War II, as long as American capitalism continued to grow and maintain its profitability, that social contract allowed for gradual welfare state expansion to more and more sectors of the American population.

It therefore was perhaps inevitable that paying attention to underlying dynamics regarding how capitalism was organized, who benefited, and how equitably such arrangements were didn't seem to matter quite so much between the mid-1940s and the early 1970s. If all boats kept rising, as unevenly as that rise was, systemic economic

---

and strategies that could bring about that transformation." In short, as Offe (1984) suggests, the theory is tenable only if it provides real answers about how people actually live. Offe's questions clarify why the modern state must be integrated into the economic system rather than standing apart from it. As such, it provides two functions: *accumulation* and *legitimation*.

Accumulation aids in the processes of capitalist investment as seen through tax credits and incentives for expanding business markets, including oil exploration in the Arctic and write-offs for new equipment. *Legitimation,* on the other hand, develops from the social fallout caused by those accepted investment decisions. The ensuing political struggle between how much to allow for greater investment—Arctic oil drilling—and how much to take care of the fallout by potentially regulating oil drilling or ending the production of coal is thus just that: political and therefore open to change. Such change is determined by the level of authority and power between contending groups within that system—in the 1930s, a more equitable struggle between worker and owner; from the 1970s onward, preeminence of neoliberalism; in 2020, a contentious period where the extreme dominance of radical neoliberalism under Trump and Republicans is being challenged by both moderate Democrats and actors far to the left of them, with growing similarities between their advocacy agenda and those found in the 1930s. (It is exciting to consider how that equation will be calibrated beyond 2020!)

Fundamental to our analysis here is that the state and its welfare-related functions (which range from education to health to welfare itself) can and will expand or contract based not on predetermined laws but political activism testing the degrees of accumulation and legitimation within the state itself—how much to help firms grow, how much to help people grow and live well. Recognizing the inevitability and necessity of these broad economic and political dynamics, it is incumbent upon social workers to understand them so that their actions better fit within those broader societal dynamics. Social work is not outside of these dynamics but an active, necessary element within them (Fabricant & Burghardt, 1992; Gough, 1979; O'Connor, 1973; Stiglitz, 2012; Stoesz & Karger, 1991).

analysis for social work seemed at best an afterthought. Capitalism was growing more profitable and the welfare state was expanding. Why not leave well enough alone?

By the late 1960s, the social unrest of the times came to be defined more by social issues and foreign policy—civil rights, the Vietnam War, the women's movement. As social work historian Robert Fisher (1994) cogently pointed out, progressive activists began to focus their energy on something compellingly vague yet inherently resonant—the problem was "the system"—southern Jim Crow, to be sure, but also any institution where the rules seemed unfair and the bosses too removed from people—colleges, churches and synagogues, welfare bureaucracies, and business big and small.

While demonstrably exciting, especially because of the genuinely heroic struggles of African Americans in the South whose legitimacy and moral authority seemed to extend to these other social movements, there were, nevertheless, two incipient problems with this generalized antagonism toward authority. First, on an individualized and interpersonal level, being "against the system" also shifted significant blame to anyone who toiled within those bureaucratic systems. Such minions—you know, social workers!—were at best dupes and more likely agents of social control (Kivel, 2000; we'll return to this issue later in the chapter). Second, lacking an analysis of how the economy and the state actually worked in tandem, by the end of the 1970s, there was little room to direct activism at either dominant economic trends or forms of state support with the same dynamic politics found in the 1930s and mid-1940s. Back then, activist social workers saw their own struggles as part of larger social movement issues, not apart from them. By the '70s, one was "either part of the solution or part of the problem." Such a stark, binary slogan required social workers to either work with client/community groups to overthrow the very welfare state they worked in, thus distancing themselves from their own working conditions, or, if they chose to focus on service interventions, to be defined as a sell-out or worse (Winocur & Reisch, 1989). It is not surprising that as the years went on, social work activism, if it existed, focused either on neighborhood organizing, solidarity movements in other countries, or electoral politics for the expansion of client/community need, not the conditions of one's own work (Fisher, 1994).

What Do We Do Now? The Global Economic Crisis and the Redirection of the Diminished Welfare State

Thus after 1973, when the seeming effortlessness of growth, prosperity, and the progressively redistributive welfare state came to an end, there was little to no effective political analysis to counter the suddenly far more competitive global markets in the world, save one: Reaganism and neoliberalism. Neoliberalism, whether from the perspective of Republican Ronald Reagan or Democrat Bill Clinton, operated on three primary assumptions: (1) the competitive nature of global capitalism required much more state support, (2) fiscal support would be garnered best by shifting the tax burden from upper to middle and lower classes, and (3) whatever was left would be distributed through an increasingly centralized welfare state system tied to dependent and working populations (ranging from the developmentally delayed to higher education, from childcare for toddlers to services for veterans). Going forward, oversight would focus more on limiting access than on expanding it (Fabricant & Brier, 2016; Lipsky, 2010).

These three neoliberal prongs have seen their pinnacle in the Trump tax cuts and the underlying analysis justifying those cuts. As economists Paul Krugman and Joseph Stiglitz have enumerated in detail, these tax cuts provided huge economic windfalls for the top 1% at the expense of further burdening everyone else, especially the middle and working classes (Krugman, 2020; Stiglitz, 2019). The justification for this largesse to the already wealthy was that such tax benefits would lead to greater investments and economic expansion, which in turn would later benefit all workers—which simply has not happened (Krugman, 2020). Given the decreased state spending on public education, welfare, and other state-sponsored services, it followed that federal oversight would focus on curtailing access and emphasizing diminished access, as occurred with subsidies for federal housing.

By the turn of the 21st century, there were also some obvious political and economic trends that had solidified over the previous 30 years into seeming truths about the now dominant information-driven global economy: First, this information-based economy, with its hedge fund–driven emphasis on abstract financial instruments using data across the web for its investment strategies, intensified levels of economic inequality as the world exploded with both more billionaires than in the history of the world and a drop in real income among Western working and middle classes (Piketty, 2014). Because economic decision-making focused on these abstract algorithms rather than concrete companies and the people who worked within them, there was little political incentive to contour any economic decision making to an actual geographic, populated place (Piketty, 2017). Furthermore, as Thomas Piketty also argued, as the level of wealth was expanding more rapidly than the actual growth of the economy, inequality could only increase—and did.

Second, this disengagement from societal responsibilities that were once built into the old social contract now uses neoliberalism to justify more extreme cost-cutting measures that further diminish the welfare state's capacity to keep expanding as it once had. After all, in this 21st-century economy, there was no sustained relationship, however fraught, between corporate managers and industrial workers. There were Silicon Valley entrepreneurs and their high-priced coders, global capitalists, hedge funders, and investment bankers—that 1%—and then that amorphous "everyone else." Who cares about a social contract when there seems to be little social relationship at all! (As the BLM movement seeks to force an even more powerful reckoning with that social contract through reparations, whether this retreat holds is a powerful question over the next 5 years.) For example, as John Wasek (2017) of *Forbes* magazine wrote, "Social Security, like Medicare and other entitlements, has benefit levels set by political vote, not economic law and … can be changed at any time." It is important for the reader not to confuse the size of legislative entitlements that must be paid such as Social Security with other welfare state functions. Social Security remains intact because of political support and the ensuing authority given to its recipients that forestalls neoliberal attempts to dismantle it. Such equivalent power does not exist—yet—to protect and expand public education, childcare, environmental regulation, or salary inequity. Whether those conditions change is a political calculation, not an economic law (Wasek, 2017).

The great challenge that BLM will confront in this old social contract is the American tax system that over the last 40 years has come to benefit the wealthy few at added financial cost to others. For perspective, under Republican president Dwight D. Eisenhower, the marginal tax rate on the wealthiest, while rarely used, stood at 91%. In 2019, that rate stood at 24.1% (Institute on Taxation and Economic Policy, 2019).[2]

This emphasis on neoliberal policy led to the second profound shift in the American political economy: More and more goods and services once seen as "public" and thus free or low-cost were now financially paid for by private citizens. While there are countless examples, the easiest way to understand this is through a brief comparative look at student debt. In 1970, the average graduating college student carried less than $1,500 of debt because higher education was seen more as a "public good" than a private one (Wadia, 2019). Today, that public good of free or low-cost college education has been replaced with students graduating from four-year programs with an average $37,7211 of debt (Baum, 2013). Such debt is a direct result of neoliberal policies designed to foster state support for further capital investment through increased burdens on working populations—whether debt-ridden students (especially people of color entering higher education); credit-burdened, middle-income workers; or the no-longer-able-to-be-retired. Rather than return to the social contract of the 1950s and '60s, the argument goes, such investment is needed for corporations to maintain their competitive advantage. What truly separates neoliberal conservatives from liberals is not economic policy but the amount of hand-wringing over the social fallout.

The aforementioned data are simple examples presented to underscore the obvious: The competitive global economy, driven by new forms of organization, is systemic in nature and thus requires *massive, sustained effort if it is to be transformed.*

---

2   While this top marginal rate was that high, that didn't mean that someone with an income of $1 million would only take home $100,000. For one thing, the top rate on capital gains, which tends to be where rich people make a lot of their money, was only 25%. Even if you made $1 million in normal taxable income, you would only pay the top marginal rate on income above the cutoff for that bracket, which in this case was $200,000. It should also be noted that $200,000 in the Eisenhower era would be well over $1 million today because of inflation.

Second, the state, in its present political configuration, now emphasizes a highly unbalanced emphasis on support for capitalist development at the expense of the vast number of working people, students, and the retired. As countless reports now document, the intensification of inequality has been greater, not lesser since 1980 (Krugman, 2018; Piketty, 2014). In 2020, it is no accident that our economic and political landscape is as volatile as it now is, from pandemic denial and increased deaths to, on the progressive side, the aspirational demands of the BLM.

This is why any social work analysis of such problems that ignores this underlying systemic imbalance does a disservice to our field and those who work within it. The charge for new social work leadership put forth by the Academy of Social Work and Social Welfare, as it emanates from the field's identified leading scholars, is especially egregious in its historical amnesia:

> For more than a century, social workers have been transforming our society. Social work interventions doubled the number of babies who survived in the early twentieth century, helped millions out of poverty from the Great Depression to today, and assisted people with mental illness through de-institutionalization, aftercare, treatment, and advocacy. (American Society of Social Work and Social Welfare, 2020)

Let's analyze the previous statement closely. Historical amnesia may be worrisome, but it does have one redeeming quality. By rewriting history to suggest that social workers acted independently in areas of great societal import, one can momentarily create a sense of grandiosity that is out of proportion with the real world: "Social work interventions doubled the number of babies who survived in the early twentieth century, helped millions out of poverty from the Great Depression to today" (American Society of Social Work and Social Welfare, 2020). What about all the public health workers? The zoning and housing activists who fought for better, less congested housing? Didn't those trade unions—the International Ladies Garment Workers Union, the United Auto Workers, the United Mine Workers—have something to do with improved incomes for working people and their families? *Framing the grand challenges with a distorted use of history shifts past social workers' vital yet interdependent roles within large-scale social movements during those tumultuous times to an illusory image of independent agents miraculously capable of transformative social change that today's social workers are not.* Such aspirational and erroneous images of the past cause further harm to today's social workers by the implicit admonition that failing to achieve equivalent results means failure. How we as a profession and as professional workers respond to the 2020 demands of BLM will be a telling marker of either new leadership capable of learning from past mistakes of grandiose overstatement or guilt-ridden understatement—both of which will lead to the further diminishment of the profession's authority.

Creating images of social work's capacity for independently instituting widespread change has played directly into the neoliberal ideology that champions the free market as the best and most efficient means for societal improvement. If social workers claim they can diminish social and economic inequality and then don't, well, whose fault is that? If violence in certain cities increases even though there are five local anti-violence projects, who's to blame? When social work leaders ignore the political economy as a way to exaggerate workers' valuable contributions, we diminish the profession's stature and erode professionals' confidence about what they can do. Make no mistake—social workers involved in, say, anti-violence projects have and will continue to make a difference in the lives of people with whom they work. Translating their "cases to a cause" (Abramovitz, 1998) can be as invaluable as it was in the days of Richmond and Addams, whether anti-violence projects, asset creation, homeless advocacy, or childhood trauma. But in the Progressive past, their cases were fit into causes of reform far beyond social work's borders—education and recreation, working-class people's health, and the need for the 8-hour workday. It was in the combination of issues, professions, and organizations that reformers of earlier days confronted both economic injustice and political malfeasance that transformed society. Ironically, by admitting to being less powerful—social workers worked openly with others, advocating for these other causes, seeing themselves as one part of a larger whole—they accomplished more. The BLM movement today provides an opportunity for a return to such a place, leaning in and learning from their demands to make them part of their own. As in the past, such a modest yet engaged relationship does not coopt or water them down but joins the BLM's push for true economic equality. Such widespread democratic equality is at the heart of their long-term demands that would benefit all Americans, including social workers (Bouie, 2020).

Today, left without an analysis that situates social work within larger political, economic dynamics, social workers end up expected to somehow achieve the unachievable. The unfortunate outcome of this void has been to demean social work and all too often blame social workers for society's ills. This painful irony is all the more problematic because so many social workers have been at the forefront alongside others to advance issues of other marginalized populations. The shifts in the nature of our economic systems did not extinguish new social problems or people's lack of collective responses to them. As women pushed to enter the service-based economy, the needs for day care, after-school programs, and domestic violence programs expanded. Likewise, in today's global economy, concerns over immigrants' rights, environmental justice, income inequality, and racial injustice have all spawned social movements that are continuing to grow nationally and internationally—of which social work deserves to be a part—and is (LeBourveay & Leslie-Johnson, 2014).

Given the earlier analysis of the push-pull relationship between the economy and the state, the modern state, in order to maintain its inherent legitimacy in providing support for global capital's continued profitability, has had to respond in some ways to address these movements' demands. The dilemma is obvious: How do neo-liberal politicians respond to these costly demands without decreasing state support for capital's needs? You can't create a PWA program to end income inequality. You can't provide free education for millions of Americans, as occurred after World War II through the GI Bill, or offer low-cost/no-cost mortgages that were provided to handle the housing crisis of that time, as was done for White Americans (Jansson, 2019). This deep contradiction—and the inevitable social and economic tensions such a contradiction spawns—is at play in 2020 as BLM and its allies force the state to consider Medicare for All, quality education, and housing supports in ways not seen since the 1930s.

In short, the growth from a manufacturing to a services- and information-based economy reconfigured the workforce (from full-time industrial workers to 21st-century part-time gig employees) and has meant that women in service industries now require more childcare, not less. Parents forced to work multiple jobs in the gig economy now need before- and after-school programs because no one can be there at 3 p.m. to pick children up when their work starts before school begins and ends twelve hours later. Likewise, familial strains wrought by unrelenting financial insecurity and the attendant stress that goes with it correlate with increases in domestic violence and drug and alcohol abuse. The social problems, community needs, and familial strains of 2020 and beyond are not about to disappear through the gig economy. Unfortunately, while in the 1930s and 1960s, equivalent needs were met with wide-scale social movements pressuring the state to respond dramatically, the fragmented activism of the 1970s and beyond has allowed neoliberalism until 2020 to successfully dominate the political discourse on how best to handle these new social needs. (It also explains why, as of this writing, BLM and its allies are aggressively pushing the Green New Deal, Medicare for All, and an End to Student Debt—all of them campaigns that focus on systemic answers to economic inequality and financial debt and thus harken back to programs initiated in the 1930s and 1960s.) As neoliberal ideology opposes the expansion of the public sector itself, it therefore drew upon the formerly modestly sized nonprofit world to legitimate how the state dealt with emerging social problems. By the late 20th century,

> there are over 210,000 human services community-based organizations (CBOs) providing services to communities across the nation. ... Over half of these human services CBOs (56%) have annual revenues of less than $250,000. At the other end of the spectrum, about 10,000 human services CBOs have revenues in excess of $10 million. These large CBOs account for nearly 60% of the sector's revenues. In aggregate,

human services CBOs receive more than $200 billion in revenues for the delivery of services to individuals, families, and communities. (Wyman, 2018)

While the next chapter will examine in detail the effect of nonprofits on the working conditions and overall well-being of social workers who labor within them, I mention this here to explain how the push-pull dynamics of the modern political economy have made the growth of the nonprofit as explosive today as the public sector was after World War II. If you can no longer totally ignore violence directed at LGBTQ teens or are forced at last to address the overincarceration of Black and Brown men and women, or the state can no longer turn a blind eye to either sexual harassment directed at women at work or workplace marginality of the disabled, what better way to deal with it than to underfund that social problem through non-profit programs staffed by the advocates who raised the issues in the first place?

SHAME ON YOU! GIVES DEEPER MEANING TO THE TERM "BLAMING THE VICTIM"

Over the last 40 years, lacking a broader analysis of the causes of socially created problems alongside actual underfunding to address these problems, social workers nevertheless jumped into the line of fire to provide help. At the same time, these same brave professionals were forced to duck at the volley of potshots whenever such service interventions proved fallible and insufficient to meet the growing need. "Attempts to Get Homeless Into Shelters Fail 99 Percent of Time, Data Show" (Kramer, 2016), "The Pernicious Failure of Child Welfare Reform" (Morton, 2017), and "Another Failure in Mental Health" (Kivel, 2018) are but three of the cascade of headlines that blare out at the inherent failure of human service reform efforts. While sometimes addressed to state funders, the workers who bear the brunt of such attacks are the social workers and other human service providers tasked with addressing these system-wide problems.

That defensiveness emerges is thus an inevitable default position for many social workers when asked what they do. For the most trenchant critiques are often from the left, as well as the right. As Paul Kivel (2000) wrote in his famous essay titled "Social Services or Social Change?," "[T]his strategy (by the state) has been to create professions drawn from the groups of people demanding change of the system, creating an atmosphere of 'progress,' where hope is kindled, and needs for change are made legitimate, without producing the systematic change which would actually eliminate the injustice or inequality which caused the organizing in the first place."

Kivel goes on to make it even more personal for the worker herself:

> The ruling class co-opts the leadership in our communities by provid-
> ing jobs for some people and aligning their perceived self-interest with
> maintaining the system (maintaining their jobs). Whether they are
> social welfare workers, police, domestic violence shelter workers, diver-
> sity consultants, therapists, or security guards, their jobs and status are
> dependent on their ability to keep the system functioning and to keep
> people functioning within the system no matter how illogical, dysfunc-
> tional, exploitive, and unjust the system is. The very existence of these
> jobs serves to convince people that tremendous inequalities of wealth
> are natural and inevitable and those that work hard will get ahead.
> (Kivel, 2000)

Golly, with friends like this, who can you turn to? Without an alternative analysis to increase confidence in the value of your work, it is sadly no accident that
social work is one of the few professions where professional shame is a hot topic,
albeit mostly through quiet conversations and asides with friends. Shame is a quality whereby a person feels the self is deeply flawed, inadequate, or incompetent
(Tangney & Dearing, 2004). Gibson's meta-review in 2017 that scoped more than
1,600 articles dealing with social workers and some of their problematic emotions,
eventually centered his work on 95 studies (Gibson, 2016). He went on to report,
"The voice of the social workers within the identified studies provide an indication
that some practitioners feel they work under a cloud of shame-based fear stemming from a culture that expects them to cope in a society that does not tolerate
mistakes" (Gibson, 2016, p. 222). The result hardly matches up with the NASW
Code of Ethics on dignity and self-determination: "The resulting negative self-eval-
uations led to feelings of inadequacy and potentially highlight how organizations,
inquiries, and inspections can promote shame in the workforce." Of course, the
Code of Ethics applies to how workers treat clients, not how they are treated! (We
will discuss more of that code in a later chapter.)

THE CONCLUDING POLEMIC: LET'S REPLACE SHAME WITH RIGHTEOUS ANGER!

Instead of shame, social workers need to feel righteous anger and a commitment
to their collective self-interest, for their detractors' assessments from the right and
far left are based on two fundamental flaws. Conservatives are unable to answer
why the social problems of the day continue to increase, not diminish. They have
neither realistic answers nor solutions for the spikes in poverty and underemploy-
ment, the growing homelessness in cities and rural areas, the opioid epidemic,
the horrific immigration crises at our southern borders, the over-imprisonment
of millions of Black and Brown people, and the systemic racism revealed (again)

since the death of George Floyd and Breonna Taylor. They have no real answers, for such problems are wrought in large part by the failures of the economy—their free-market answer rather than state intervention—to create sustainable work at a living wage for millions of people. Such problems aren't going away through political indifference masquerading as "balanced thought." This chapter's analysis would suggest that the contradictions and dilemmas wrought by the intensified competition within global capital and the state's neoliberal contraction from progressive interventions gives lie to the conservative's romanticized desire for less state support for human services.

Likewise, the far left has an equally romanticized notion of what social workers should do. To proclaim that social workers should either go elsewhere for work or that they need to rewrite their job descriptions as singular warriors for social justice is both elitist and unrealistic. Where exactly is a caring person seeking to improve the conditions of the world supposed to go to find work? If your skill set precludes work as a Silicon Valley coder for the latest Minecraft app and you have no desire to be Elon Musk's first paid passenger to Mars, what do you actually do? As this chapter suggests, developing an analysis of the dynamics between the economy and the state alters the over-responsibility of one group of actors—social workers—for transformative change. It also allows social workers to break away from the assumptions that their efforts with a small segment of an oppressed population turns them into agents of social control. The far left ignores the ever-present reality that a lot of people will suffer without services, as limited as they might be. There are young people with trauma being helped, older folks no longer isolated, veterans being served the way they deserve to be, and women freed from the prison of domestic violence because of social work programs. Sure, they don't do enough and reach all in need, but they sure as hell do something for the greater good.

The economy does too little, the right demeans too many, the far left asks for too much. As the previous analysis of the global economy makes clear, understanding the world and the people who toil within it through a political-economic framework can be freeing. The BLM is confronting these hard truths as their work moves from mobilizing to achieving their aspirational and long overdue demands. Through such an analysis, a social worker neither has to fearfully ignore larger social realities nor guiltily accept the shameful burden of over-responsibility for society's ills. However, to connect this analysis to their own working conditions and the need for collective action requires another deeper discussion of the actual work of social work. For that, we turn to an explanation of why and how the nonprofit sector has been created—in great part through the loss of the financial and physical well-being of those workers who toil within it.

CHAPTER 3

FROM ISLANDS OF POSSIBILITY TO WORKPLACES OF BELEAGUERED LABOR

Fragments for Reflection

NASW Ethical principle: Dignity and Worth of the Person

Social workers respect the inherent dignity and worth of the person.

Social workers treat each person in a caring and respectful fashion, mindful of individual differences and cultural and ethnic diversity. Social workers promote clients' socially responsible self-determination. Social workers seek to enhance clients' capacity and opportunity to change and to address their own needs. Social workers are cognizant of their dual responsibility to clients and to the broader society. They seek to resolve conflicts between clients' interests and the broader society's interests in a socially responsible manner consistent with the values, ethical principles, and ethical standards of the profession.

"There are 15 social workers in our agency's services program. Every one of us has a part-time job somewhere to make ends meet" (youth development worker, interview, 2019).

"I have too much student debt not to take a part-time job. Given my salary (working with older adults), I figure my loans will be paid off in 2035. I'll never own a home" (recent graduate working with older adults).

"I was paid 30% more when I was head of our hospitals training and professional development program than when I was director for all of social services. And my social services staff was three times larger than my training staff" (Judith Trachtenberg, retired hospital social services director and adjunct professor of social work who works part time to supplement her modest pension).

"Working a half-day today, Ms. B?" (night receptionist to a child welfare executive leaving work at 5 p.m. rather than late in the evening per her normal workweek).

THE RISE AND FALLING OF THE STARVING NONPROFIT

As the previous chapter made clear, the increased competitiveness of the global economy post-1973 elevated a set of neoliberal policies that emphasized a retrenchment from welfare state interventions through the public sector itself. Of course, that neoliberalism espoused anti-welfare-state intervention didn't mean that the needs of a society's people magically disappeared. With more women entering the workforce, childcare needs grew; the growing housing crisis in cities across the land, combined with new policies on deinstitutionalization of the mentally ill, exponentially increased the number of homeless; the fight against AIDS led by enraged and mobilized LGBTQ activists led to an expansion of AIDS preventive services, as well as LGBTQ programs; and the racist "War on Drugs" policies leading to the mass incarceration of Black and Brown men and women that wrought familial and economic havoc on communities of color were but some of the social issues crying out for wholesale societal interventions *before* the BLM call for addressing systemic racism. Neoliberalism might be able to justify the state's unwillingness to respond to social needs, but sweeping such problems under its patchwork rug of indifference was impossible.

In European social democracies, such societal problems were ameliorated through public-sector institutions and programs. Of course, such programs were then administered through unionized and salaried state employees, whose benefit packages contained the same 6-week vacations, pensions, paid parental leave, and health insurance coverage as their private-sector counterparts. Neoliberalism didn't simply espouse anti-statism; it also preached austerity measures that saw such worker benefit packages as anathema to their "balanced budget" credo. Given the soaring social needs that wouldn't go away, there was an obvious answer: farm out the programs to nonprofits and let them develop these needed programs. If things didn't work out so well—families left untended, programs nonresponsive, waiting lists too long—there'd be new actors to blame: the ineffective nonprofit managers and their seemingly indifferent staff.[1]

---

1   A powerful analysis that began in the 1970s by both neo-Marxist and feminist scholars evaluated how the state and its nonprofit subsidiaries vitiated the socially charged nature of most social problems. Rather than focusing on economic dynamics, they addressed organizational

Before we get to who is really to blame for service shortages, let's look at the size of this farmed-out growth. Where in the early 1960s there were few social service nonprofits beyond Progressive Era charities and settlement houses, by 2017, there were more than 210,000 human service nonprofits across the United States (Wyman, 2018), accounting for more than $200 billion in revenue throughout the economy. Sounds impressive, right? Out of those 210,000, there are 10,000 nonprofits with revenues in excess of $10 million. Large numbers of these more corporate entities are sprawling medical centers with myriad outsourced programs targeted for populations with specific needs where social workers can be found: preventive outreach programs, post-maternity care, etc. As for the rest of those 210,000, 56% of those nonprofits had revenues of less than $250,000. This means that such agencies operate on shoestring budgets with few staff members, have little to no property, and are able to provide a narrow range of services. Nevertheless,

---

processes: *bureaucratization, centralization, and professionalization* (Morgan, 1983; Schechter, 1982). They focused on how gender-based violence was reframed over the years, as 93% of all physical violence was male to female. Situating this violence as an extreme form of sexism itself, the initial programs (almost 50 years before the #MeToo movement) had a layered approach to intervention: protection, to be sure, but also education on the socialized strictures of patriarchy, legislative advocacy promoting more economic opportunities for women otherwise unable to leave a terrifying marriage, etc. Shelters were thus a sanctuary and a means to a larger end for changing the norms of patriarchy itself.

Forced to address a surging social problem made even more powerful as a part of the second wave feminist movement of the 1970s, the state through its professional minions began to carve up the programmatic response to this powerful social analysis by funneling funds to particular bureaucracies that would be programmatically responsible. Results would be measured by centralizing oversight and allowing only certain professionals to run them. "The growth of non-feminist shelters ... changed the relationship between shelters and social services ... . Untroubled by political consequences ... these organizations have begun to demand they include domestic violence services ... unrelated to advocacy" (Morgan, 1983). Shifting the language from "male violence" to "domestic violence" vitiated much of the social character of the attacks, thus resituating the problem as within the family alone. Such a refocus allowed professionals disinterested in the gendered critique of this violence to instead focus on family dynamics alone (Schechter, 1982). In turn, as millions of dollars began to flow to address this issue, centralized oversight began measuring results by numbers of families seen and referrals made. With the widespread growth, by the 1990s, of shelters, domestic violence programs, and established (if poorly implemented) police protocols the underlying issues related to the social causes of such violence were all but dropped. What first animated the feminist movement—patriarchy and the deepening alienation bred by the commodification of relationships under capitalism—was no longer woven into analyses of the problem. That segments of the analyses, deepened by queer theorists like Judith Burton, have resurfaced in the #MeToo movement wrought by the revelations of sexual violence and the norms of "toxic masculinity" are of great importance. Whether the critique of "toxic masculinity" extends to a deeper and sustained assessment of causality for such toxicity beyond "bad boy norms" remains to be seen (Burton, 2006).

while often struggling, over the last 10 years, the nonprofit sector has grown an average of 2%–3% a year—about 5,250 new nonprofits a year (Wyman, 2018).

Such growth, alas, does not always mean health. The Wyman report looked at the fiscal health of more than 40,000 community-based nonprofits as measured by their federal tax filings, and the results are unsettling (Wyman, 2018):

1. Nearly one in eight human services (community-based organizations [CBOs]) are technically insolvent, with total liabilities exceeding total assets. Like many of the clients with whom they work, this means such agencies couldn't pay their weekly bills, let alone plan ahead. What kind of stress gets created within both management and staff when there are fears about not paying something as basic as weekly expenses?

2. In addition, "more than 40% of CBOs lack the liquidity to meet their immediate obligations, with short-term liabilities exceeding short-term assets. Many of these organizations limp along from payroll to payroll with limited resources on-hand, often delaying payment of other short-term obligations and dipping into restricted funds to cover their immediate costs" (Wyman, 2018). Change the words about an organization to a family, and a social worker's empathy goes into overdrive at their plight: We all know clients who have had to choose between food for their children and paying the rent or older adults forced to choose between prescription drugs or three meals a day. Not enough of us realize that many agency managers are making the same heartrending decisions. Keeping the lights on while living with antiquated computers that force staff to work later hours is a choice one makes not out of indifference but because there are no other options. Overwork becomes a norm for survival, cloaked uncomfortably but proudly as a hair-shirt badge of honor.

3. Furthermore, "nearly half of all human service CBOs reported a negative three-year operating margin, with the bottom quarter reporting a three-year margin of -5% or less. These CBOs lost money, impacting their ability to remain solvent and build financial reserves … . Conversely, about one third of CBOs reported an average 3-year margin greater than 5%, providing for the ability to cover liabilities, make investments, and add to reserves. 30% of human services CBOs have virtually no margin for error with cash reserves that cover less than one month of operating expenses—the absolute minimum required to demonstrate financial health" (Wyman, 2018). Change the financial language from "organizations" to "people" and who are we talking about? Strapped families, people without savings never able to retire, and an inability to send their children to college. The problems of inequality, it turns out, apply not only to the 99% of our population but also to many human service organizations.

And which programs were most likely to operate in these settings with limited supplies, overstretched budgets, and personal stress? "CBOs facing more financial stress include those delivering services pertaining to: Housing and shelter; mental health; and general human services—programs at the heart of social work (Wyman, 2018).

Such financial conditions are not just about balance sheets and cash flow ledgers. They are the basis for a simple biopsychosocial assessment applied to an organization. Long-term, weak financial resources create an uncertain organization-in-environment approach. Therefore, such an uncertain environment means that the people working under those conditions are stressed and potentially traumatized over time. As the Mayo Clinic wrote,

> When stressors are always present and you constantly feel under attack, that fight-or-flight reaction stays turned on. The long-term activation of the stress-response system and the overexposure to cortisol and other stress hormones that follows can disrupt almost all your body's processes. This puts you at increased risk of many health problems, including:
>
> - Anxiety
> - Depression
> - Digestive problems
> - Headaches
> - Heart disease
> - Sleep problems
> - Weight gain
> - Memory and concentration impairment (Mayo Clinic Bulletin, 2019)

It may be hard to accept, but almost every agency-based social worker reading the previous list of stress-related symptoms will recognize that their own personal health-related strains have far more in common with their clients than they'd like to think. Dignity and worth may be ethical badges of professional honor, but they are difficult to experience when working in the newest form of the poorhouse—but not one for clients. It's been created, brick by neoliberal brick over the last 40 years, for the workers toiling away within it.

Part of the difficulty in acknowledging that one's own agency is the source of such stress is that by 2019, it all seems so normal and routine. As the National Institute of Mental Health (NIMH) acknowledged, "Routine stress may be the hardest type of stress to notice at first. Because the source of stress tends to be more constant than in cases of acute or traumatic stress, the body gets no clear signal to return to normal functioning" (NIMH, 2019). Thus, the resulting coping strategies used across the profession place an emphasis on day-to-day work that has more in common with Social Darwinism than empathy. To be a good social worker means "you'll stay later ... work harder ... if you cared, you'd go the extra mile ... if you're in social work, get used to the 50 hour week." (I will return to the ideological use of "how our service norm is used as a weapon for exploited labor" in the next chapter.) In too many agencies, "survival of the fittest" applies to those who agree that to sacrifice their work-life balance for the greater good is worth it. Whether personal well-being survives over time is another matter. How much dignity can one maintain with ever-present anxiety, hypertension, and heart disease?

A PROPOSED ADDITION TO THE NEXT DSM: FUNDING FEARS AND THE ACCUMULATION ANXIETY OF THE FRAUGHT SOCIAL WORK EXECUTIVE

A discussion about frontline workers and supervisors will occur in the next chapter. This section addresses the effect austerity has on agency executives and managers and how "austerity" expresses itself in the ways that agencies go about their work. In so doing, we can locate the actual sources of programmatic dysfunction that course throughout human services: the state system of contracting and its seemingly progressive partners and foundations.

The Wyman report (referred to earlier) documented the financial strain that so many nonprofits operate under. What it doesn't address is the byzantine, counterproductive, and erratic approaches that too many funders take in overseeing how their monies are spent. As the late human services executive and anti-AIDS/HIV champion Janet Weinberg once stated, "First they want us to address historical and multi-generational forms of trauma with the people we work with. Then they expect us to show on-going improvement every three months. It would be a joke … except it's not funny" (personal communication, July 1, 2017).

Pettijohn and Boris (2014) made clear why state and foundation oversight isn't a laughing matter. First, state contracts don't simply pay less: They often don't pay on time. Both federal and individual states are notorious for requests for proposals (RFPs) being offered at the last minute and with tight turnaround times, thus forcing executives and their development teams (if they have them) to work late hours to meet the deadline. However, that nonprofit executives must scurry about under an enormous time crunch doesn't mean their corresponding state actors must do the same. Their "response" deadlines all too often move further and further past the expected response date, thus further destabilizing the agencies (as well as increasing the direct pressure on the financially strapped executives).

If the whiplash from the RFP process ended there, executives' blood pressures might return to normal, but it doesn't. Federal and state funding arms also often pay late, erratically, and sometimes not for months at a time. An experienced yet exasperated executive put it this way, "I received our major government contract in July. Guess when the funds arrived? June! You think the landlord would put up with that late payment, or other vendors? We had to float a bridge loan with interest to meet our monthly obligations." Unprompted, she went on. "It gets worse. We also received a grant to work with homeless young men who were fathers. While it was a three-year grant, it had to be renewed each year. Because the funds did not come, we were required by law to send our staff termination letters each year until the grant was re-approved. Some stayed, but some couldn't live with the financial insecurity that letter created. It was crazy-making."

Stories like this make one ask: *What exactly is a struggling nonprofit's leadership to do here besides worry?* Again, pause and recast this discussion into familial terms. How do we expect a hardworking parent who is "living paycheck to paycheck" to behave when needed wages from a part-time job are withheld? While mindful breathing exercises might be a short-term answer for some, the more likely response will be tension-filled as one doubles down on existing resources—no movies, no desserts, "new" children's clothing from thrift stores only, feed the kids just a little less, fret during the day, and lose sleep. Agency leaders confronted with equivalent conditions will do the same—forego software upgrades, cut back on custodial services, delay hiring a needed professional or administrative staff, ask the rest of the staff to address staffing gaps through added work—fret and lose sleep too. What keeps one from a new DSM diagnosis—accumulation anxiety, a fear of not meeting one's desired payroll accumulated from multiple sources—is that it all seems so normal because other agencies' leaders are experiencing the same thing. A chronically abused child or adult often experiences their battering as "normal" for all too long also.

As in any family dynamic, accumulation anxiety soon spreads from the parents to other family members, even if they do not recognize its source. In agencies, anxiety spreads not from family dysfunction but from the accumulation of paperwork (or, in today's world, data entry). As Pettijohn and Boris discovered, the average nonprofit has six state contracts. Six contracts mean six different reporting deadlines, six different sets of measures on success, and six potential audits on outcomes. While agency leadership can work wonders with spreadsheets to handle overlapping measurements, no one can disguise the increased oversight that creates bottlenecks on service and longer hours for staff. The primary reason people leave the field is not because they have come to dislike people but that they dislike the accumulated numbness of data entry required for state compliance. The churning caused by job turnover becomes an accepted way of agency work life: Staff members are trained, finally learn their jobs, can't stand the focus on data entry and mechanistic oversight, and then leave. In turn, managers then ask the experienced staff to take on the increased workload, leading to overwork, fatigue, and the slow but steady increase in health-related problems—weight gain, sleeplessness, and free-floating accumulation anxiety passing for heightened commitment. Asked to train the next round of hires, they do so and try to hide their hard-earned fatalism along the way. Even agencies nationally famous for their progressive work can run into the problem of staff churning and the conditions that fostered such rapid turnover. In 2019, Housing Works, famous at its founding for its militant, social justice approach to the AIDS crisis, found itself facing a militant walkout by staff seeking unionization. Part of the problem was high turnover, with an annual staff turnover of about 30%. As one walkout stated, "Over the course of a year, I saw (a client) shuffled to three new case managers. ... I wonder what we could have done better to assist her (as she became homeless)" (Liebson, 2019).

The source of accumulation anxiety extends beyond state contracting. Anxiety is also increased, albeit with a mix of gleaming board rooms, warm smiles, and a patina of open progressivism, from the philanthropic foundation world as well. What makes the form of their oversight even more disturbing than that of the state is that many such foundations have a stated opposition to neoliberal ideology—professing commitments to more verdant, equitable, and inclusive worlds. While professing egalitarianism, their actual investment in the poor is circumspect. The most recent data finds such focus on the poor to be about 31% (Rosenman, 2013).

Furthermore, oversight from the philanthropic foundation world can be even more brutal, seeking responses on cultural and social measures, participation rates from marginalized populations, and other measures related to multigenerational oppression and trauma that perhaps can't be altered in 3- to 6- or even 12-month time frames. A young Latinx social worker, charged with working with young, middle school Black and Brown boys who were seen as "at risk," succinctly summed up the problem. "These kids have been through hell in one way or another, and then they meet me. I'm supposed to get their trust and engage with them. But I can't relate to them on their terms because my supervisor let me know the quarterly assessment was due on their goals. This 13-year old starts opening up to me about this and that, but as soon as I ask him about his goals, his eyes suddenly changed. 'So you're just getting a report on me? Why would I tell you about a goal when I don't even know you? That goal s--- is for somebody else. That's not about me.'" This doesn't just relate to client measurements—foundations have funded grassroots organizations and required a stated measurable outcome as the number of participants at each rally held. Whether their research design controlled for rainy weather, snow, or transit failures in outcome measurement is another matter. In short, all too often, foundation reporting on measurable results about diminishing opression actually signifies nothing. They instead undermine the kind of long-term relationship building required in working with the oppressed and marginalized that, over time, might otherwise signify transformative possibility. Numbers alone, quantified in easily digested, short-term data, will never be a measure of trust between the oppressed and those who seek to work with them.

What? No accountability? Doesn't the critique imply foundations would soon be throwing good money after bad? Well, before becoming too incensed, consider this. What exactly is the *strategic purpose* of progressive grant giving? Is it to truly diminish poverty by a concerted, layered effort that develops the power to alter income inequality, thus serving as a counterweight to the neoliberal ideology and its market-driven focus on profitability that intensified inequality over the last 40 years? Or is it to foster a new grant-making class of program officers and foundation leaders who can then carry forward the mantle of 19th-century do-goodism dressed in anti-oppression, culturally conscious clothing? For at least 30 years, thoughtful analysts have suggested that progressive foundations have focused too much on an ephemerally exciting yet piecemeal approach to grant giving that their conservative counterparts have consciously outplayed. These progressive thinkers have urged grant makers to examine the success of conservatives and use it as a guide to their own grant making: "Sally Covington, a researcher at the National Committee for Responsive Philanthropy, had support from a few small foundations in 1997 and wrote a report showing the way conservative strategists had directed their money over three decades, calling it 'an extraordinary effort to reshape politics and public-policy priorities at the national, state, and local level.' That unabashedly political strategy shaped the grant-making patterns of about a dozen foundations working to shrink the size and authority of government, to roll back regulations and public safeguards, and to cut public spending, especially for the needy. Their single-minded objective was to extend the number and power of extreme conservatives. And as we know today, they were successful" (Rosenman, 2013).

In short, conservative foundations and other sources of right-wing funding streams have been funneling hundreds of millions of dollars to conservative think tanks and social programs since 1964 (after the defeat of Goldwater, perhaps the nadir of conservatism in the 20th century) with an underlying consistency that created leverage through programs, policy proposals, and electoral campaigns that garnered power, not just publicity. They also did so by letting those programs go about the long, hard work of fostering genuine political change and power: "Their grant making was guided by a commitment to strengthen and sustain a coordinated network of conservative organizations, and then trusting them to make program decisions without grant-maker interference" (Rosenman, 2013).

As Rosenman documented, their measures of success were tied less to quarterly reports and far more to creed. Conservatives' 50-year ascent to political might by the end of the 20th century relied less on bureaucratic oversight and more on tightly adhered to, strategic alignment on what mattered: free markets, anti-statism, centrality of the patriarchal and heterosexual family, and pro-life, anti-abortion positions (Fisher, 1981). Imagine this: A core set of beliefs was the demonstration of need, measurement was action on those beliefs based on whatever arena in which one worked (thus allowing for variability across regions and states), outcome was the accrual of power and program (rewritten history books; closing down abortion centers; electing right-wing conservatives to water commissions, school boards, and state legislatures; and conversion counseling for LGBTQ folks), and ascension to a majority of local, state, and national offices that further control the purse strings for social programs.

While there are exceptions that are willing to give programs yearly latitude in overall oversight, most progressive foundations do little of the same, unlike their highly conservative counterparts. Most all too often prefer to foster the same grueling oversight and reporting mechanisms as their state equivalents, complete with the demand for short-term, measurable outcomes on, for example, historical trauma affecting Native Americans or the multigenerational effect of incarceration on African American communities. Instead of combining efforts for, say, a 10- or 20-year approach to eradicating poverty in urban and rural America through a mix of both programmatic innovation and growing political power necessary to sustain any kind of structural change, these foundations find it better to fund 500 discrete, unconnected, albeit initially inspiring, efforts on youth development projects, domestic violence prevention programs, and Black male initiatives that, however worthy their intent and focus, have altered little on the larger economic and political landscape.[2] As a result, agency executives, battered by state grant requirements and desperate to make up their shortfalls through foundation dollars, understandably pursue the latest foundation flavor of the month. While progressive foundations can point to unending innovation focused on cutting-edge issues, complete with glossy photos of the oppressed populations of the year in their annual reports, can they demonstrate shifts in the political landscape with the staying power to confront and defeat the right's political power? Not exactly.

THE NEAR-PAUPERIZATION OF THE COMMITTED PROFESSIONAL SOCIAL WORKER

Remarkably, non-profit agency leaders and their staff manage to carry on despite the excruciatingly unstable financial stress under which so many of them work. (Understanding why they do so without serious collective complaint will be

---

2   There are some exceptions in terms of long-term efforts to address systemic problems. For example, Casey Family Programs has had a 10-year plan for reducing the number of children in foster care by 50%. See https://www.casey.org/who-we-are/2020-building-communities-of-hope/. Some interesting steps have been taken by the Marguerite Casey Foundation (2016), which seeks out already established community groups for long-term partnership, and the Baltimore collaborative between Johns Hopkins and the Open Society Institute–Baltimore that is combining child welfare and anti-poverty and job-business creation efforts. See https://www.caseygrants.org and https://www.aecf.org/resources/responsible-demolition-a-baltimore-case-study-with-national-implications/.

addressed in the next chapter.) It's important here to put to rest a leftist shibboleth about social work and social workers functioning as "buffers" who keep oppressed and working people from rising up against the capitalist state through their mollifying presence. Over the years, Western European workers and other social groups, even though they are sustained by rich social democratic traditions, services, and benefits, have consistently and militantly challenged state and economic policies, whether fighting the incursion of Uber into their Paris transit system or cutbacks to their pensions in Italy and Spain. What has dampened American militancy and collective action can be traced far more easily to the weakness of its trade unions, with its emphasis on business unionism (focusing only on contracts and not on other social issues, as occurred in the 1930s through the mid-1940s) and the ever-present stain of racism and White supremacy that undercuts collective action among working people against state and economic interests. Social workers would serve themselves and their clients/community members far more effectively by militantly joining with them on fights over income inequality—including their own—than spending another guilt-ridden minute that they are even a partial cause of working and poor people's lack of militancy directed at neoliberalism. Professionals working 50-hour weeks at less than $50,000 a year are fortunate if they have time to buffer their own shoes! Controlling the working masses seems to be done somewhere else, far away from their own agencies' doors.

Meanwhile, whether working with the homeless, engaging with the mentally ill in supportive housing, or supporting families in child welfare or adults living in lonely isolation, social workers carry on as they must, for the needs of so many remain ever present. To do so, however, leaders must make their own Faustian bargain, but one not of greed but of well-intentioned goodness. Agencies will be built, services rendered, programs expanded. What will be eaten away, however, will not be a person's soul. It will be an agency staff's well-being beginning with their financial health.

One can best understand the dire state of financial affairs for so many social workers by making a brief historical comparison with the field's previously categorized "sister professions." Fifty years ago, the "sister professions" of nursing, teaching, and social work were aligned in a focus on helping others largely through their female-gendered workforce (Ozawa, & Law, 1993). They also had equivalent incomes: in the 1960s, the average registered nurse's salary was $5,200 (Greenwood, 2019), while teachers made $6,485 (National Center for Education Statistics, 2007). While comparable figures for all social workers are incomplete because of a lack of federal requirements for reporting nonprofit wages, available data suggest salaries of around $6,000 (Ozawa & Law, 1993; Ozawa et al., 1988).

Now, let's jump ahead 50 years. In 2019, the national average income of a nurse with a master's degree was $72,000 (Greenwood, 2019). For a teacher with an equivalent degree, it was $61,780 (National Center for Educational Statistics, 2007). For a social worker with a master of social work (MSW) degree, it was $47,000.

(Bureau of Labor Statistics, 2018). In 50 years, social workers have gone from a slightly higher salary than nurses and an equivalent one with teachers to two thirds to three-quarters of their sister professions' salaries.

The field's contraction cannot explain this stunning downward trend. The Federal Bureau of Labor Statistics projects an increased demand for social workers of 16% over the coming 3 years, "higher than average" compared to other occupations (Bureau of Labor Statistics, 2019). Comparatively, growth of workers in the health field is expected to be slightly higher at 18%, while for teachers it is 8% (Bureau of Labor Statistics, 2019).

Equally important, it's not like nurses and teachers have been working within sectors unaffected by neoliberal cost cutting. Both of these professions have confronted direct threats to their members' autonomy, wage compensation, and benefits. Health care has changed dramatically because of health-care consolidation that has led to a smaller number of more corporatized entities competing for ever more scarce public dollars (Geyman, 2017). Likewise, the rise of charter schools has contributed to privatized education (Fabricant & Fine, 2012). In short, none of these professions has escaped fundamental challenges to their members' well-being. If such material factors like growth and consolidation/competition within these three fields do not explain the average social worker's relative decline in income and professional standing, what does?

A primary argument advanced for this change is gender based, stating that the percentage of men in other fields has grown relative to social work, thus justifying larger salaries. The gender trend in social work is indeed startling: just 13.3% of present students in MSW programs identify as male as compared to 42.1% of MSW graduates in 1964 (Kramer, 2016). The trends in other professions, however, are not dissimilar. For example, while the number of men in nursing has grown, the percentage over the last 5 years has plateaued at 12% (Egan, 2019). The data for public education reveals that the percentage of women since 1987 has actually increased from 71.4% to 76.1% in 2012 (WIA Report, 2017). Gender issues provide little explanatory power in understanding the relative standing of teaching, nursing, and social work.

Poor salaries are only part of the financial problem. While many agencies do offer both health insurance and standard vacation packages (although nowhere near those of their European counterparts), the pension plans have either been curtailed or are at such a modest rate as to portend future financial struggles for any retired social worker. While most social workers have an aversion to math, it's important to pay attention to what the future holds here. Indeed, all too often, social workers, because they are indeed well-intentioned and focus more on client needs than their own bottom lines, rarely take a hard look at their long-term compensation and its implications for their future well-being. The detailed analysis that follows on a standard social work pension is offered here as a stark reminder that developing financial literacy is not just for clients.

A review of various state offerings, for example, show state's contributions to 401(k) and 403(b) pensions being between 2% and 4% of a person's annual salary. Two percent of $50,000 a year is $1,000! Being generous, let's say 10 years later, the social worker is making $65,000 a year—a fairly accurate expectation given national data (NASW, 2020). Now the contribution has risen to 4%—$2,600 a year. Multiply that number by another 20 years—we're up to $52,000 in pension savings. Add that on to the approximate $15,000 from the previous 10 years—we're up to $67,000. If you then compound that at a generous interest rate of 4% over the next 20 years, that social worker will have about $214,000 in retirement savings. Assuming this person lives another 20 years, that means they will have about $10,000 a year to live on from their pension—before taxes.

Of course, having worked those 30 years, the social worker can also count on Social Security. Assuming the person's salary averaged $60,000 a year over that 30-year span, the social worker can expect their monthly Social Security benefit to be $2,113.30, or $25,359.60 a year—as long as they don't collect it until they're 70. Combining that with the yearly pension, and the social worker now has a pretax income of $35,359.60. Using standard inflation rates of 2%, that means the person's actual purchasing power in 2035 will be slightly below $27,000. In other words, the retired social worker will be living below the level at which they began their social work career. When looked at closely, those golden years don't have much glimmer for social work professionals.

PAUPER VERSUS PROFESSIONAL: WHAT, ME COMPLAIN?

While the previous data on pensions is troubling, I would argue that the actual level of total benefit compensation for social workers is not only worse, but it may be perniciously so. I invite you to review the content at Career Trends, an established and well-regarded website that documents career opportunities, salaries, and benefits for almost every profession in North America, from engineers to plumbers to physicists, through a careful vetting of trade associations, professional groups, academic institutions, unions, and federal labor statistics (see https://careertrend.com).

A quick comparison between nurses and social workers is more than unsettling. Here is the way they frame and then list the benefits for nurses: "As full-time employees, nurses are eligible for a variety of benefits that, when broken down into monetary value, can make a substantial difference in salary. From medical benefits to paid time off, these benefits make an already attractive job even more desirable … They include: Insurance; Vacation; Sick Time; Education; Retirement Plans."[3]

---

3   Another website listed these nurses' benefits: job security, better job opportunities, varying job areas, flexible work schedules, career flexibility, high salary packages, mental satisfaction, traveling assistance (Registered Nurse, 2020). There is no equivalent list for social workers to be found on their web page or anywhere else.

Now notice how they frame social work benefits:

> Whether you work as a clinical social worker and counsel people with problems or as a direct-service social worker that people rely on to find resources to solve their problems, you are in the business of helping. *The rewards are both internal and external* [emphasis added]. You can find meaningful work in a variety of arenas and know that your efforts are appreciated while you earn a decent living. (Ray, 2017)

As for concrete benefits, the list looks a little different.

Pay: Well, that's already been presented, hasn't it?

Fulfillment: "Both clinical and direct-service social workers help people solve challenging problems ... .The career can be fulfilling knowing that you make a real, tangible difference in the lives of children and adults struggling with various issues ... often overwhelming for clients who turn to social workers for guidance and assistance."

Action-Oriented: "Social work differs from other helping professions because you seek tangible results for your clients."

Training (not "education"!): "You can get into the profession with just a four-year degree."

This comparison would be laughable if it didn't hurt so much. Nurses are asked to consider their jobs in terms of material benefits commensurate with their stature. Social workers? Well, their pay is two thirds of nurses, but they get to be fulfilled through their dedicated work, nourished because they advocate for others, and trained—not educated—at least for 4 years. Nurses deserve a generous, concrete wage and benefit package. Social workers deserve what? A pat on the head for their dignified forbearance on behalf of the downtrodden? And, by the way, who exactly are these social workers living well off the *internal benefits* of good works? Extended family members living off the substantial inheritance from Jane Addams's father? Or progeny of Mary Richmond's Park Avenue benefactors? Probably not.

THE CONCLUDING POLEMIC: STOP THE CHURN RATE!

The crisis wrought through neoliberal, anti-state ideology helped foster the rise of nonprofits over the last 40 years in ways that its leadership could not foresee and its frontline workers cannot tolerate. The accepted 30% churn rate of frontline staff at so many nonprofit agencies is a symptom not of worker fragility but of a system whose leadership now assumes that the Faustian bargain of dignified suffering—for themselves and their frontline workers—is worth it given the good work undertaken. Promulgating the Social Darwinist norm that surviving the agency's fiscal instability, diminished working conditions, and rapid turnover is somehow a noble badge of honor has been a fundamental mistake that translates into little that is dignified or worthy of one's staff or one's self.

Social workers at every level of the profession must reflect on the events that led its members, who were paid equal to or better than members of their counterparts in education and nursing 50 years ago, to now be far behind in compensation. Why is it that individual and collective self-interest so common to its sister professions are absent from social workers' vocabulary? What could cause a profession's members to become even more atomized and isolated, seeking succor from their agencies alone? If self-directed, would self-care be seen as the answer to their chronic stress and physical exhaustion?

The answer to these and other questions tied to professional well-being will be found in the next chapter as we examine the actual working conditions of agency life that explain how and why the rise of private practice is so closely correlated with the rise in the nonprofit sector itself.

CHAPTER 4

FIGHT OR FLIGHT

The New and Updated Forced March from Exhausted Professional to Part-Time Clinician

Fragments for Reflection

Pro Bono Service, Self-Sacrifice, and the Search for Options: How Much Is Too Much?

NASW. Value: Service

Ethical Principle: Social workers' primary goal is to help people in need and to address social problems.

"Social workers elevate service to others above self-interest. Social workers draw on their knowledge, values, and skills to help people in need and to address social problems. Social workers are encouraged to volunteer some portion of their professional skills with no expectation of significant financial return (pro bono service)." (NASW Code of Ethics, 2019)

"Social workers average 45.9 hours a week—much higher than the average of 37.2 hours they are contracted for work ... . Fifteen per cent of their time was in face-to-face contact with service users" (Butler, 2012; Munro, 2011).[1]

"A United Way report of social service agency directors found that over 30% did not want staff development training as such training was "a threat to staff retention" (Birdsell & Mazzio, 2003). If an agency provides them the respect and dignity of further development, why would workers want to leave? How could staff training become a threat to the good of an agency? Are they not worth professional development?

---

1   https://www.theguardian.com/social-care-network/2012/sep/25/social-workers-longer-hours-survey

WORKING CONDITIONS AND THE FATIGUED STATE OF THE PROFESSIONAL SOCIAL WORKER

Low salaries alone do not account for the frontline worker's exhausted and increasingly alienated state. People do not go into social work to get rich—of course! At some point, every social work web page, generalist textbook, and training manual mentions this bromide. Such generous self-sacrifice almost always elicits a comforting affirmation from reader or trainee alike, initially secure in the self-knowledge that helping others somehow makes up for much of the difference between their paychecks and those of other professionals.

Acceptance of diminished pay perhaps—just perhaps—might be tolerable if the work met their student aspirations of sustained relationship building, healing, community engagement, and serving as social change agents. Recent BSW and MSW graduates may beg to differ given the level of student debt that they now carry.[2] However, neoliberal austerity is not just about dollars. It's also about the rationing of services in shorter and shorter chunks of time and the narrowing of what passes for service outcomes. If, as the Munro report found, more and more social workers are spending only 15% of their time on direct client contact, what exactly are they doing that makes up for diminished income? Data entry, repetitive phone calling, texting clients back and forth, audits, and staff meetings on regulatory changes rarely appear as primary focal points of social work textbooks, and yet they lie at the broken heart of too many social workers' daily experiences.

It is thus sadly no surprise that a nationwide study commissioned by the British Association of Social Workers and the Social Workers Union in 2017 found that "61% of social work practitioners and managers surveyed were looking to leave their current positions in the next 16 months" (Haynes, 2018). Why the dissatisfaction? "A large workload was cited as the cause of increased stress … (resulting) in 11 hours more work a week" (Haynes, 2018). Eleven hours a week translates to more than 2 hours more a day—such as 9 a.m.–7 p.m., which means arriving home for dinner no earlier than 7:30 p.m. A similar study in Ottawa, Canada, of 1,000 social workers found that "60 per cent reported stress in their work place, with 40% reporting … depression and frequent illness" (Baines et al. 2009). It is important to underscore that there have been few studies of U.S. agencies' working conditions undertaken by social work professional associations or academic institutions.

While the length of the workday was an obvious stressor, other studies reveal equally troubling causes of stress. A detailed study of more than 2,800 New York social workers by Abramovitz and Zelnick—one of the few to address stress related issues—found workers with a variety of other work-related stressors:

---

2   The average master's level student leaves school with a combination of undergraduate and graduate debt of more than $57,000. That means if you're thinking about getting an MSW, given your starting income, your return on investment is going to be negative if you borrow the entire cost of school (Meyer & Financial Finesse, 2018).

"More than 60% of respondents reported they have less professional autonomy related to 1) faster pace of work, 2) the standardization of practice interventions, and 3) the lack control on the job ... over 80% said that they 'have to work too fast'" (Abramovitz & Zelnick, 2018). This includes having to see more people and open cases more frequently, leaving less time for seeing clients and building trust with them. In addition, more than two thirds expressed deep concerns about the "standardization" and "routinization" of their work. Over 60% agreed that they "don't have enough control over their job." As one worker in the report stated, "*I remember when it was possible to sit with my clients and develop a relationship without having to type in the middle of an interview. Now, if I have a client who is in crisis and need to focus on their immediate needs I am left with hours of paperwork and phone calls*" [italics in original] (Abramovitz & Zelnick, 2018).

The authors also found that "many workers also reported significant threats to their well-being and that of their co-workers. Almost 73% experienced their job as stressful 'often/very often.' There also were other, profoundly troubling numbers: 85.8% experienced burnout and 83.1 % had low morale. 68.3 % identified growing routinization of their work, 58.2 % had experienced ethical dilemmas" (Abramovitz & Zelnick, 2018). I'm citing these data in detail for a simple reason: Whether in the United Kingdom or the United States, *too many social workers are miserable.* Too often, data are presented dryly to make important policy and programmatic arguments that do not stress the lived experiences of the workers themselves. Sixty-one percent want to leave the field? And 85.8% feel burned out, while 83.1% have low morale. These are not just troubling findings for the profession: They are devastating because they speak to a quiet, unyielding fatigue, emotionally and physically, at play in the lives of far too many social workers.

While I will address this more thoroughly in Chapter 5, it's important to contextualize what has created such astronomical numbers related to social workers' alienation and defeat. A worker's context begins at entry into the profession at a social work school's doors. Based on their own experiences and beliefs in helping, they arrive hoping to make a difference in the lives of other people. While at school, they are exposed to frameworks of interpretation about the world, models of practice on how to act upon it, and an aspirational code of ethics that espouses core values in action—social justice, dignity and worth of the individual, empowerment. While recent graduates are perhaps a bit unsteady because of a mixture of modest experience and newness to the profession, they then walk toward a new set of doors—the agency that has hired them—hoping that at last they indeed can make a difference in the lives of people who have been marginalized and oppressed. "To make a difference" isn't easy; it requires practice innovation, creativity, cultural humility, and enough autonomy to build and sustain relationships with people who at first understandably may be reluctant to do so. It is the kind of aspiration that is indeed noble—principled, moral, and, yes, self-sacrificing. However, for self-sacrifice to be enriching and not completely exhausting, one must be able to act on those principles with enough consistency that cancels out the added hours—that proverbial "extra mile" has to be worth it, not devalued or ignored.

What the previous data reveal is not just stress and fatigue; it's heartache. When one works under conditions where too much stress is the norm and danger to one's well-being are accepted practices, "social justice" becomes a forgotten value necessarily better left unexamined. There is sadness underscoring the fact that 61% of frontline workers and their supervisors wish to leave the field. The sadness grows when you consider some of the reasons for increased heartache that underlie this desire to escape. For example, just like nurses, doctors, and firefighters, many social workers are first responders. Not that the wider public is aware of this, as the pandemic of 2020 has shown. When firefighters or nurses are so identified, they are rightly honored for their bravery and self-sacrifice. Social workers? Social workers don't even make the list of the most respected professions.[3] Yet look closely at what a first responder in social work does:

- In child welfare, a social worker may be standing in a cold, dark apartment with a highly distraught, often high, parent enraged at her presence while a 2-year-old baby, terrified by the emotional upheaval underway and familiar only with her mother's world, shrieks in terror as the social worker moves ahead with a mandated removal.

- In adult services, a social worker sits with a weeping, disoriented 88-year-old who has wet herself because she can no longer get to her bathroom because of the piles of hoarded papers blocking its entrance. The social worker gently coaxes the old woman, with little success, to prepare for her relocation to a nursing home that she is loath to enter later that day. This intervention takes 5 hours into the evening.

- In homeless services, a social worker is visiting a homeless encampment on the far side of the city park where homeless people have been living for about a year. A recent city ordinance has proposed the encampment's removal, and the worker, having worked with many of the residents over the year, wants to alert them about what may happen. While some of his clients are upset, his fear is directed at two men he does not know who are increasingly angry and hostile at his presence.

The list could go on and on—work with the suicidal teen, the despondent undocumented immigrant, the trans person beaten for a third time and unable to return to their supportive housing. They are all scenarios filled with an intensity of

---

3 "More than four in five Americans (84%) again rate the honesty and ethical standards of nurses as 'very high' or 'high,' earning them the top spot among a diverse list of professions for the 17th consecutive year. Telemarketers joined members of Congress as having a majority of low/very low ratings" (Brenan, 2018).

physical and emotional stress for the worker and client alike. Such experiences are not 10-minute stressors but sustained events of unrelenting pressure that are far beyond the normal range of daily human interaction.

First responders are understood to accept that such events are part of the job. But what is the organizational response to a first responder's event? Firefighters at each fire have an assigned rehab officer who monitors their on-site well-being and is responsible for reporting in writing what steps were taken to protect any identified firefighters who are at risk (Sonoma County Fire Chief's Association, 2010). Police officers are put on paid administrative leave and must see a counselor before they return to work if they have discharged their gun for any reason (Emberlin, 2013). Yes, both firefighters and police officers in these examples may be in great physical danger as they perform their duties. As they report, the intensity of the event—a 3-hour fire or a 3-minute shooting—necessarily requires such post-event attentiveness. But what do social work agencies do for their workers? Twenty-four hours of paid leave post-removal of a weeping child who has been traumatized for years to come? The same paid leave time after the removal of a frightened, disoriented older person from a home they've lived in for 40 years? Half a day after escaping a dangerous homeless encampment?

In the modern world of social work agency life, the answers to such questions are too ludicrous to dwell on, let alone respond to. They *are* ludicrous—as long as one assumes such extreme stress is "normal" and thus acceptable for some people—frontline social workers of the world should shoulder such burdens and get back to work!

Not that the profession's leadership hasn't noticed. Monthly newsletters of NASW chapters, as well as the national office, consistently post actions to overcome burnout, heightened stress, and difficult working conditions through *practitioners' mindful self-care!* For example, the 2018 CSWE's Annual Program Meeting had 18 presentations by academics that focused on self-care, meditation, and self-compassion as a response to the increasing probability of professional burnout.[4]

Self-care, like empowerment, is a wonderful thing—as long as it is placed in context and its purpose is understood. So let's look at self-care *out of context*. What exactly is self-care? "Self-care is an approach to living that incorporates behaviors that refresh you, replenish your personal motivation, and help you grow as a person. Creating time for yourself each day is vital in maintaining energy, concentration, and overall wellness. There are three components of self-care: physical, mental/emotional, and spiritual" (Kim Foundation, 2019). Well, who wouldn't like that as a way to live? Buy the spandex referred to in Chapter 1 and away you go! A mindful life for sure.

---

4   CSWE Annual Program Meeting (2019) https://cswe.org/getattachment/Events-Meetings/2019-APM/2019APM_FinalProgram_WEB72.pdf.aspx

Unfortunately, back in the office or out in that cold apartment or finishing up that paperwork later in the evening gets in the way of sustained self-care. Furthermore, it places the responsibility for relieving workplace stress completely on the workers themselves. As one experienced social worker put it, "Why does the extra work of self-care fall on those of us who are already doing extra work?" Exhausted by those additional uncompensated 15 hours a week? Breathe them away! Stressed out over your suicidal client or your grieving older adult, feeling the managerial pressure of more data entry and a lack of timely payments from the state? Chant for 10 minutes at the start of the workday—for the next 10 years! Just as on the macro level social workers are blamed for the failure to eradicate poverty, on the mezzo level, it's up to individual workers to overcome difficult working conditions through their own personal efforts. As for the micro level, accept the norm of updated Social Darwinism applied to agency life: survival of the fittest through your own effort alone. And if you complain, well, maybe you don't care enough.

IT GETS WORSE: THE UNREQUITED PARTNERSHIP BETWEEN THE PROFESSION'S ETHICAL DEMANDS AND ITS MEMBERS' SELF-SACRIFICE

As you will have noticed by now, the emphasis in this book is on the actual lived experiences of the social worker and not on mounds of data. If the reader wants more evidence on the degradation of social work agency life, there are additional references listed at the end of this chapter about the work itself. This section addresses a different, more puzzling set of questions: *Why has there been so little emphasis on collective self-interest throughout social work? How could a profession that pridefully centers itself as "the social justice profession" so readily ignore "justice" as applied to social workers themselves? Why would the pivotal answer to burnout and worker exhaustion be the nostrum of individual self-care and not self-organization?*

Many of the answers, I will argue, are tied to an unexamined dynamic at play throughout the field. First, the NASW Code of Ethics, unlike that of other professions, is focused exclusively on client well-being, often at the expense of the workers. The case example at the beginning of this chapter underscores this point:

First Ethical Principle: Service. "Social workers elevate service to others above self-interest. Social workers draw on their knowledge, values, and skills to help people in need and to address social problems. Social workers are encouraged to volunteer some portion of their professional skills with no expectation of significant financial return ('pro-bono service')" (NASW Code of Ethics, 2019). Given the diminished pay of most social workers and the reams of data revealing uncompensated overtime work, why would the profession's code espouse even more self-sacrifice?

In fact, most professions don't espouse pro bono work. A review of various codes of ethics makes that clear. Doctors don't. Nurses don't. Teachers don't. Legal services and legal aid lawyers don't. For example, psychologists are "also encouraged to donate some of their time to the betterment of the community." Let's see. That can encompass baking for Parent-Teacher Association bake sales at your neighborhood school, participating in a charity golf tournament, or picking up litter at your community riverbank. As for psychiatrists, "a physician shall recognize a responsibility to participate in activities contributing to the improvement of the community and the betterment of public health" (American Psychiatric Association, n.d.). To wit, volunteering is fine. It's just not defined as pro bono work!

However, you will find one other profession committed to pro bono work: corporate lawyers. The American Bar Association highlights pro bono work: "Our mission is to ensure access to justice through the expansion and enhancement of the delivery of legal and other law-related services to the underserved through volunteer efforts of legal professionals nationwide. We foster the development of pro bono programs and activities by law firms, bar associations, corporate legal departments, law schools, government attorney offices and others" (American Bar Association, 2019).

Of course, the average corporate lawyer makes about $114,000 a year—before bonuses (Glassdoor, 2019). How can it be that a profession whose membership makes just slightly less than *one half* of what lawyers are paid would exact a proportionate financial sacrifice of its members? The ghosts of friendly visitors drawn from the volunteer ranks of the early 20th-century middle class are all too alive and well inside a profession whose 21st-century members are barely scraping by.

An overemphasis on self-sacrifice is only part of social work's outdated code. While aspirational in its focus on client needs, dignity, and worth, the NASW Code of Ethics manages to completely—no overstatement here—ignore any focus on how such ethical principles and standards apply to social workers themselves. For example, when speaking of work in interdisciplinary teams of professionals, "social workers who are members of an interdisciplinary team *should participate in and contribute to decisions that affect the well-being of clients* by drawing on the perspectives, values, and experiences of the social work profession. *Professional and ethical obligations of the interdisciplinary team as a whole and of its individual members should be clearly established*" [emphasis added] (NASW, 2017).

Compare this standard with the American Nurses Association, the most conservative of the nurses' organizations, and how nurses look at their ethical duties "[ANA] advances the nursing profession by establishing high standards. Promoting a safe and ethical work environment, bolstering the health and wellness of nurses, and advocating on health care that affects nurses and the public" (ANA, 2019). Framing their ethical imperative on its members' needs and their well-being as much as the public's is a powerful statement reflecting nurses' sense of self- and collective efficacy. Such efficacy can also be found as they apply their ethical standards to interdisciplinary work: "The complexity of health care services requires collaboration ... . Nurses should provide collaborative planning to provide safe, high quality patient-centered care. *Nurses are responsible for articulating, representing, and preserving the scope of nursing practice, and the unique contributions of nursing to patient care*" [emphasis added] (ANA, 2019). Notice that professional and patient care and well-being are framed as equally deserving.

Furthermore, rather than the passive "standards (of collaboration) should be established"—which can be almost anything, by anybody—nurses are expected to be "representing and preserving" the "unique contributions" of nursing throughout any collaboration. Just as the salary differences between lawyers and social workers are no small matter when exhorting each to *work for free*, framing language as an active participant in one's ethical code is a critical distinction between those who act as their own "subjects of history," capable of acting on their own behalf, as opposed to those who cautiously serve as mere receptacles of others' history (Freire, 2018). Ask yourself this question: How does one promote self-determination for clients and community members (as articulated in the NASW Code of Ethics under "Dignity and Worth of the Person") when not expected to model self-determination for oneself and one's fellow social workers?

To understand how a 21st-century profession could still be articulating 19th-century nostrums of financial sacrifice and passivity toward its membership's well-being, it is important, albeit painful, to address an unspoken yet easily understood reality within our field about almost all of us. *The background stories of social workers are used to reinforce personal hesitancy toward self-interest, discomfort in asserting material needs, and a lack of confidence when confronted with professional difference, competition, and misuses of power directed at them.*

The personal stories of social work's founding mothers, Jane Addams and Mary Richmond, along with that of Ida B. Wells[5], are suggestive of who is drawn to social work: people who for good reason have a powerful sensitivity to the slights, suffering, and hurts that course through the lives of the poor, the marginalized, and the oppressed. All three founding mothers had tragic losses of parents and siblings at an early age: Addams, most of her siblings; Richmond, her parents and her siblings; Wells, her parents and a brother. That such heartbreaking losses occurred during their early formative years and subsequently left them with a predisposition for caring for others will not be a surprise to almost any social worker reading this book.

---

5   Ida B. Wells, an African American journalist and lifetime civil rights activist, while not a social worker, was a good friend of Jane Addams and worked with various settlement houses and community groups in pursuit of the same programs and services for Black Americans as were provided to White poor people.

The modest research on the backgrounds of social workers brings to light equally revealing results. Black and her colleagues found that "social work students reported a high frequency of family trauma in early life that was significantly greater than that of the business students" (Black, et al.,1993). Twenty years later, Thomas had similar findings for social workers, where "results reveal rates of adverse childhood experiences are much higher than those found in a general population sample" (Thomas, 2010).

Let me underscore that this is not leading to an argument that social workers, because of their childhood scars, are living and working as more damaged, less capable human beings than those in business or any other sector of the world. I am arguing that, just like our founding mothers, almost all of us chose this field because of events in our early lives—substance abuse, divorce, domestic violence, loss of a sibling or parent, best friend killed in an accident, incarceration of a parent, learning disabilities, forced immigration, the list is endless—that predisposed the vast majority who do this work to be highly observant about our social environment and more than ready to assist anyone at risk within it. As the literature on coping and defense strategies of adults who experienced trauma as a child make clear, the aforementioned qualities are *healthy forms of adaptation* to what had once been a painful event or events in a person's life[6] (Littleton et al., 2007). *Observant, care-taking behavior directed toward others is admirable—as long as one is not taken advantage of within the systems in which one finds oneself. That is exactly what the social work profession all too often has done to its members:*

- A profession's leadership cannot tell its underpaid workers who struggle with affirming their own value that a good, ethical professional should also work for free.
- An agency's leadership cannot establish a norm that working 10 to 20 extra hours per week is the measure of a good worker and in turn direct their displeasure at those who work what they are contracted for and label them as "not committed." Such norms intensify guilt in people long socialized to first take care of the needs of others before their own.
- It is irresponsible for a profession's leadership to ignore the secondary trauma of their first responders who day-in and day-out handle the personal ravages of poverty—child abuse, elder isolation, domestic violence—which

---

6   I want to flag the growing overuse of the term "trauma," which is all too often applied to every kind of stressful life event: There are traumatized children separated from their parents at the Mexican border who are living in cages and children traumatized by divorce whose parents have joint custody and share childcare. Likewise, there are children traumatized by sexual violence by a predator living in their homes and others traumatized by bullying at a summer camp. We need a more stringent and clear use of how we define and act upon actual trauma as opposed to genuinely stressful and difficult events that may require interventions of a far different kind.

is an integral part of their work week. Seeing the solution to such accumulated trauma through social workers' own self-care is like asking a sailor on a sinking cargo ship to bail with a tin can. One's own effort may be admirable, but it's far more likely that the water will keep rising. Given his past, of course, the sailor is likely to blame himself for not having bailed hard enough. Almost no one in a formal position of authority is likely to tell him otherwise.

Low wages, overwork, secondary trauma—all of these are the preconditions for burnout. While there have been innumerable articles on burnout—almost all of which propose as solutions a mix of self-care away from work and mindfulness while at work (Shresher, 2019)—their failure to address the working conditions themselves and the norms that reinforce such abuse leave workers with little to fall back on other than their own resolve. And resolve they do, combining a remarkable capacity to compartmentalize their own pain, fear, and personal exhaustion with an unwavering commitment to their clients.

A well-seasoned professional's Facebook post beautifully and poignantly captured the daily life of too many social workers:

> I suspect it is hard to be a social worker. We get up early and don't have time to drink coffee over the newspaper. We come home late and are too tired to cook. We work extra because we know there are families/clients who need us. We don't get too excited over a minor crisis because we deal with massive crises all day. We have seen far worse. We don't want to talk when we come home. We have talked all day. We don't want to move when we come home. We have moved all day. It may seem that we have left all our caring, our heart, and our love at work, then come home to you empty. We probably have. But we don't tell you that many times at work we are scared. Scared we are missing something. Scared that we let our clients/families down or leave the children unsafe. Scared to go into homes or heads of unknown people and scared what we might find. We have to deal with angry families, loved ones and victims, and all the while do our best to help them. We don't tell you how the trauma we see and hear about affects us, and how stressed we are for the pain our families/clients are going through. I expect it is hard to love a social worker but know this: Your social worker needs your love. Needs your understanding. Needs to know you 'get it.' Needs to be taken care of. Needs you to do the hardest work you may ever do, which is to love a social worker (Anonymous, 2019).

The painful relationship between early 20th-century codes of normative, voluntarist behavior and the keenly observant, self-effacing and care-taking temperaments of most 21st century social workers has left too many in our profession personally hollowed out rather than collectively determined to better their own lives, as well as their clients. Deference has been created by first imposing an exclusively client-focused Code of Ethics and its backbeat of self-sacrifice working off the quiet elevated heartbeat of people seeking just to help. It is then reinforced through organizational norms of agency Social Darwinism that make "survival of the fittest" a measure of committed endurance rather than a cry of despair.

For the social worker who is all too attuned at quiet adaptation to others' needs, the initial response of self-care means stepping back from other more collective options. This approach puts off the accumulated exhaustion and burnout for another time. Deference to agency Social Darwinist professional norms then continues apace, replenished with new, younger professionals.

PRIVATE PRACTICE AS A MARKET-BASED RESPONSE TO ALIENATED LABOR

However, there has been one other alternative for the exhausted social worker that has been widely embraced throughout the profession: the turn to private practice. As Specht and Courtney (1995) documented more than 25 years ago, social workers have been moving into private practice at a rapid rate greater than found in any other profession (p. 47). Indeed, by 1985, social workers outnumbered psychologists two to one (Goleman, 1985). Twenty-five years later, there are so many social workers in private practice that they account for 60% of all clinical work in the United States (New York State Society of Clinical Social Workers, 2020).

Specht and Courtney (1995) rightly pointed out that much of the reason for this shift was the sheer interest and need for mental health services that grew exponentially from the 1960s onward (p. 6). That there was a growing societal need does not fully explain why so many social workers moved into private practice itself, for the option to do individuated work was ever-present in social work, even in its origins. Specht and Courtney (1995) relate an amusing story of Mary Richmond herself receiving a knock on her door in 1896 from a volunteer who requested her services and at the end of the unexpected session paid Richmond $3 for her clinical efforts pp. 107–108). They document the occasional use of private practice over the next 50 years as well.

While it was a sporadic interest for some social workers, it was not until the late 1960s that the exponential growth in private practice began. At that same moment, nonprofit agencies expanded and with this growth increased oversight and monitoring by the state. As the previous chapter made clear, explosive growth did not mean a better practitioner experience, as state oversight rationed services, shortened worker-client interactions, and expanded data collection on more and more practice outcomes. I would argue that social workers' movement into private practice has been caused as much by the increasingly degraded structure of agency work life over the last 50 years as by the expansion of the mental health market.[7]

Harry Braverman's seminal *Labor and Monopoly Capital*, written more than 40 years ago, and still a primary source for understanding the dynamics of work, deskilling, and managerial centralization, provides a powerful explanation for this argument. He analyzed how capitalism evolved from a skilled crafts, small manufacturing, and mercantilist model of work (think of Paul Revere the silversmith and all the neighborly tradespeople selling their wares) to one of monopoly capital (think of Huawei producing, Amazon selling, but don't even bother thinking of a well-known crafts worker). Braverman focused on how work itself changed over time, more and more removing *the autonomy and creativity from the worker's hands—and mind*. His opening pages capture the contradictory dynamics of not just "labor" but also of changes in social work agency work life over the last 5 decades: "The more I read ... on occupations ... I became aware of a contradiction. ... On the one hand, modern work ... requires even higher levels of education, training, the greater exercise of intelligence and mental effort. ... At the same time, a mounting dissatisfaction with the working conditions of ... office labor seem to contradict this view ... . That work has become subdivided into petty operations that fail to sustain the interest or engage the capacities of humans with current levels of education" (Braverman, 1975, p. 21).

This brilliant insight allowed Braverman to assess work as a labor process dynamically tied to managerial oversight, where the push-pull between worker and manager was primarily focused on two concerns: (1) *the degree of autonomy to conduct one's work* and (2) *the amount of creativity in the ongoing development of that work.* Autonomy and creativity: nothing could be both more fundamental and aspirational about what any professional seeks to do and the way they do it. A professional—nurse, doctor, teacher, social worker—wants the time to assess, engage, and intervene with the client or community member(s) and, through that time together, use the mix of informal and formal skills, experience, practice wisdom, and technical knowledge to creatively respond to the issues at play in their ongoing relationship.

It is this professional autonomy and creative discretion that every new regulation, oversight outcome, process measurement, and ration of time created by every RFP and foundation grant has undermined over the last 50 years in every profession. Where Braverman situates the resultant centralization within a smaller and smaller sector of powerful managers, for social work, it can be found among the

---

7   Specht and Courtney briefly allude to this as well. Courtney identified the issue in 1992 as well (Courtney, 1992). See also Brauner (2015). Bogo (2015) addresses these problems from the perspective of field education and the loss of quality fieldwork assignments.

state and foundation caste of program officers and audit reviewers whose ability to annually or quarterly intimidate and overwhelm agency staff when they arrive at their doors is matched by an equivalent, albeit more circumspect, trek—the flight of agency staff into private practice.

Confronted with working conditions far more degraded than their aspirational expectations when first leaving their professional programs, other professions have opted for a more confrontational approach based on collective self-interest. For example, since 2017 there have been at least five statewide teachers' strikes, as well as city-wide strikes in Los Angeles and Chicago (Rossman, 2018). Nurses struck in four states in 2019 alone (Ortiz, 2019). For social workers, however, the only option seems to be much more individualized and free-market based: private practice.

If one has been socialized to see self-interest as hostile to professional norms, private practice understandably becomes the best option for making a professional middle-class income. Pew Research defines middle income as "those whose annual household income is two thirds to double the national median. For a family of three, that ranges from $42,000 to $126,000 in 2014 dollars" (Pew, 2018) So, assuming we seek a safe median level, that income would be $84,000—an income 50%–75% higher than what the average social worker now makes. Furthermore, such an income would give the worker the autonomy and independence to work as they saw fit, able to diagnose and treat their clients based on their hard-earned professional expertise—the very qualities Braverman saw being whittled away under monopoly capitalism. If social work agencies were to provide an equivalent set of financial and creative options, does anyone doubt that far more staff would seek to stay rather than desire to leave?

But desire to depart they do, and in doing so, those who develop a full-time private practice leave behind their social work commitments to social justice, human rights, and self-determination. A review of three different state clinical social work associations finds the complete removal of any mention of social justice, empowerment, or even the poor. For example, note the loss of social work's stated values in the California Clinical Social Workers Association:

> Strengthening IDENTITY ... When is the last time you called yourself a licensed clinical social worker?
>
> - YOU are part of the largest group of professional mental health clinicians.
> - YOU deliver Bio-Psych-Social Assessment and psychotherapy services and supportive services for children, teens, adults, couples, and families.
> - WE are your voice working to protect the future of the clinical social work profession at the national level.

- None of us can do it alone ... together WE can make a difference.
- LCSWs maintain and enforce ethical professional standards.
- CSWA unites the profession in the delivery of high-quality psychotherapy, counseling, and related services.
- CSWA is working to implement mental health parity within the healthcare delivery system.
- CSWA strives to ensure fairness of pay for all licensed clinical social workers. (CSSW, 2020)

As for NASW, in its national newsletter, there are triple the number of articles and ads connected to licensure than to social workers' rights and working conditions. What was written 25 years ago is still, unfortunately, accurate: "On one page of the national newsletter—usually the first page—they present a picture of social work as concerned about the poor, public services, and the need for social change. The following pages are filled with stories of legislative progress made in winning third-party payments for social workers to do psychotherapy, advertising for social workers to attend conferences (on psychoanalytic issues) ... and economic and legal issues on starting a private practice" (Specht & Courtney, 1995, p. 168).

As Specht and Courtney (1995) presciently identified 25 years ago, entering the world of private practice is to set aside the core values of the field—service to the poor, a commitment to social justice in deed and not just words. That the web pages of each clinical social work association are devoid of social justice–related content is perhaps not surprising when other data reveal that the overwhelming number of fully independent private practitioners are White—about 90%—and that the overwhelming number of clients are not poor (Lord & Judice, 2012). While devoid of social justice content, it is quite striking that these professional groups do not shy away from direct political advocacy on behalf of their members. It's as if freed from the yoke of normative self-sacrifice espoused within the dominant professional associations, these smaller, yet at times more politically astute, groups are wholly comfortable in addressing members' concerns front and center. Of course, unlike teachers and nurses, they do not connect worker interest to client well-being as well. Perhaps NASW and CSWE might take half a page from these clinical associations and connect them to the other half about clients—a professional's self-interest and client concern belong together!

Equally important, the Janus-like duality of espousing work with the poor while a majority of licensed social workers seek to practice with the nonpoor has had an unforeseen outcome: *The further diminishment of the authority of the profession itself as the convergence between word and deed that marks professional integrity is diminished.* Integrity is easily defined in many dictionaries: "The state of being whole and undivided" (Merriam-Webster, n.d.). If page 1 of your newsletter is all about helping the poor and pages 2–4 are figuring out better ways to secure reimbursement from your obviously nonpoor clients, how "whole and undivided" do you think the larger public would view the social work profession?

There is an added strain created by this internal contradiction for most clinical social workers: While the desire to leave agency work may be strong—62% is a large number—most find they cannot do it full time. An NASW Workforce Study published in 2011 found that the private practice–based median income for clinical social workers was $45,000 (NASW, 2011). If one factors in costs for rent, insurance, health care, and social security payments, such an income is inadequate to sustain a middle-income standard of living. The result is private practice becomes a part-time option on top of full-time agency work. Given the degraded working conditions and diminished autonomy that confront one inside the agency, the added work hours, even with their remuneration and autonomy, inevitably fuel further burnout.

Finally, if the *implicit bias* within the profession is all about private practice—unstated but ever present—such bias helps explain why there's so little *explicit focus* on addressing the quality of work life for agency workers. If anything, this detachment from agency workers helps explain the profession's reinforcement of deference and passivity among those who continue to carry out social work's stated mission. After all, if agency staff members don't make waves, the present neoliberal focus on stringent state oversight and diminished worker autonomy, cloaked in a mix of 19th-century moralism and the free-market individualism of private practice, will grow unchecked.

THE CONCLUDING POLEMIC: ENOUGH!

This chapter is filled with the untreated pain and unexamined suffering of the agency social worker. That the stark data on burnout, turnover, and stress are reported with the annual frequency of a New Year's resolution and just as quickly ignored is an indictment of the profession's leadership. The social work profession's drop in public respect and status over the last 50 years is the result of a pronounced absence of integrity between what our field espouses for its clients and what it does for its membership. That years have gone by while agency members grow physically and emotionally exhausted is unconscionable. Its implicit yet all-too-evident commitment to private licensure over worker safety and well-being explains why we are a profession divided against itself.

Our field must rewrite its professional norms so that self-interest is not regarded as selfishness and collective self-interest is seen as a legitimate, powerful way forward for the good of its members and not a threat. To do otherwise is to allow neoliberal ideology to continue its domination over the poor and those who serve them—thus both deserving less. One cannot decry income inequality and ignore the harsh working conditions and underpayment of its workforce. One cannot stand for social justice and disregard that exhausted worker living with secondary trauma by simply "thanking them for their service" and recommending self-care as a cure-all. As the BLM movement pushes for a reallocation of services from the police to other professions, social work's opportunity to embrace this historic change requires new ways of reimagining itself as well—with worker autonomy and respect alongside that of their clients and community members.

Finally, professional integrity is compromised when the difference between stated aspirations of public service and the concrete emphasis on private practice is as profound as it now is throughout the profession. It is not simply that the pages of every professional newsletter, whether national or statewide, use three times as much print on licensure, insurance, and marketing. Over time, such implied yet ever-growing emphasis creates an unstated cultural focus within the gateways to the profession—the schools of social work that are expected to train them. That far too many students attend social work programs with the unstated yet obvious desire to obtain their license for private practice seems self-evident by now. Whether schools of social work seek to alter that trend or not will be the focus of the next chapter.

CHAPTER 5

THE EVIDENCE IS IN

Expedited Core Competencies and the Fast
Track to Diminished Social Work Education

Fragments for Reflection

The Bureau of Labor Statistics listed the following as skills of the average professional social worker:

- Identify people and communities in need of help
- Assess clients' needs, situations, strengths, and support networks to determine their goals
- Help clients adjust to changes and challenges in their lives, such as illness, divorce, or unemployment
- Research, refer, and advocate for community resources, such as food stamps, childcare, and health care to assist and improve a client's well-being
- Respond to crisis situations, such as child abuse and mental health emergencies
- Follow up with clients to ensure that their situations have improved

From the Susan Dworkin University of California School of Social Work Web Page:

> If you already hold a Bachelor of Social Work (BSW) degree, you may be eligible to earn a Master of Social Work (MSW) degree in just 12 months through the MSW@USC Advanced Standing program. With the same leadership focus as the traditional MSW curriculum, the Advanced Standing curriculum enables you to bypass the first-year foundational requirements and start classes at the second-year level. As an advanced standing student, you will: (*) Earn your MSW full time in three semesters or part time in

five semesters … (*). Complete 37 credits that will prepare you to pursue professional licensure."

"Higher education calls for higher order thinking on the part of the student. Whether engaged in propositional thought or in professional action, students should be enabled to develop the capacity to keep an eye on themselves, and to engage in critical dialogue with themselves in all they think and do … . It is a reflexive process in which the student interrogates her/his thoughts or actions. The learning outcome to be desired, for every student, is that of the reflective practitioner." (Barnett, 1997, p. 198)

TALK IS CHEAP. EXCELLENCE ISN'T.

The primary mission of the social work profession is to enhance human well-being and help meet basic and complex needs of all people, with a particular focus on those who are vulnerable, oppressed, and living in poverty. If you're looking for a career with meaning, action, diversity, satisfaction, and a variety of options, consider social work. (NASW, 2020)

Well, okay then! Meeting "basic and complex needs of all people," especially the "vulnerable and oppressed"; that's a worthy and righteous challenge. Combine it with "meaning, action, and diversity," as well as "a variety of options" (whatever that means), and one is committing to a profession where the quest to achieve such aspirations should be as demanding as it eventually will be satisfying. Such challenges carry with them the implicit expectation that the educational rigor required to meet them will be exacting as well. For that to happen, it's necessary to take a momentary step back and review what exactly higher education is meant to provide to an emerging professional committed to such demanding work. After all, the definition of a profession is as straightforward as it is exacting. Merriam-Webster defines a profession as "a calling requiring specialized knowledge and often long and intensive academic preparation" (Merriam-Webster, n.d.). The Oxford Dictionary is equally clear: "A type of job that needs special training or skill, especially one that needs a high level of education" (Oxford Dictionary, n.d.).

While social work has never attempted to equate itself with the medical training and was long ago labeled along with nurses and teachers as a "semi-profession" by sociologists (Etzioni, 1970), there is significant value in aspiring to pedagogical excellence for those who seek to work with the poor, marginalized, and oppressed. The frenetic pace of today's world need not diminish what is required for "higher learning" to be just that—*higher, not in the sense of distancing elitism but in the notion of offering something of distinctive value*. NASW'S introductory statement on its web page makes that clear:

> Social work is different from other professions, because we focus both on the person and their environment. Social workers deal with the external factors that impact a person's situation and outlook … . We help guide people to critical resources and counsel them on life-changing decisions. (NASW, 2020)

It is hardly elitist if one aspires to work effectively with the poor and marginalized on *both* "external factors that impact a person's situation and outlook" and "counseling them on life-changing situations." Developing skills that both can assess a turbulent external environment while also maintaining the internal capacity to counsel people on *life-changing situations* are higher order tasks for sure. It is thus important to recount what educational theorists wrote about the underlying purpose to higher education: "Higher education calls for higher order thinking on the part of the student. Whether engaged in propositional thought or in professional action, students should be enabled to develop the capacity to keep an eye on themselves, and to engage in critical dialogue with themselves in *all* they think and do … it is a reflexive process in which the student interrogates her/his thoughts or actions. The learning outcome to be desired, for *every* student, is that of the reflective practitioner" (Barnett, 1997, p. 198).

Ahhh, *reflective practice*. Doesn't every foundational text on social work detail that capacity to think critically on the world, one's perceptions of it, and to mediate between them both for sound assessment and action? Doesn't every social work text get around to addressing the topic? "The ability to think critically would appear to be a defining feature of competent social work practice" (Hagan, 2004). As Gambrill (2014) also noted, "Clients may be harmed more than hurt by the decisions we make if we do not think critically" (p. 4). Likewise, Kirst-Ashman and Hull (2018) noted, "Critical thinking is essential because … CSWE accreditation standards requite critical thinking (or critical evaluation) to make informed, ethical decisions and judgments in practice and behavior on (*no less than seven core competencies-SB*)—EPAs 1, 2, 4, 5, 7, 8, 9."

As critical thinking is fundamental to developing a reflective practitioner, we can't escape how demanding such a pedagogical task that will be. Donald Schon, perhaps the most noted writer on the pedagogy required for a professional's reflective skill sets, identified the challenges a teacher faces if a student were to develop the *sine qua non* of professional practice: *critical thinking*. Those challenges are "(1) finding time to reflect; (2) (the) fear of surfacing unmanageable complexity; (3) infinite regression of reflection over action; and (4) the apparent incompatibility of reflection with action" (Schon, 1992). Such challenges are what make teaching as exciting as it is exacting. Overcoming these challenges will not occur through checking off simple "competency" markers or noting what behaviors are to be mastered. Such an educational process of inquiry will mix reflection, new knowledge, and growing self-awareness that makes learning an end in itself. (We will return to each of these challenges throughout this and the next chapter.)

Both Barnett's and Schon's writings serve as aspirational opportunities and a riveting challenge to social work faculty, students, and professionals alike who seek to claim "professionalism." As John Dewey likewise stressed to those preparing students for "investigative learning" as opposed to "externally imposed requirements,"

> The alternative to furnishing ready-made subject matter and listening to the accuracy with which it is reproduced[1] is not quiescence, but participation, sharing in an activity. In such shared activity the teacher is the learner, and the learner is, without knowing it, the teacher. (Dewey, 1916, p. 160)

These theorists thus imagine a classroom environment where the ease of give-and-take is matched by the paradoxically *willing discomfort of teacher and student alike* to encounter each other through unresolved dilemmas and ambiguous problems that foster ongoing *reflection on action* in the classroom that lays the basis for future *reflection in action* outside it (Schon, 1992). (for an exhaustive and engaging analysis of reflective learning in higher education, including facilitation tools and practice guides, see Brockbank and McGill [1998]). As such, these authors therefore provide standards for learning, including the struggle to maintain them, that can guide any academic program seeking to develop critically thinking students to become lifelong learners, adept at the always-shifting, ever-changing dynamics of 21st-century practice.

What exactly is "critical reflection"? Before turning to whether today's sped-up classrooms have the structural capacity to develop such a dynamic learning environment, we still need a clear definition of what "critical reflection" or "critical thinking" means—and why it seems to matter so much in social work. There have been numerous works that have deepened our understanding of critical thinking that affect classroom learning for practitioners (Ennis, 1962; Facione, 2011a, 2011b; Fisher, 2001; Freire, 2018; Halpern, 2003; Nisbett, 1993; Schon, 1992; Sternberg, Roediger, & Halpern, 2006).

While the works range from the philosophical to the cognitive psychological, our interests here are centered on what critical thinking "looks like" and why it matters

---

1 Paulo Freire developed these ideas with his emphasis on critiquing the "banking system of education" and replacing that with education through dialogue and "problem-posing" (Freire, 2005).

in the practice of social work as a distinctive profession working with the poor and oppressed. Using the previous authors' words as a guide for the 21st-century practitioner and professor, there are three important domains of critical practice:

1. *Being able to analyze and interpret data, evidence, and facts as they present themselves,* whether results from a recent research study on child-rearing stressors for homeless families or the actual conditions in a neighborhood to which a homeless family has been relocated;

2. *Having the capacity to evaluate and interpret actions and events for both their manifest and latent content,* including possible unstated psychological conditions and defenses in individuals and groups, as well as, on the macro level, underlying trends in community and political behavior (ranging from voting to support for various initiatives and programs that may or may not be controversial in a neighborhood, such as new supportive housing, drug programs, or community policing programs); and

3. *Using the practitioner's own internal capacity for self-awareness and self-reg-ulation, with an emphasis on both awareness of causes for personal discomfort and attention to possibly unintended dynamics of social power and privilege that may or may not be at play* in various practitioner-client, worker-community, and staff-to-staff relationships.[2]

All three domains are important to sustained, effective professional practice. Aligning with the classic works of Bateson (1972) and Schon (1992), they closely correspond to *what one can concretely know* (the world as it manifestly presents itself), *what one doesn't know* (how we interpret actions and behaviors as those "facts" and actions present themselves, even in clouded or uncomfortable ways), and *what one doesn't know that one doesn't know* (how one's own positionality and social identity may or may not be interpreted by other actors in the setting in which practice is taking place).

Within the 21st-century classroom, the content of each of these three domains is increasingly more demanding. As Brockbank and McGill (1998) explained, the first domain is "factual, a consequence of the transmission of knowledge and information ... often drawing on 'expert' sources and received wisdom/knowledge" (p. 41). Such factual information is, of course, foundational to any learning environment: A good practitioner needs to know the stages of human development; identify the difference between stress, coping, and adaptation; understand explicit and implicit bias; know a community's resources and forms of social capital; and comprehend

---

2   Facione's excellent synopsis of a study by 46 experts on critical thinking distills six key skills: (1) interpretation, (2) analysis, (3) inference, (4) evaluation, (5) explanation, and (6) self-regulation. With the exception of "explanation," or the ability to explain one's reasoning and thinking to others, his work guides the aforementioned analysis (Facione, 2011b).

how the economy of a city or state is affecting the types of jobs available for unemployed community members.

The second domain begins helping the student assemble those facts or knowledge in differing contexts, "encourage[ing] multiplicity, subjectivity, and the realization that a variety of other sources may impact how one interprets those 'facts.'" A crying child in a doctor's office may have a cold, thus causing no real alarm; the same child crying in a school hallway or playground may mean something very different and require a more engaged professional response. This domain requires the student as a potential practitioner to assemble and reassemble facts with attention to subjectivity—how people feel and react in varying contexts—that facts alone cannot ascertain.

Finally, in the third domain, the student is awakened to the process of how facts are assembled and interpreted by and with others, including their very presence in that assemblage. Subjectivity expands to include not only different forms of interpretation but also how power is constructed and reconstructed in that relationship. Furthermore, as Facione explained, within this final domain is a further cognitive skill: *self-regulation.*

> Maybe the most remarkable cognitive skill of all is ... self-regulation. This one is remarkable because it allows strong critical thinkers to improve their own thinking ... what self-regulation does is look back at all the dimensions of critical thinking and double check itself ... . You can monitor and correct an interpretation you offered. (Facione, 2015, p. 7)

This capacity for self-review carries with it the willingness to subject both facts and interpretations as well as one's own process of inquiry to a rigorous review for possible shifts in actual facts, breakdowns in context, misinterpretations of actions, and, of course, one's own fallibility with all of these. This seems to be exactly what is underway within White America as it realizes the depth and breadth of systemic racism directed at Black Americans and other people of color. For example, the murder of George Floyd, which took place for 8 minutes and 46 seconds on stunning video seen around the world, awakened Whites to an awareness that the way they are treated by the police and how Black Americans are treated is vastly different, biased, and historically long-standing. They didn't know what they didn't know about how pernicious and systemic such policing practices and that Whiteness was given greater value until after they witnessed this racial horror. To take a very different example, social work professors relying exclusively on the old psychoanalytic paradigm of transference-countertransference dynamics alone would be equally out of date and not in the know in today's fast-paced, cognitive-behavioral world.[3] In 2020, the discomfort of self-regulation over what was once unseen or long out of date seems an existential quality of these modern times.[4]

Furthermore, exemplars of self-regulation are not easily taught from textbooks or case studies alone. Indeed, Schon, Facione, and others make clear that the primary way self-regulation can be "taught" requires the professor to model their own struggle with such changes—including the shifting power changes within the classroom that occur over the years (Facione, 2011). The young, untenured faculty member close to the age of their students has a very different set of power dynamics to negotiate than when that same faculty member is older and tenured 15 years later. One classroom dynamic is neither better nor worse than the other; the younger teacher may be closer to students and understand their motivations and interests more easily, but their authority is more open to challenge from them; the experienced faculty may not understand them as well but receives fewer unnecessary challenges to her expertise. In either case, the key teachable moments available are through the ensuing struggles for each professor: one to remain engaged but not be disrespected and the other to better engage but not be overly deferred to. Thus the necessity of ongoing reflection on action is ever present and changing one year to the next—and one classroom from another—if the capacity for critical reflection is to emerge and be sustained within students and teachers alike.

As Facione goes on to explain, the importance of self-regulation, therefore, cannot be underestimated within the classroom itself. Self-regulation carries with it the humbling insight for professor and student alike that self-monitoring is the key to avoiding what he named the *dominance structure* in human thought—the replication of hierarchies of thought and the implicit baggage of misused power and unearned privilege that all too often substitute for classroom wisdom and inevitable student deference that stands to be replicated in their own practice with clients.

In short, developing critical thinking through the classroom is a demanding and humbling experience that can only happen over time.[5] Facts, arguing over interpre-

---

3   Cognitive behavioral therapy itself is becoming outdated as well, as a variety of apps are being developed to monitor physiological responses and individual stress so that the smartwatch on your wrist serves as your clinical guide, not an actual clinician.

4   Perhaps one of the most frightening aspects of today's public discourse is the espousal of "fake news" as a rejoinder to any facts, scientific or otherwise, that do not conform to one's worldview. Such loss of even elementary assessment and evaluation lays the basis for the spread of authoritarianism and White supremacy, which operates through power alone, not facts or democratic institutional norms and logic.

5   As learning theorists Schon and Argylis likewise argued, such experiences are fraught with learning demands that require student and teacher alike to examine assumptions, contexts, and actions so that a "dominance structure of certitude is not overly imposed on the actual variability any professional experiences in her or his work" (Schon & Argylis, 1978). Such a classroom environment requires an exploration of ambiguity and inevitable discomfort for teacher

tations, acknowledging one's struggle to avoid unintended domination without sacrificing one's beliefs—no wonder higher education is "higher"—not "better than" but demanding exertion, internal effort, and growth.

STEP RIGHT UP! MASTER'S LEVEL SKILLS IN 12 MONTHS! FROM THE COMFORT OF YOUR OWN HOME!

Can today's academic settings provide the space for such learning?[6] If Schon and others are right, developing reflective practice will require time that allows for multilayered inquiry, not only of the facts and the interpretation of those facts but also of the interpreters themselves. What does the actual 21st-century classroom look like for students and faculty? Are our social work classrooms promoting this multilayered, reflective approach to learning?

The trends aren't just discouraging; if you believe professional education must provide a foundation on which to build critical thinking skills, they're deplorable. The rapid expansion of so many accelerated programs, such as at University of Southern California's School of Social Work have occurred at the unfortunate, historic juncture of exploding costs, a diminished cadre of trained academicians, and the substitution of mechanistic "competency" criteria for standards of accountability. These factors combine to seemingly legitimate the acceptability for accelerated social work programs—while instead further diminishing the standing of the profession itself. (And all of this occurred *before* the pandemic and the need for remote learning exploded.) Dedicated social workers truly do amazing work that most of the world never knows about. The Bureau of Labor Statistics' relatively narrow list of six skill sets noted in this chapter's introduction is hardly exhaustive. Among many things, the list ignores socially charged content tied to oppression and marginalization and doesn't distinguish the number of fields of practice where social workers labor—child welfare, mental health, education, community services, domestic violence, etc. That said, it suggests enough to let anyone interested in the field to realize that social *work* is *complex, demanding, and challenging*:

---

and student. As Schon and Argylis suggested, "There are areas (*in teaching practice—author*) where the meanings of publicly observable performance remain stubbornly ambiguous—when the content of a student's learning is in question ... or when learning bonds occur. There are (classroom) cases where a coach helped students by eliciting from them a description of their difficulties and confusions, *acknowledging his own uncertainties, or describing his picture of the changing experience of the practicum* (the classroom itself)" (Schon, 1987, p. 301; [emphasis added]—author).

6   Many writers on reflective practice further argue that such dialogical learning "in and of itself is neither necessarily empowering nor transformational in nature if not positioned to challenge large social, cultural, and political relations and practices that exploit some and privilege others" (Ashwin et al., 2015; McLaren & Guttierrez, 1998).

- **Complex.** "Assessing a client's needs and strengths" isn't easy, as Gambrill also noted (Gambrill, 2014) —a battered woman crying at the shelter has an obvious need, but locating her strengths in ways that can help her persevere when so vulnerable won't happen through a checklist.
- **Demanding.** "Helping clients adjust to change" means getting that isolated older person to consider moving from the only home they've known for 60 years. That won't happen through a one-time visit and a follow-up phone call.
- **Challenging.** "Responding to crises" when considering removing a child from their home is emotionally wrenching, requires social and cultural awareness to distinguish poverty from abuse, conflict mediation skills, and an acute sensitivity to differences between mental illness, addiction, and trauma. It's not a skill set one gets at the ready in 2 years, let alone 12 or 16 months.

Today's social work educators and leaders cannot have it both ways here. One cannot argue that such noble work, if it is as complex, demanding, and challenging as it is—and it is!—should result in speeding up one's professional education to begin practicing such work. While there are modest exceptions, lawyers still have a 3-year program. Doctors, the seeming pinnacle of professional status, still require 4 years of medical school and between 3 and 7 years of internship *before* licensing— just as their profession required 50 years ago.

Would you sign up for surgery with a doctor having any less preparation before operating on you? Could you tolerate an urgent care's nurse practitioner with a year of school and a couple of terms of internship instead of the 4 or more years now required, even for their hybrid (online/in-person) programs? What exactly is "professional" about a 12- or 16-month degree and who is creating professionally accountable field placements? Given the explosive size of so many online programs, schools are not relying on their trained field department staff but farming out agency selections to for-profit companies, such as 2U. How can there be professional social work competencies applied to fieldwork when the fieldwork agencies are selected by corporations operating from a business model?

As the previous section on pedagogy makes clear, the implicit connotation of "professional" is a person with a mix of substantive knowledge, self-awareness, reflection on action (in classrooms, in supervision), and reflection in action (the actual professional work). That heady, demanding mix of reflection, personal awareness, and application of skill elevate a professional-client encounter into something beyond a rote or mechanistic set of techniques. The argument that a faster program can ensure a foundation to the development of such refined skill sets and reflective practice frameworks is more than suspect. It's outrageous. Higher education shrinks in size accordingly—while its tower was never ivory, it shouldn't be a fast-track tunnel to mediocrity either.

THE CRUMBLING IVORY TOWER

While first mentioned in "The Song of Solomon" as an image of purity, "the ivory tower," by the late 19th-century, had morphed into its present-day usage for academia, used mostly by conservative pundits as a serene place for unrealistic, perhaps dreamy, scholars not able to work comfortably within or relate to the rough and tumble of the "real world" (Quinion, 2007). It's a handy, binary trope to sling around any academic issue: "ivory tower" versus "real world," the romantic against the pragmatic, the politically correct rather than the politically astute, the ethereal pitted against the concrete, and the soft as opposed to the hard. It is never a term of approbation; when mentioned, it suggests at the very least the singular incapacity to understand and work with life as it actually is lived. Implicitly, of course, it has the whiff of privilege and the sanctimonious air of the otherwise disengaged. Such assumed distance from the give-and-take of real-life experience also means that reflection, if it exists, is an end in itself: *reflection without action.*

A closer look at almost any academic institution today reveals a very different set of images: For most, the ivory is at best stained, if not chipped away. Comparing the turn of the 20th century to the 21st, Bok (2012) wrote,

> In 1899–1900, according to the National Center for Education Statistics, there were 23,868 faculty in degree-granting institutions. In 1999–2000 there were 1,027,830. Likewise, students increased from 237,592 to 14,791,224 in the same period—a factor of almost 63 times, whereas the population rose slightly more than 3.5 times. The university is a hub institution of our time, touching the lives of almost every American, reaching them as students or through any of its other spokes.

Perhaps paradoxically, tuition, rather than keeping pace with the democratizing trend of enrollment, has exploded in alarming ways. The average cost of tuition and fees at a private, nonprofit, 4-year university this school year was $31,231—up sharply from $1,832 in 1971–1972 (*in current dollars*). At public, 4-year schools, tuition and fees cost about $9,139 this year. In the 1971 school year, they added up to less than $500 in *current dollars*, according to the College Board. The rate of increase since 1978 is so large as to seem satirically inflated: 1,120%. That's not a misprint: *one thousand, one hundred and twenty percent.* It makes the 601% increase in medical expenses almost meager in comparison (Jamrisko & Kolet, 2012). The result, of course, has been both a loss of greater public subsidy and an enormous increase in student debt.

As Fabricant and Brier (2016) documented, over the last 20 years, public support for higher education has diminished greatly. "The real dollar value of per capita student funding that states provided to public colleges and universities declined 2.3 percent between 1990 and 2010. The US inflation rate over that twenty-one-year period averaged 2.7 percent per year, totaling more than 56 percent over the course of those two decades" (Fabricant & Brier, 2016). In short, with increases in tuition, diminished grants, and other state subsidies came increases in both student debt and the need for students to work part or full time.

Today's Tired and Financially Stressed Student

The average graduate of a baccalaureate college in 2016 carried $29,000 in debt. That alone was troubling, but racial and class issues intensified the problem. As Fabricant and Brier (2016) explained, the racial and class issues at play in higher education intensify the financial inequality—and the ensuing pressure for many students of color while on campus. "The Pew Research Center report indicating that the bottom 25 percent of the population ... accumulated 58 percent of the total amount of student debt. Alternatively, the top 25 percent ... accumulated only 6 percent of the total debt" (Fabricant & Brier, 2016).

With debt growing and tuition inching higher each term, poor and middle-income students also have had to work more and more outside those ivory walls as well. The proportion of full-time students who are employed has increased from 34% in 1970 to 50% in 2000 (Cauthen, 2009). Just as important, in 1970, only about 15% of students worked more than 20 hours per week, the standard definition of part-time employment. More than 30 years later, that number had doubled (Fabricant & Brier, 2016). (There are multiple reasons that explain the explosion in tuition that can be found in Fabricant and Brier's [2016] seminal *Austerity Blues: Fighting for the Soul of Higher Education*. As we are focused on the effect of such changes on the classroom environment, such structural and political causes are not detailed here. I refer you to their work.)

This combination of increased tuition costs, rising student debt, the necessity of full- or more than part-time work cascade together in ways that negatively affect more and more students even before they enter a classroom.[7] Another jagged piece of ivory appears between the haves and have-nots: the added physical, emotional, and cognitive toll wrought by the stress of overwork and financial hardship. Tired from toiling away at a full workweek, recognizing that family resources do not include financial support once graduating, and nervous that future increases in

---

7 ProPublica, a policy think tank, noted in a recent report that "from 1996 through 2012 public colleges and universities gave a declining portion of grants—as measured by both the number of grants and dollar amounts—to students in the lowest quartile of family income. That trend continued even though the recession hit those in the lowest income brackets the hardest" (Fabricant & Brier, 2016).

tuition will lengthen their stay in college, *a student's learning capacity to analyze, interpret, and reflect is, therefore, compromised before the class begins*. Neuroscientists explain why:

> Stress hormones produced during worrisome times can shape the developing circuitry of the brain. They influence the neural connections in the prefrontal cortex … that house our executive functions, include[ing] our working memory, self-regulation and cognitive flexibility … (these functions) are critical for reasoning, planning and problem solving, and for regulating emotions and attention. They are essential to academic success. (Blair, 2010)

Through no fault of the student, they thus arrive in the classroom hoping to learn but physiologically depleted and thus underprepared for the deep dive of analysis, interpretation, stimulation, and ambiguity that sustained critical reflection requires. As we shall see later, their exhausted predisposition for shortcuts neatly dovetails with the push toward compressed academic programs emphasizing speed, work/life credits, and technically measured, competency-based outcomes. But before turning to that subject, let's look at the other side of the classroom aisle: the professor.

The Anxious, Tenure-Track Professor

As noted both in the United States and Europe (Curtis & Thornton, 2013; Fabricant & Brier, 2016), the most significant trends in higher education over the last 30 years have been an expansion of enrollment, an expectation of grants writing as a funding source for the university, and increasing budgetary deficits that destabilize the learning environment. While a vast majority see teaching as a primary part of their job, the study found that faculty "get little support in improving how they teach and spend less time in class than in the past" (Barrett, 2012). The ensuing stress that faculty identified was caused by the mismatch between their own expectations for quality teaching and the institution's increasing demands for research and administrative duties that interfered with quality time inside and outside of the classroom (Barrett, 2012). Whether an assistant professor anxious about the tenure clock or the tenured associate professor demoralized by continuing administrative duties (Wilson, 2012), their ability to focus on the demands of reflective learning is being squeezed by academic settings more focused on the financial bottom line than academic quality.

The Exhausted Nontenure Track Professor

Of course, compared to contingent faculty, tenure-track academics have it relatively easy. Thus, while college costs have risen exponentially, the other exponential growth in higher education has not been in academic salaries or the promotion of more and more full professors but in part-time faculty. "Between 1975–76 and 2011 the rate of growth for part-time instructors was 221.7 percent as contrasted with an increase of only 23.4 percent in full-time faculty during that same period" (Curtis, 2014, p. 21). Fabricant and Brier (2016) quote from a Congressional Budget Report of 2014, "[The report] 'The Just-in-Time Professor' notes that 'more than one million people are now working as contingent faculty and instructors at US institutions of higher education, providing a cheap labor source even while students' tuition has skyrocketed'" (p. 149).

As with other sectors of contingent labor in North America, the work is not only part time: It is poorly paid. "The Coalition on the Academic Workforce recently estimated that the median pay for a standard three-credit course is $2,700" (House Committee on Education, 2014). The House report found that "a large number of respondents [to the Congressional survey on contingent faculty] reported making between $15,000 and $20,000 per year, at or mostly below the federal poverty line for a family of three" (Fabricant & Brier, 2016, p. 159).

For many social work programs, some of this problem is mitigated because many full-time social work practitioners seek both the needed added income and the stimulation of the classroom by teaching an additional course or two. However, such academic work comes on top of their full-time jobs. Their preparation may be well intentioned but cannot match what Schon and others demonstrated is needed for the development of critical thinking. Equally important, colleges provide little space for these part-timers. As many receive notice only weeks before their class begins, preparation is all too often minimal and rushed. As a *New York Times* editorial observed, "This practice in turn erodes instructors' abilities to properly prepare their courses ... it is linked to a lack of support, financial or otherwise, to invest in developing a syllabus or course notes" (Lewis, 2013). Equally important, the *New York Times* reported,

> The lack of compensation for holding office hours for students ... also affect(s) the quality of instruction. Although contingent workers often carve some time out of the classroom for student meetings, they are hard-pressed to sustain such contact because of their own pressing financial and time obligations. (Lewis, 2014)

In other words, the exhausted, anxious student walks into a classroom with better than a 50% chance that they will meet their counterpart in fatigue, worry, and stress. Elite universities are well aware of what they offer instead of part timers. Under its marketing materials, Harvard University makes its point of view clear with its subheadings [italics added]: *"Do You Like Being Taught by Full-Time Teachers? Then You're Picking the Right School:* Harvard University's utilization of full-time teaching staff is ranked among the highest in the nation, with 87.0% of instructors employed full time ... . *Not Many Adjunct Teachers Here:* At Harvard University, only 13.0% of the teaching staff are part-time non-faculty or non-tenure-track faculty. This use of adjuncts is far below the national average of 48.5%, which could be indicative of Harvard University's commitment to building a strong, long-term instructional team." Why is such a commitment to "a strong, long-term instructional team" marketed as extraordinary? Meanwhile, if lucky enough to get full timers, over the years most students at non-elite schools (where most social work students will be found) will be less attentive to the classroom as well. The classroom, therefore, has hardly become a more robust arena for contemplative study filled with ambiguity, discomfort, and eventual growth.

Of course, given the enormous effort by teachers and full-time working students alike, classroom learning can still stimulate analysis and interpretation of new ideas and challenging issues. Such stimulating learning, however, will cry out for follow-up. For today's student, such follow-up, complete with after-class discussion and quiet reflection, is relegated to at best an occasional moment and at worst a distraction from life's seemingly larger worries. Better to spend your time figuring out the quickest route to your after-school job or, if you're the teacher, how to get back to your grant proposal or next administrative meeting. For so many inside today's classrooms, the brain's "executive functions" required for critical thought may be sought after, but too much fatigue, stress, and worry on the way to and from the classroom will have gotten in the way. Academic inequality takes on a new dimension beyond the financial: the inequitable advantage some are provided simply to find the time to think straight.[8]

THE EROSION OF ACADEMIC EXCELLENCE: INFLATED PROMISES AND THE WASTEFUL ENERGY OF DOGS CHASING THEIR OWN TAILS

It is thus no accident that the corresponding drop in classroom preparation and academic readiness for reflective learning is tied to the dramatic shift in higher education toward metrics that focus on the timeliness of completion and outcome measurements of technical knowledge over rigorous analytical skills. Today's higher education environment devolves around the student burdened with debt

---

8   There is no cutting corners inside or outside the classroom either. At elite institutions, which see themselves charged with preparing the next generation of a nation's leaders, developing critical thinking skills is the primary objective. See Tara Westover's *Educated* for a riveting account of her education at Cambridge University, where her professor grilled her on the meaning behind not only her ideas but also her choices of a sentence's punctuation (Westover, 2018)!

and overworked outside the classroom alongside the stressed professor confronting either underpay or nonteaching demands for labor outside the classroom. It thus is a context ripened to shrink academic programs by focusing on knowledge-based learning that speeds up graduation rates (Fabricant & Brier, 2016). Twelve-month and 16-month *exclusive* online social work programs, therefore, become conveyor belts of convenience, not corridors of academic excellence.

Not that such programs don't sound appealing. For example, USC's 12-month online program for BSW students offers three sequential courses connected to practice: "Assessing Wellness to Improve Recovery in Integrated Care," "Social Work Practice in Integrated Care Settings," and "Advanced Practice with Complex Social Work Cases," as well as two terms of fieldwork through "Integrative Learning for Advanced Social Work Practice" (established by those corporate folks over at 2U; USC, 2020). Sounds pretty impressive, right?

Unfortunately, recent research *sympathetic to online teaching* does highlight an important caveat to effective online learning programs. As Xi and Xi's exhaustive national report in 2019 concluded, "While some students may benefit substantially from a well-organized online course with high levels of peer interactions and student-faculty interactions, maintaining these high-level interactions requires instructors to devote a substantial amount of time throughout the courses" (Xi and Xi, 2019). Thus the first challenge Schon posed in developing "reflective practice" skills is undermined by the simple reality that such *expansive use of time* required for effective online learning no longer exists for the vast majority of students or faculty.

Other findings also sympathetic to online learning further document the limits in developing effective professional practice. As McKurtry (2016) summarized her findings on effective online teaching, "Two key themes emerged in the findings: human connection and organized structure. Exemplary online instructors seek to connect with students so students know and feel the care, support, and respect of the instructor. Exemplary online instructors also maintain a clearly structured environment that is logically organized, delivered in small chunks, and sufficiently repetitive to keep each student focused on the content." The first corresponds to Xi and Xi's work—"care, support, and respect" are indeed necessary—and consume the kind of time faculty don't have anymore. As for "logical organization, small chunks and constant repetition," this is indeed important—as long as such learning rules out ambiguity, discomfort, and self-monitoring—the other qualities Schon emphasized in developing reflective practitioners.

Just to be clear, the social work students these programs will turn out will have expanded their debt load while nevertheless getting a job with a "social worker" title. They will be hired primarily to handle mostly "externally imposed requirements" that John Dewey opposed rather than "investigative learning." This means filling out forms, responding to legal regulations, and data collection—the very work highlighted in Chapter 2 that later drives so many people from the field. Such mechanistic practice does have one advantage. It more easily justifies lower salaries.

However brief and mechanistic the academic work may be, these truncated online programs, nevertheless, are careful to tout their credentials: each makes certain to exclaim that they are certified by the CSWE. Professional accreditation through demonstrated use of core competencies throughout school curricula, including fieldwork, is a grueling process that schools undertake every 7 years, resulting in thousands of pages of materials and the inevitable exhaustion of every program director, associate dean, dean, and other staff as they await their final evaluation. What's of interest here is not the accreditation process itself but whether those touted core competencies actually measure what they purport to and, if not, what damage such poor measurement does to the legitimacy of the profession itself.

In 2008, CSWE made the educationally sound decision that school programs needed to demonstrate not only what the content and structure of their curricula entailed but also what the learning outcomes were. As CSWE wrote at the time of their latest revision in 2015, "A competency-based approach refers to identifying and assessing what students demonstrate in practice. In social work this approach involves assessing students' ability to demonstrate the competencies identified in the educational policy" (CSWE, 2020).

What's important here is this process of "identifying and assessing what students demonstrate in practice ... students' abilities to demonstrate the competencies ... in the educational policy" (the EPAs). Those EPAs are (1) demonstrate ethical and professional behavior; (2) engage diversity and difference in practice; (3) advance human rights and social, economic, and environmental justice; (4) engage in practice-informed research and research-informed practice; (5) engage in policy practice; (6) engage with individuals, families, groups, organizations, and communities; (7) assess with individuals, families, groups, organizations, and communities; (8) intervene with individuals, families, groups, organizations, and communities; (9) evaluate with individuals, families, groups, organizations, and communities (CSWE, 2020).

This is an impressive list—one that I'm sure all of us hope to have accomplished to a modest degree by the end of our first decade in the field! Temporarily leaving aside the enormous breadth of these expected competencies, CSWE also ties these EPAs to evidence; that is, the competencies themselves are evidenced-based. While there has been an epistemological debate long underway throughout all of social science as to what exactly constitutes evidence (Schorr, 2019), for more than 30 years, Eileen Gambrill has been the leader in assessing whether actually reliable and tested evidence informs and guides social work practice (Gambrill, 2014; Thyer & Pignotti, 2015). After decades of research, her point of view is clear: "We must keep in mind the gravity of problems that confront many social work clients, often related to environmental circumstances ... as well as the uncertainty that may surround what is effective. Helping takes place within an interpersonal encounter with all the complexities of such an encounter. Most social work interventions have not been tested … [w]ithout the values, skills and knowledge needed to handle the inequities and uncertainties involved in helping people, professionals are likely to fall for pseudoscience or quackery. There is pressure to offer something … . In the absence of needed material resources and knowledge regarding a well-tested theory and related empirical data … social workers [in order to] reduce uncertainty and helplessness, they may seize on the latest pseudoscientific … intervention" (Gambrill, 2014, p. xi). She goes on to conclude, "Thus, the very reasons that encourage people to become social workers, a desire to help and to decrease inequities, may encourage use of dubious methods"[9] (Gambrill, 2015, p. xi).

But wait! Perhaps CSWE and others have developed a way to overcome both the pressures and uncertainty, as well as the need for the rigor that Gambrill, Schorr, and others state is the foundation for reliably tested evidence. Look at the elevated language the council asserts in how it expects programs to develop their assessment process:

> Assessment is an integral component of competency-based education. Assessment involves the systematic gathering of data about student performance of Social Work Competencies at both the generalist and specialized levels of practice. Competence is perceived as holistic, involving both performance and the knowledge, values, critical thinking, affective reactions, and exercise of judgment that inform performance.

---

9   Leading social scientists underscore the limits of what passes for "evidence-based research." Lisbeth Schorr, a leading analyst on the subject wrote, "For example, The latest winner of the Nobel Prize in, Economics, Princeton's Angus Deaton, argues that because 'a particular government intervention worked is no guarantee that it will work again, or in another context.'" Evaluation guru Thomas Schwandt also urged caution in how we approach documenting effectiveness. In the 2015 book, *Credible Evidence in Evaluation and Applied Research* (Donaldson, Christie & Mark), he wrote, "The field of evaluation seems captivated by discussions of methods needed to produce evidence of impact … [distracting] us from carefully attending to a variety of important issues related to evaluative evidence and its use." From a philanthropic perspective, Vivian Tseng, vice president of the WT Grant Foundation, wrote, "A narrow focus on evidence-based programs encourages people to run after silver bullet solutions that are not necessarily aligned with the myriad other interventions that they are running." Schorr concluded, "There seemed to be considerable agreement that a narrow focus on trying to identify which *programs* 'work' is actually keeping us from getting better results and that the social sector's program-centric focus has been based on several erroneous assumptions … . No one questions the importance of evidence. But it is time for all of us to think more expansively about evidence as we strive to understand the world of today and to improve the world of tomorrow … . As Don Berwick, wrote, 'the world we live in is a world of true complexity, strong social influences, tight dependence on local context—a world of uncertain predictions, a world less of proof than of navigation, less of final conclusions than of continual learning'" (Schorr, 2019).

Assessment therefore must be multi- dimensional and integrated to capture the demonstration of the competencies and the quality of internal processing informing the performance of the competencies ... . Programs assess students' demonstration of the Social Work Competencies through the use of multi-dimensional assessment methods (CSWE, 2020).

So what exactly does occur here to capture this "holistic, multi-dimensional involving both performance and the knowledge, values, critical thinking and affective reactions"? It's here where the emperor's clothes begin to fall out of the closet. First, CSWE simply requires faculty from each course to choose two professional competencies (such as demonstrating ethical behavior or assessing individuals, families, groups, organizations, and communities). The faculty then must highlight concrete exemplars within the class that demonstrate the competency (e.g., a paper on ethical dilemmas in one's practice). As Gambrill makes clear, such a measurement cannot be of the students' actual practice but of their capacity to do a paper—at best an indirect, heuristic measure of a student's ability, confined to by the classroom, their writing skills, and the comfort of engagement between themselves and their laptop. There is no actual evidence of competent practice at all.

From here, the review process goes from Gambrill's and Thyer and Pignotti's "pseudoscientific" to preposterous. At the end of each academic term, in accordance with CSWE accreditation mandates, faculty must rank each of their students on their degree of competency—from "not competent" to "highly competent—the student is fully able to perform the practice behavior with a wide range of client types and situations without any direction needed." Who is kidding whom here? It takes *years* to be competent at this kind of demanding practice, let alone with a "wide range of clients." Unfortunately, this all gets more outrageous. To remain in good academic standing, *programs must rate themselves* so that 80% of all students are "competent" or better in their classes. Faculty have a pseudo-Solomon-esque task—tell the reliable truth about students' competence (as measured by the classroom cocoon of written papers and cagey role plays) and risk a program being out of compliance or check off high competency scores and live with the guilt that you haven't measured anything of value. Since there's no one to contradict your evaluation anyway, hopefully, the guilt will diminish over time. That you may feel like a tired dog with its tail between its legs is just something to get used to.

As bad as all of that is for legitimating a student's competency and a profession's standing, let's circle back to those 12- and 16-month exclusive online programs being taught primarily by either adjuncts or very junior faculty. How will they address these evaluative criteria? Pressed to focus on the course's primary competencies, as constrained by time pressures as ever, and expected to provide learning through manageable chunks of information, overstretched faculty members meet their overstressed students with an obvious mandate: emphasize the mechanics of competency through abstract measures of "classroom" performance that reinforce quick chunks of knowledge. Schools will get their needed measures, students their grades, and faculty members their required workload. But deep learning that prepares new professionals with the capacity to assess, reflect, self-regulate, and critically analyze their work and the needs and strengths of their clients won't happen. Perhaps they someday will, but it won't be because of their academic preparation. Both their professional legitimacy and that of the profession itself can expect to suffer accordingly—as it has.

The contagion effect for traditional 2-year programs is obvious. As another expert of higher education analyzed, more universities are emphasizing "institutional outputs ... (so that they) define their success ... in terms that they have been sustained as an institution ... (such outputs) may have very little to do with deep learning. More of the assessment becomes transactional ... where the proof of success increases an emphasis on easily measured indicators" (Campbell, 2016). C. G. Schneider, a scholar of higher education and 2015 president of the Association of American Colleges and Universities noted, "It seems to me that the completion engine has hurtled down the track with a lot of states putting in financial rewards and penalties for speeding up completion and cracking down on excess credits. Then there's the quality engine, still struggling to get out of the shed" (Fabricant & Brier, 2016, p. 149). All of the stressors affecting the learning process of online education detailed earlier affect classroom learning in traditional programs as well.

Whether faculty members committed to preparing students with a foundation for reflective practice and lifelong learning will remain viable across their schools and programs depends on their willingness to confront its leadership, on campus and nationally, with the profound and inequitable limits underway in how academia is shortchanging both its students and those who teach them. For that to happen, academics will have to demonstrate a commitment to collective self-interest and mutual support for such a campaign. We'll return to the feasibility of such a campaign in the last chapter.

THE CONCLUDING POLEMIC: THE DIMINISHED CAPACITY TO THINK DEEPLY AND THE EROSION OF PROFESSIONAL LEGITIMACY

As this chapter makes clear, a set of economic and social conditions has expanded the numbers inside higher education while diminishing the overall quality of that educational experience. Outside of the elite 5% of colleges and universities, which are still comprised primarily of children of the upper middle class, college has become more costly for the overworked student and more stressful for the teacher. The academy now focuses on the speed of completion for the student and the heightened expectation that academics will devote more of their energy to grants and administrative responsibilities wrought by outside stakeholders' compliance demands tied to funding and accreditation. Except in elite institutions out of reach for the vast majority of students, the context of 21st-century academia is replete with unreliable, pseudoscientific outcomes, rewards for speed, and measures of complacent, reductionist behavior. "Critical thinking" and "reflective practice" have all the operational heft of the remainders at an antiquated bookstore.

Such a context has bred reactive thinking among students who seek defined answers, quick learning, and a desire for descriptive measures rather than analytical reasoning. Through no fault of their own, when they show up in a senior year BSW or MSW practice classroom, their unease wrought by case studies filled with ambiguity, discomfort, and open-ended curiosity is going to be palpable. They probably won't be alone.

There is, unfortunately, one final glint-filled lining in this discouraging scenario that, as you are about to incredulously learn, is less silver than lead. If you are a good test taker in a traditional program and live in the right state (e.g., going to school in New York while taking the exam in New Jersey 4 or 5 months before graduation), *you can take your licensing exam to be a licensed master social worker (LMSW)—a seeming pinnacle of professional achievement—and pass it* **before** *the last term of your academic program!* The explicit and implicit messages here are as damning as they are obvious: Many programs' last-term courses include research, advanced practice, advanced material on human behavior, and a capstone course. Given this slipshod bridge to licensure (those who pass do have to wait until they graduate to receive their actual license through the mail), either the licensing exam is too easy and not based on what schools offer, or the social work academic programs' content doesn't much matter. Such disregard for one's own professional academic integrity may make it easier to keep passing debt-laden students through their programs and into the social work field, but make no mistake what the cost has been and who will bear it. The exhaustion, disillusionment, and financial strains that await too many caring social workers discussed in the earlier chapters of this book are the carriers of this disingenuous slide into academic and professional mediocrity. It turns out that talk isn't cheap after all.

CHAPTER 6

FROM CULTURAL COMPETECY TO FIGHTING SYSTEMIC RACISM IN 500 NOT-SO-EASY STEPS

Fragments for Reflection

From the CSWE after the death of George Floyd:

"Social workers are called to address racism and all forms of social injustice. The education provided by more than 800 accredited programs is meant to prepare students to act on this ethical principle. Therefore, we must take this moment to honestly examine how social work curriculums go beyond teaching an appreciation for physical or cultural diversity and empower the next generation of social work practitioners to dismantle institutional racism." (CSWE, 2020)

"A historic and defining feature of social work is the profession's focus on individual well-being in a social context and the well-being of society. Fundamental to social work is attention to the environmental forces that create, contribute to, and address problems in living ... . Social workers promote social justice and social change with and on behalf of clients .... Social workers are sensitive to cultural and ethnic diversity and strive to end discrimination, oppression, poverty, and other forms of social injustice." (NASW, 2020)

CSWE Competency 2: Engage Diversity and Difference in Practice

Social workers understand how diversity and difference characterize and shape the human experience and are critical to the formation of identity. The dimensions of diversity are understood as the intersectionality of multiple factors including but not limited to age, class, color, culture, disability and ability, ethnicity, gender, gender identity and expression, immigration status, marital status, political ideology, race, religion/spirituality, sex, sexual orientation, and tribal sovereign status. Social workers understand that, as a consequence of difference, a person's life experiences may include oppression, poverty, marginalization, and alienation as well as privilege, power, and acclaim. Social workers also understand the forms and mechanisms of oppression and discrimination and recognize the extent to which a culture's structures and values, including social, economic, political, and cultural exclusions, may oppress, marginalize, alienate, or create privilege and power. Social workers:

- apply and communicate understanding of the importance of diversity and difference in shaping life experiences in practice at the micro, mezzo, and macro levels;
- present themselves as learners and engage clients and constituencies as experts of their own experiences; and
- apply self-awareness and self-regulation to manage the influence of personal biases and values in working with diverse clients and constituencies (CSWE & CSWE Commission on Education, 2015).

AND:

- Competency-based education is an outcomes-oriented approach to curriculum design. The goal of the outcomes approach is to ensure that students are able to demonstrate the integration and application of the competencies in practice (CSWE & CSWE Commission on Education, 2015).

AND YET:

- "The complexities of race, gender, and sexuality make the examination of cross cultural issues in supervision a rare topic" (Hall & Spencer, 2019).
- "Social work faculty have become increasingly conscious about how to teach in today's social work classrooms without committing microaggressions or triggering racial trauma … . Students and faculty are disengaging from transformative learning, decolonization and healing in the classroom" (Edwards & Lerner, 2019).

"TWO STEPS FORWARD, ONE STEP BACK," DONE OFTEN ENOUGH, CAN MAKE YOU DIZZY

On paper, no other profession other than social work should be better prepared to address through word and deed the systemic racism again revealed through the death of George Floyd. As the previous section of the preamble to the NASW Code of Ethics rightly describes, there's a lot of history of social workers' engagement in fighting for social justice, embracing diversity, and working to end discrimination against a variety of marginalized groups. Founding mother Jane Addams started Hull House in the slums of Chicago purposely to serve immigrants who were otherwise mostly ignored by traditional charity organizations. In the 1930s, Russell Sage Research director Mary van Kleeck and voluntary social service activist Jacob Fisher and case worker for the Seamen's Union Bertha Reynolds were well-known for joining the fight for the rights of the working class. By the 1960s, Black social workers Whitney Young and Dorothy Height were fearless in their push against racist practices both within the social work field and elsewhere in the North and South. (Height also championed the rights of women). Barbara Lee (now a member of Congress) had been a social worker before entering the fight against AIDS as well as homophobia, as did well-known activists Dennis Levy, Joyce Hunter, and countless other social workers throughout the 1980s.

Indeed, a careful review of NASW's premiere journal *Social Work* over the last 40 years would suggest that by 2008, there had been an explosion of articles related to activism, analysis, and program innovation tied to our profession's fight for social justice and against oppression of any and all marginalized groups, especially related to that most unsettling of social topics: race, racism, and White supremacy. Looking at articles published in a 3-month period (volume 3 of each decade1978–2018), the journal had one article in 1978, two in 1988 (along with some lively editorial observations on race and culture by the African American editor at the time, Dr. June Hopps), followed by four in 1998, and then *bam!*—a seeming avalanche in 2008. Consider this sampling from April 2008 alone:

- "A Social Worker's Reflections on Power, Privilege, and Oppression," by Michael C. Spencer
- "Has Social Work Met Its Commitment to Native Hawaiians and Other Pacific Islanders? A Review of the Periodic Literature," by Noreen Mokuau, Jessica Garlock-Tuiali'I, and Pamala Lee
- "Race, Resistance, and Restructuring: Emerging Skills in the New Social Services" by Donna Baines
- And this list is leaving aside such implicitly and explicitly intersectional articles on demographic trends in an increasingly female profession and sex trafficking in the United States! (And, lest we forget, Barack Obama hadn't even begun to run for the presidency when these articles were first written.)

Such depth and breadth gave concrete meaning to the profession's aspiration to be the "social justice" profession. Curiously, however, by 2018—only a few years after the well-publicized deaths of dozens of African Americans at the hands of the police, the birth of BLM and the upsurge in activism to end the prison pipeline for African American and Latinx young men—the uptick in numbers had not simply decreased but moved downward rapidly. All of volume 3, 2018 had one article on Trayvon Martin and racial profiling and an ethnic-racial socialization scale connected to Latinos, and that was about it—save one at the end of the year: "Is Social Work *Still* Racist: A Content of Recent Literature" by Nicole Corley and Stephen Young in which the authors reviewed 1,690 articles published in four mainstream social work journals between 2005 and 2015 and found that only 123 met established criteria for inclusion. It's enough to make your heart ache. After so much progress, how could this have happened?

Corley and Young's (2018) point was not that these journals should publish articles only on racial matters but that less than 8%, for a profession locating social justice at its core, seemed more than paltry. Likewise, their further content analysis revealed that the few works published primarily focused on micro-interventions with little replicability to larger social issues affecting the communities that social work purports to serve. One has to ask, what causes a profession to move ahead on these vital issues of race only to fall back into either seeming indifference (avoiding the subject of race altogether) or abstraction (submerging racist dynamics under a gloss of broader, seemingly neutral terms—groups less integrated, populations still needing expanded services, etc.)? How could the good work that the profession could champion seemingly be ignored just as it arrived at the mountaintop? What does such history augur for our future focus on systemic racism within our own field?

Equally perplexing, how could it be that even with the championing of diversity, human rights, and dignity of the individual over decades, there would continue to be annual topics at our national conferences year after year such as those cited in the beginning "fragments" of this chapter? Are faculties fearful of teaching about race and supervision failing to address cultural issues on race? Indeed, there were 11 presentations at the 2019 CSWE Annual Program Meeting on racially charged classroom and supervisory issues (implicit bias, teaching while Black, addressing White fragility, etc.) *on one day alone* (Friday, October 25, 2020). That a profession could be embracing such social justice aspirations while remaining so fraught about the very topics "social justice" seeks to address could be described as a puzzle, but it's not. When you look at our more recent history and some of the substantive theoretical and practice-based accomplishments buried within it, it's a mark of shame. Such history must be addressed if the BLM demand for attending to systemic racism in all American institutions is to move past the window dressing of proclamations of heartfelt, paper-thin support.

A BRIEF LOOK AT RECENT SOCIAL WORK PRACTICE HISTORY AND WHAT MIGHT HAVE BEEN, PART I

Name a recent social work writer whose work advanced the field's reputation for innovative, sustained practice models. Dennis Saleebey comes to mind for his work on strengths-based social work. Others have impressive fragments related to singular populations or issues. These and many others are substantive additions to a segment of the profession and the people with whom you work.

As Bernice Simon (herself one of the last nationally known writers on practice) wrote, theories of practice, if they are to work, "link knowledge about an identified problem and its context with knowledge about an intervention with a conceptual format that is oriented toward action and rooted in previous research" (Simon, 1994). That's quite a conceptual and operational mouthful—a social worker is involved in *understanding a problem in context* (not just a "problem"), *using knowledge with a conceptual format* (practice that's grounded in ideas and concepts), and *designing action in the present without ignoring research* on which to build that action.

Now, name a recent, nationally recognized social work writer whose work advanced the field's reputation for innovative, sustained practice models. Besides Saleebey (2007), others have impressive elements: Lawrence Shulman's and Ruth Middleman's work on groups (Middleman & Woods, 1990; Shulman, 2015); Jack Rothman on models of community organizing (Rothman, 2007). Other examples include Jama Shelton on LGBTQ issues inside and outside the classroom, Michael Sherraden on community assets, Ellen Baxter and Kim Hopper on rediscovering homelessness, and Susan Schechter on the battered women's movement (Baxter & Hopper, 1981; Schechter, 1982; Shelton, 2019; Sherraden, & Gilbert, 2007). A quick check of the most-used theories in social work and others come to mind: Erickson in human development, systems theory from Parsons and Bateson, and adapted first in social work by Pincus and Minihan and others (Pincus & Minihan, 1973). Is it really possible that with so many accomplished thinkers, writers, and skilled practitioners that our field has lacked equivalent theoretical heft of all-encompassing practice models? Did it all really come to an end with the likes of Grace Coyle, Bertha Reynolds, Gordon Hamilton, and Helen Harris Perlman? All were significant contributors to social work practice who maintain their influence today—and whose most important works were completed before 1960.

Actually, it turns out we have had such practice theorists whose work is easily resonant with today's socially charged world. The groundbreaking work of one of these authors appeared in the mid-1970s. There is thus a slightly personal reason why I chose 1978 as the starting point for the previous review of *Social Work*. That was the first year I attended the CSWE's national conference to present on efforts to organize laid-off city workers reeling from the newly identified "city crisis." It was an exciting moment, as it is for anyone attending their first national conference. While the primary theme of the day has been long forgotten, at the time, it was wonderful to know and meet other like-minded people who were working on responses to the fiscal crisis and the attack on social services. Equally important was the buzz in the air about topics on race, with a special emphasis on something that sounded exciting and interesting: "Black empowerment," which had been developed by an African American professor, Barbara Bryant Solomon (Solomon, 1977). As I attended various workshops, it seemed she had combined social science theories on racial segregation, social psychology on self-esteem, her own practice on working with poor African Americans in need of services, and enough research where there had been breakthroughs on how a social worker could work more effectively with people who otherwise might be estranged from social service encounters.

As one reviewer at the time noted, Solomon's breakthrough began "within the social work paradigm (by defining) 'empowerment' as a process whereby the social worker or other helping professional engages in a set of activities with the client aimed at reducing the powerlessness stemming from the experiences of discrimination because the client belongs to a stigmatized collective" (Lucas, 1978). Notice where the emphasis is within the work: *a process using activities "aimed at reducing powerlessness."* By itself, this could be no different than any practice model from the color-blind 1950s, again locating the use of *power primarily within the worker.* But Solomon was careful to not fall into the privileged trap of locating power solely within the practitioner. Grounded in the most recent social science literature, she went on to write, "[This model] provides an opportunity for the client to step out of the supplicant role of one who seeks service into the more favored position of helper ... . The broader the conceptualization of the client as helper can be interpreted, the greater the probability the clients will be able to perform multiple roles" (Solomon, 1977, p. 354).

Her breakthrough was clear: Social workers had to know—and thus learn from—the poor Black people themselves before attempting any active intervention. Responding to the basic knowledge that White practitioners needed at the time, she also placed special emphasis on the variety of African Americans within the Black community, thus necessitating (for White social workers) a developing awareness of the complex humanity of the people with whom they were working (e.g., the mix of social classes within the Black community). If you reflect on this for a moment—especially if you now seek to address systemic racism in our and other fields—such awareness would had to have been hard won: A White practitioner would have to note their own biases or ingrained ignorance, stumble awkwardly toward new information and personal insight, and begin to craft a new, more "partnered" approach to their practice. Solomon had developed a practice model that met all of Simon's earlier requirements for rich practice theory—plus one. The "design of a conceptual format" for practice intervention wasn't going to simply be an intellectual process—it was going to be an emotionally humbling one as well.

Because her work was grounded in research, as well as the hard-earned wisdom of years of practice, Solomon provided uplifting examples of how such work could and did unfold without prolonging guilt and the ensuing immobility such guilt intensifies. For example, Solomon, in positively describing a practitioner's ability to see beyond her own story in school, successfully worked with a young Black high school junior whose home life was filled with upheaval through a recent transfer. Having gone from a mostly Black high school to her new, integrated, predominantly White school, the teenager was depressed, perceiving her new high school peers as actively discriminating against her. While the social worker believed her recent move, heightened stress, and real loss of a former peer group were more at play than active discrimination, she accepted the girl's interpretation, believing these other issues would surface over time (Solomon, 1977, pp. 303–306). By respectfully accepting the girl's perspective as a starting point, the social worker relinquished power in the assessment phase of the relationship, which soon paid the dividend of a young person much more engaged in her own treatment plan.

For many young social workers at the time, her theory of practice centered on "the nonracist practitioner" and the potential power of the clients to help themselves. This Black empowerment approach provided an avenue of exploration and renewed possibility for socially charged interventions resonant of earlier, more radical times, such as the 1930': clients as partners, a liberating recognition of racial and ethnic differences that placed everyone at the service table, a chance to work *with* communities and not just *for* them.

And then a not-so-funny thing happened as the years went by. A book that had appeared on so many academics' bookshelves and course syllabi began to disappear, if not from the shelves but definitely within classrooms. By the early 1980s, the term "Black empowerment" had been whitewashed (literally) into "empowerment"—as more a nostrum for personal self-care and intellectual enlightenment than a socially charged practice redefining worker-client relationships. Need to empower yourself? Join that local health club! Feeling uninformed? There's a book club for you! With the elevation of "empowerment" across American culture came the erasure of "Black empowerment" within social work. The loss of a single word, just one syllable long, and the socially charged practice of the profession, while not disappearing, by the mid-1980s, it no longer seemed to matter much. (Not coincidentally, the late 1970s and early 1980s saw an upsurge in clinical social work associations and more and more social workers entering private practice.)

While widespread use of Solomon's important work had dissipated, there were still numerous practitioners and academics influenced by her work, using her insights on powerlessness, the diversity within the Black community, and the possibility of creating a more dynamic relationship between client and worker to inform these progressive social workers' own research and theoretical interests. These efforts, seemingly piecemeal and disparate, continued at national conferences, workshops, and symposia often led by the growing number of Black and Brown faculty sprinkled across schools and universities. While their numbers remained small at most schools and received little national attention, their collective activity (often supported by an equally small but distinct group of White radical academics whose politics had been shaped by 1960s activism) grew throughout the

1980s. It is within this numerically modest yet deeply committed milieu that the next extraordinary contribution to practice theory emerged, Elaine Pinderhughes's *Understanding Race, Ethnicity and Power: The Key to Efficacy on Clinical Practice* (1989). Pinderhughes, an African American social worker practicing since the 1940s whose clinical brilliance and personal resilience in the face of institutional, interpersonal, and (as she wrote) daily "insanity" of racism (2004) had elevated her to clinical director of a large counseling agency by the 1960s.

As the director charged with not only clinical supervisory responsibilities but also personnel issues, Pinderhughes quickly noticed the variable ways that her White and Black staff responded not only to similar clients but also to each other. Rather than either avoiding the social tensions or dictating rigid clinical protocols, she spent years in the painful, often personally lacerating, task of bringing together her multiracial staff to confront and overcome their divisions. Think about this for a minute as you go about your present-day work combating systemic racism: *years* of team meeting after team meeting, filled with racial tension, tears, anger, and frustration, and yet Pinderhughes was skillful and tenacious enough to lean in rather than run from such emotionally draining work—work clearly not in her job description but undoubtedly central to her core values and personal identity.

Such Herculean effort paid powerful dividends for her developing practice model as her insights on both staff development and clinical effectiveness merged into a singular contribution for our field. First, it became clear to her that working on racial issues required a facilitator who could handle the tensions that emerged rather than smooth them over. As she later wrote regarding these classroom discussions, "[My] knowledge gained at the inner-city child guidance clinic ... helped keep before me the necessity of creating a safe-enough environment for students to engage in some useful, substantive discussion of their differing perceptions and experiences. Of course, I sometimes failed but I became unalterably convinced that while conflict can interfere with learning, it also can become an effective tool for growth when people feel safe enough to speak honestly and are required to do so with respect" (Pinderhughes, 2004).

Make no mistake, Pinderhughes's inherent modesty cannot disguise the demanding skill set required to forge and sustain these necessary conversations: differences will be in the room, both of perception (how people interpret their world) and experience (how people have actually lived in that world, with often markedly different degrees of privileged ease and access in that world). Such social differences, allowed into the open at last, will cause *tension*, a nice-enough word that in actuality translates to acknowledging hurt, upset, tears, and anger that a facilitator, whether professor, director, or consultant, cannot shy away from. Finally, at the same time one is handling participants' visible upset, one is also fostering a required level of respect among them—a seemingly paradoxical stance for facilitator and participant alike.

How did Pinderhughes do this? As she admitted, she "sometimes failed." Nevertheless, her humble modesty was constructed alongside her indefatigable efforts *over years* to work within these tensions rather than put them aside. Her ability to surface obvious and not-so-obvious differences, reflect on their meaning, handle the inevitable upset, and still expect and require mutual respect throughout this work was obviously hard earned. Of course, such capacities could seem impossible for others to emulate, thus dooming such efforts from entering the larger mainstream. Perhaps Pinderhughes and Solomon could do this kind of work but not you or me! Better to remain safely ensconced within the warmer confines of one's specialization than enter this hornet's nest.

It is here where Pinderhughes's clinical and pedagogical brilliance came together in ways that can allow any dedicated social worker, whether academic or professional, to emulate her work. While never ignoring the centrality of race in so many of these discussions, she came to understand that underlying so much of the variability in people's insights and capacities to work with charged topics, such as race, gender, and sexuality, was the dynamic of *power*. As she explained, power is always being constructed in new contexts and thus has varying effects on people and their own interpretation on how to act on their world. As she wrote,

> It was soon becoming clear how power and powerlessness were significant not only in terms of racial dynamics, but in any situation where a power differential exists such as in roles and behavior related to ethnic group status, class status, sexual identity, and sexual orientation. Therefore, in what was clearly emerging as a model for diversity training [*and as she wrote elsewhere, teaching—SB*] the focus expanded to include experiences related to class identity, sexual identity, or other experiences related to identity and connectedness where power had been significant. The constellation of feelings and perceptions that people identified in relation to these experiences became known as one's 'power gestalt' (Pinderhughes, 2004).

Meeting Simon's expectations for practice theory building, Pinderhughes's work thus allowed every classroom student or professional trainee access to their first experience with difference without fear of judgment based on an implicit hierarchy of greater oppression being more noble (often called the "Oppression Olympics"). As she explained, the social psychological experience of recognizing difference—whether on race or hair color or gender or physical size—depended in part on a young person's reaction to it *and* significant adults' later interpretation of that difference—was it "good"—and thus cause for comfort and easy adaptation to difference, or "bad"—and thus a likely source of discomfort and anxiety. Her research found that most people's initial experiences were negative, leading to an inevitable socialization *to unconsciously fear difference itself.* Building on Berger and Luckmann's (1967) work on the social construction of reality, she found a way to make sense of professionals' discomfort with working with different social groups without too easily casting blame: If difference itself, replicated throughout one's life, creates unconscious anxiety, then when "difference" walks into the room, discomfort tags along beside it. The professional relationship is thus compromised even before it begins.

However, Pinderhughes had suffered far too much racism in her personal and professional life to let Whites—or anyone else—off the socially constructed hook. Her work made clear that this initial insight also served the purpose to free people to examine how those on the receiving end of difference's discomfort in schools, agencies, and on the street therefore confronted conditions far more painfully than those who experienced it either rarely or not at all. Replicating negative difference throughout one's life leads to a power differential of unearned privilege for some, unearned suffering and marginalization for others. It is this unfair power differential that she challenged everyone with whom she worked to recognize, confront, and change—a challenge again being magnified in 2020 and beyond by BLM activists in 2020.

The easiest way for a straight, White person to understand this is to reflect on what happens when an all-White, cisgendered group suddenly has a person of color or an openly nonbinary queer person enter the group. The overwhelming reaction is that then and only then do group members recognize that the group has been monochromatic all along. The ensuing discomfort creates a power differential within the group that has automatically privileged everyone except the new arrival. After all, when "difference" is a problem, as W.E.B. Dubois wrote almost 125 years ago (Du Bois, 1897), even an unconscious one, that "problem" resides in the very presence of the person of color or openly queer individual. When replicated inside organizations, the person of privilege is more easily promoted not because of merit but because they keep the executive board room comfortable for everyone. The seemingly minor experience of initial difference, when cloven to the dynamic of race, institutionally and culturally replicates White supremacy and its four horsemen of objectification, marginality, discrimination, and violence—too often by people who believe they are committed to social justice.

Pinderhughes's brilliant work helped social work professionals understand that power, privilege, and positionality could also change and shift through the day for many as one's role changed—more power with a client, less with a supervisor, perhaps ambiguous with peers in a work group. Ever the astute clinician, she saw this variability as opportunity for reflection and action over time, providing those safe enough spaces for a person to shift their "power gestalt" from one of fragments and hierarchy to a more fluid and liberating one capable of freeing worker and client alike to more fully engage in the work at hand. Such fluidity still had room for mistakes similar to her own but mistakes to grow not hide from. By situating her theoretical insights of power dynamics within the worker as much as the client, her practice model was designed to free both actors to acknowledge difference, expect discomfort, and get on with the work at hand. What enormous possibilities her work created for the social work profession!

Like Solomon, Pinderhughes was lauded for her work when it first came out in 1989; many years later, her book was central to her receiving the CSWE lifetime achievement award in 2017. And yet, why are their seminal theories no longer woven into today's practice models? Our field still openly builds on the problem-solving models of Perlman and Coyle and the person-in-environment theories of Richmond, Hamilton, Hollis, and others. The explicit reason for the disappearance is obviously connected to their race, but the problem is deeper than that alone (not that it would be discounted). The implicit reason is more pernicious: that because they focus on either Black clients and/or issues of racism, their work does not have the theoretical heft to be generalizable to all of social work and those who toil within it. The insidious racism here is exactly what Pinderhughes was writing about as to how privilege is ascribed to certain people and not to others, thus replicating lessened status and power. Hamilton's work on person in environment and, say, Hollis's on clinical work is more privileged and ascribed more theoretical power because of the unconscious "comfort" its authors create simply because of *what* they are—White female academics. That Solomon's and Pinderhughes's work is as valuable for White professionals as much as it is for their Black and Brown colleagues is just too "uncomfortable" to consider.

We, um, will return to this topic of profession-wide racial discomfort later in this chapter.

PUSHING THAT RACIAL SISYPHEAN BOULDER UP THE MOUNTAINTOP: WHAT MIGHT HAVE BEEN, PART II

No one can review all of the remarkable literature on race and racism that has been written over the last 40 years in North America and not be in awe at the depth and breadth of the work. That awe extends to efforts inside higher education, as well as social work itself. It hardly began with Solomon or ended with Pinderhughes. While the profession's mainstream journals may have ignored the subject, there's been a veritable underground railroad of powerful material appearing through workshop presentations, published research anthologies, study groups, and textbooks. There is insightful, nuanced work to be found on everything from trauma-informed treatment with oppressed populations to nuanced developmental assessments of children of color to models of participatory research with marginalized groups to anti-oppression tools for educators, all of which place issues of race, as well as other intersectional identities, at the heart of their work. If you google it, they will come to your inbox ready for use in your class or your program.

That said, there are a few powerful texts that synthesize many of the other authors' efforts, which can serve as foundational texts for future generations' efforts, especially with attention at last focused on systemic racism. One of the most prominent historical texts is *Racial Formation in the United States* by Michael Omi and Howard Winant (2015), with over 800 references. Their work analyzes the vagaries of racial construction and the pushback against marginality over the last 400 years, including the 21st century. Another important, more pedagogical work focuses on the struggles and possibilities within American academia: *Engaging the Race Question* by Alicia Dowd and Estella Mara Bensimon (2015), with 255 references (almost all of them published in the 21st century; Down and Bensimon's work is but one of more than 50 texts in the Multicultural Education Series edited by James Banks at Teachers College Press at Columbia University).

These works, and the scholarship developed by so many other authors that informed them, left me pondering. Since 1978, there have been so many titles, names, and conceptual terms applied to this American racial project: multiculturalism, racial and ethnic diversity, cross-culturalism, cultural diversity, cultural competency, racial equity, cultural humility, anti-racism, anti-oppression, intersectionality, restorative justice, anti-colonialism, and diversity, equity, and inclusion. Wow! So many different names, each parsed a little more than what came before, all seeking the same result: that the genuine fullness and complexity of all peoples be embraced, that past wrongs are finally corrected, and that we get on with working together so that this human prospect can be redeemed, not doomed by what otherwise awaits us in the 21st century (Heilbroner, 1974). What do all those name changes signify? Could it be that all those shoulders, instead of pulling us toward shore, are simply taking their turn at pushing that racial Sisyphean boulder toward a mountaintop that can never be reached?

If so, it will not be for either the lack of effort or an uninformed analysis. Omi and Winant's well documented historical work, while cognizant of the social forces at play that make up intersectionality, puts forth the claim of race's central role in the shaping of our culture:

> Since the historical encounter of the hemispheres and the onset of transatlantic enslavement were the fundamental acts of race-making ... that constituted the (creation) of the modern world, race has become the template of both difference and inequality ... The concept of race as a marker of difference has permeated all social relations. It is a template for the processes of marginalization that *continue to shape social structures as well as collective and individual psyches.* (Omi & Winant, 2015, pp. 106–107; italics added)

Their work situates race as a central social construction on this continent from the moment Columbus, Cartier, and other Europeans stepped on the Native lands now known as North America. With their arrival began the interpretation of "others" in terms that placed those Native peoples in positions of marginality and oppression. As they document carefully, this construction of racial superiority for some and marginality for all others has continually shaped and reshaped North American life since the 1600s. The authors go on to document the historical struggles that then have ensued over centuries: to reassert White, colonial domination, as well as the valiant fights against such subjugation. Their work brilliantly breaks away from the false, binary categorization of race as either a simple biological determinant or a totally illusory construct. As their work makes clear, while these forces are literally and figuratively neither Black nor White, they also have had the very real power to racially dominate, marginalize, and do violent harm.

Omi and Winant's scholarship clarifies how dynamic this racial struggle has been in each and every generation. As they went on to write about national mythmaking, "the 'American people' ... (necessitated) not only equality but community ... . But to create community required a social reorientation, a reinterpretation ... of the American nation and the American people. The movement (for racial progress) asked *'Who is included, and who is excluded from our community?'*" (Omi & Winant, 2015, p. 185). Their work is helpful for anyone seeking the kind of progress as that sought by previous generations as groups situate their own answers to that same question of who belongs: BLM's intersectional demands are forged from 21st-century relations with the dominant White culture that are necessarily distinct from those created by W.E.B. Du Bois in the early 20th century. Each has fought to reshape "social structures and collective and individual psyches" to better answer that question of community membership, building on the past successes, and inevitable incompletion of previous struggles.

Thus a profession and its leadership that professes a singular historical commitment to social justice and racial equality in 2020 and beyond must ask, *Why does this question still have to be asked again and again within our community?*

It is here where Dowd and Mara Bensimon's work on how to actually teach on these topics becomes so important. (Their work can easily be applied within agencies as well.) They, too, have sought ways that diminish racial inequity and foster community inside classrooms—the central social movement themes that Omi and Warner described. At the beginning, they set themselves a seemingly modest objective: "to share what we have learned, by doing action research focused on racial equity, about *promoting accountability* in higher education to address the race question *with wisdom*" (Dowd & Bensimon, 2015, p. 4; italics added). Building on the work of the philosopher John Rawls, they have sought the "creation of a fair educational system that demands, besides the equitable distribution of material and financial resources ... (to include) liberty and self-respect" (Dowd & Bensimon, 2015, p. 11). In other words, they seek to create classrooms that in a microcosm transform "social structures," as well as "collective and individual psyches," through learning and teaching together—just what Omi and Winant documented was at the center of American racial history. In developing their social equity scorecard for assessing a school's implicit and explicit curriculum and commitment to racial equity, they built off a powerful insight—that it was not enough to "critique discriminatory ideologies and practices" but it was also necessary to support practitioner's capacities as change agents and to develop a commitment to "*inquiry as a stance*" (Dowd & Bensimon, 2015, p. 17; emphasis added).

This certainly seems positive and affirming enough—such a process ought to be straightforward, right? However, their research poses a particular approach to teaching and learning that builds on "contradictions" and "critical disturbances" that allow practitioners and academics to "see and act on the gaps between their espoused theories of action and their actual practice" (Argylis & Schôn, 1978; Dowd & Bensmon, 2015, pp. 23–24). Such disturbances in the classroom, they go on to posit, can be technical in nature—a scheduling mishap, even a mis-phrased concept or idea, which can be addressed by an obvious and equally technical correction—correct the date or apply the information to the correct source. More importantly, other issues that rise to the level of critical disturbances in classrooms reveal "substantive differences, fears or other indicators of systemic contradictions" (Engestrôm, 2008). As Dowd and Mara Bensimon found in their research, these more fundamental conflicts are what will engage learners in the deeper reflection and thought needed to handle Omi and Warner's historical issues of both structural inequality and its impact on the "collective and individual psyches" that show up in our classrooms and agencies. It's what's meant to explore systemic racism wherever it shows up—in the community, in the classroom, and within one's self.

Dowd and Bensimon (2015) succinctly lay out a cycle of learning that, if consistently followed in the classroom, would use such disturbances as a way forward to deepen both a learner awareness of systemic issues and an increased personal openness in response to "difference" of all kinds. A learner must seek knowledge of "historical structures" and awareness of the effect of such structures on one's own "psyche." Redlining by banks that purposely lowers the value of Black-owned homes fosters economic hardship for people of color while elevating Whites' wealth, intensifies segregation, reinforces negative difference, and fosters racial fear. Long-term structures of racial history collude with short-term psychic anxiety to present such gaps as extraordinary moments to learn, not run away from. Such an active, open embrace of gaps and "disturbances" when they appear would paradoxically create a flexible openness to the lifelong learning and adaptation needed for individual and societal transformation.

As they explained their learning cycle:

> Practitioners Acquire Adaptive Expertise through the Cycle of Inquiry: Knowledge—Beliefs—*Social Interactions (where contradictions emerge and critical disturbances occur)*—Reflection—Problem Identification

Through Data Analysis—Experimentation/Problem Solving—Action/ Experience-Adaptive Expertise—*(Repeat Cycle)*. (Dowd & Bensimon, 2015, p. 23)

Their masterful work develops a diversity scorecard that applies elements of this cycle to all sectors of an academic institution—admissions, hiring, and promotion, as well as the classroom itself. In 2020 and beyond, it points a way forward for any academic program or agency to strengthen its approach on diversity, equity, and inclusion. Their work helps a program develop the adaptive capacity to handle the complexities of intersectionality and the weight of American racial history without losing sight of other elements of an institution's core mission.

There, of course, is far more to their analysis and the tools they provide than can be summarized in this chapter. I strongly recommend anyone seeking a powerful framework to shift social dynamics inside their school, program, or agency as they approach systemic racism should study their work in-depth. The issue at hand for social work is more immediate: *Why have so few social work programs adapted such an approach to their work?*

WALKING ON EGGSHELLS WILL NEVER GET US UP THE MOUNTAINTOP

There are at least three reasons for the paucity of engagement in this kind of deep learning inside social work academia and the profession at large. All of them are at least partially solvable with the right leadership. The first is the most obvious: As discussed in Chapter 5, today's overstretched faculty (especially the 50% or more who are adjuncts) are meeting financially and personally stressed students in their classrooms. Therefore, there is no longer much internal capacity in most academic settings for "critical disruption" let alone deep reflection. The ensuing focus on "content" as a survival mechanism necessarily has relegated "gaps" to simply referencing others' written works—when in doubt or distress, refer students to those readings by bell hooks or Patricia Hill Collins on page 6 of the syllabus (Collins, 2008; hooks, 1994).

The second is more pernicious and equally pervasive: the over-reliance on competencies as a measure of practice performance. As Brigid Carroll and her colleagues brilliantly distilled in her award-winning 2008 article, competency is "an underlying characteristic of an individual that is causally related to an effective or superior performance on a job" (Boyatzis, 1982; Carroll et al., 2008). As she cogently argued, "Competence thus 'can appear as a desired measure to replace the actual discomfort and complexity of practice in an organizational milieu which has long privileged rationality, control, clarity and simplicity'" (Caroll et al., 2008, p. 36). Remember all those grant and RFP funding requirements for quarterly measures and yearly results discussed in Chapter 3? As long as the desired state is a future goal—no matter how abstract that goal is in actuality—the pristine image of "competency" will always trump the daily mess of lived experience. That a practitioner actually works within the mess and not the measure is conveniently sidestepped—or, more likely, overwhelmed by the mounds of "competency-defined evidence" that further contribute to the harried mess itself.

And let's face it, social work practice, day in and day out, is demanding, relational, complex, and offers little control over what comes at you—especially when you factor in issues of race or any other socially constructed identity of that person sitting across from you. In other words, it gets messy—a lot. An obvious practitioner in her own right, Carroll powerfully distills the distinctions between competency and a social worker's actual practice:

Competency	*Practice*
Rooted in objectivism	Explicitly constructionist
Individual level of analysis	Inherently relational and collective
Quantifiable and measurable	Discourse, narrative, and rhetoric
Unanchored in relationship or context	Situated and socially defined
Privileges reason	Privileges lived, day-to-day experience
Assumes intellect predominantly	Incorporates embodiment and emotion

(Carroll et al., 2008, p. 366)

All of these differences are worthy of their own explication when applied to racial dynamics:

- *Constructivism* recognizes Omi and Walton's dynamic struggle between privileged and less-privileged groups while *objectivism* seeks ahistorical neutrality
- The *relational* poses learning as interactive and changing between people with more or less power interacting throughout the day as Dowd and Mara Bensimon suggest, not *individualized* and solitary: as we all know, individualism was a central organizing principle of 19th-century Social Darwinism)
- *Discourse* prizes the process of learning with others over *measurable outcomes* applied to individuals and groups
- Actions are analyzed through *socially created situations*, not *unanchored* to them and "objective" as if social differences did not apply to such actions
- *Lived experience* and its messiness is prized over *reason*

Such distinctions are no idle matter; taken together, "practice" allows for the messiness afforded the actual work of social work—changing, adaptive, humbling, real. "Competency," on the other hand, reifies objective, "competent" outcomes requiring practice to reveal itself in narrowly constrained buckets of superior performance that few attain before a number of years of actual practice—and no one sustains with the mark of perfectibility. (Remember Pinderhughes's modesty?) Rather than deepening legitimacy, the false narrative of abstracted, unrealistic results diminishes the actual quality of work within the classroom, agency, and profession.

To understand why this is no small problem for a profession's standing, let's look more carefully at the practice issues embedded in the final "competency versus practice" distinction: *intellect* as opposed to *embodiment and emotion*. If you accept the framework of competency, "intellect" must predominate because it is rational and measurable—you either know something or you don't: Erickson's stages of development, for example. "Emotion" is perhaps slightly measurable—degrees or types of feeling, abilities to moderate or self-regulate either negative feelings (hostile "triggers') or romanticized reactions (unrealistic hopes or desires). But "embodiment"? *Embodiment cannot be an outcome, an event, or an idea*. It manifests both as a physical and emotional experience in an immediate context, not as an outcome. Such presence is revealed in the midst of those "social interactions" of Dowd and Bensimon where "contradictions emerge and critical disturbances occur." Pinderhughes had to have embodied it in all those group meetings with her staff, revealing a capacity to live and respond to the mess of the work among people struggling to get it right. As she admitted, sometimes she failed. The key was that she never let momentary failure stop her—it was her lived experience, again and again, to remain in that difficult struggle that led her to embody a practice capacity far behind "competency."

What does that kind of *practice mess* actually look like in a classroom or agency—and how does one embody a powerful stance to work within such a mess? For all of Dowd's and Bensimon's own modesty, their "social interactions" can't be comfortable for anyone to respond to. As Jeffrey wrote, "Most definitions of 'good' teaching (or 'good' social work for that matter) mean that 'crisis is averted, that lessons are doable'" (Jeffrey, 2007, p. 130), "[but] anti-oppression teaching requires the disrupting of comforting knowledge, that students will always need to confront what they do not want to confront … (therefore) crisis should be expected in the process of learning" (p. 130). Jeffrey uses the example of variations of racial privilege among students that can prove unsettling for almost everyone, especially those with previously unexamined advantage. She notes that one's marking of privilege is a good "starting but not end point of one's self location." Left at the level of simple self-awareness, a student (or professor or practitioner!) "creates a daisy chain of naming differences but not with a critical awareness of its incompletion ... . Student or practitioner must get assistance on exploring professional selves without a stable solution, resulting in on-going action" (Jeffrey, 2007, p. 138).

Golly, that's a lot to swallow! And how does all that happen? *This is where the embodiment of one's incompletion and willingness to relearn "identity," privilege," and other racial and anti-oppression qualities in teacher or leader must appear—the very opposite of "competence."* It is the quality of becoming "comfortable with discomfort" that is required in addressing systemic racism, of accepting struggle as prerequisite to lifelong growth, that a professional embodies on the trek up that mountaintop. As a skilled, seasoned African American clinician and adjunct professor, Chanda Griffin wisely responded to my questions about competence: "I seek grounding, not competence for myself and my students. If I'm grounded, I can adapt to whatever appears—transference, counter-transference, microaggressions." She paused. "If students leave grad school thinking they're 'competent' to practice, we haven't done our job. If they're grounded, they can keep growing." As her fellow clinician and clinical professor Sherwood McPhail added, "It's a journey, not an arrival. When I realized that, I finally became a clinician."

Grounded, not competent. What a profound distinction: the latter an end point to arrive at and the former, a humble stance from which to adapt, reflect, learn, and grow committed to the journey, not the destination. By embodying a grounded approach to their own learning, Griffin and McPhail exemplified a willingness to struggle in the midst of disruption, not shy away from it by quickly returning to the content at hand. Unfortunately, the over-reliance on "competency" when applied to anti-oppression and anti-racist work in one's practice sets students and practitioners up for one of three outcomes: (1) a sense of abject failure because they know they will never arrive where they hoped comfortably to be; (2) constricted positionality, where one is not so much grounded as encased in using one's narrow definitions of what "good" practice looks like so as to ward off the humble reflection of self-discovery that those with less power and privilege might otherwise provide; (3) delusion, leading to future burst bubbles, fear, guilt, and the wringing of hands.

The third reason is as obvious as it is painful: *As the work ahead on systemic racism demands, either professional leadership commits to this work as central to a program's mission each and every day on racial and social justice—empowerment, dignity, human rights—or its mission is composed of abstract and false categories of competence, not preparation for the uncomfortable yet fulfilling journey that awaits a social work practitioner.* The present-day frustrations, conflict, and tensions that are common to the "walking on eggshells" phenomenon of so many classrooms and agencies exist *because* of the exalted mission toward social justice that every social work school and agency espouses. Such commitments are emblazoned on the printed page and heralded across websites (is there any social work program's web page that doesn't lead with a picture of at least one person of color, preferably smiling?). And yet by being unattended throughout their programs, such schools and agencies forever fall short of the racial grounding that would allow them to adapt and grow as new issues arrive and discomfort once again staggers into the room. The equivalent defensiveness of the professor, supervisor, and executive meets the resulting frustration of the student or entry-level professional. The smashing of eggs soon follows.

In 2020 and beyond, a profession cannot promise so much and until now do so little. Lorraine Gutierrez, a lifelong social justice educator and present associate dean charged with diversity, equity, and inclusion oversight at the University of Michigan School of Social work, recounted how a joint MSW/MBA student, while upset by the indifference of his business school to racial issues, was enraged at some of the social work school's failure to fully address issues of White supremacy. "He knew they both should be held equally accountable, but his expectations of the business school were much lower than what he expected in social work. 'But social justice is central to this profession!' His anger grew because he couldn't see how it was possible that everyone at our school didn't take social justice and racial justice seriously." How many countless enraged young professionals will it take for its leadership to start paying attention?

Gutierrez's vignette succinctly captured our field's central dilemma on race, racism, and other social issues for teachers and agency leaders alike: *Don't preach what you won't practice.* Removing the Oz-like curtain of social justice rhetoric, history reveals a leadership unwilling to vulnerably learn from and value those with less power and privilege. They instead stake a program's claim to legitimacy on false measures of professional "competency" that individuates and separates students and staff from a commonly shared grounding in our mutual humanity. To locate our mutual humanity, however, most of our profession would have to confront perhaps our deepest source of incompletion: that the historical harm of racism—past, present, and future—only affects people of color and not White people.

To make such a statement will raise many readers' immediate concerns, but please bear with me. There is no binary construction of thought here nor an attempt to recenter this discussion on White people—as the rest of this chapter has hopefully made clear, the intensity, duration, and scope of American racism inflicted on all peoples of color, including the genocide of Native Americans; the robbing of land and citizenship of Mexicans who had been here for centuries; the enslavement, rape, and subjugation of African Americans; and the enforced servitude, internment, and marginalization of multiple Asian-Americans—as an animating, central theme of American history. At the same time, such oppression does not blot out the White fragility that White supremacy fosters, as dissected by Robin DiAngelo. It is a fragility created through forms of denial, guilt, and irrationality whose harm to the "collective and individual psyches' of White Americans is as ever-present in our communities as are the opioids, heroin and fentanyl used to disguise so much white misery" (DiAngelo, 2018). By not recognizing *how racism curdles so much of every Americans' lived experience*, it allows some to construct racism and its impact as always somewhere else, happening to "other" people. As such, campaigns all too often become a moral, not material, concern for most progressive-minded White people. Historic wrongs can pull at our conscience and nightly cable shows on the latest act of racial violence cause momentary outrage, but live with it as an ever-present condition? Donate money, provide occasional awards, but recalibrate the varying lived experience of people of color *and* one's self as a permanent condition?

When tragedies occur and the inevitable crises of every generation repeat themselves, this pattern of cloistered White responses after momentary, collective action, as DiAngelo documented, is almost always the same. Because of the previous inability to acknowledge and live within these "multiple truths" wrought by White supremacy, Whites, *"especially white liberals,"* respond not through competency (!) but through its exact opposite. As DiAngelo wrote, "White people's defensive anger, guilt, and fear, result in 'sputterings' about oppression that work to reinstate white equilibrium as they repel the challenge, return to our racial comfort, and maintain our dominance with the racial hierarchy" (DiAngelo, 2018).

This critique applies directly to our profession. With a few exceptions in academia (most notably Smith College School of Social Work), almost all established social work programs have gone through cycles of student upset at a lack of racial content or hiring or diverse field placements, followed by committees being formed and modifications of some kind being made—required readings on diversity in every syllabus, a course being added in the next cycle, the purposeful hiring of people of color and openly LGBTQ folks (mostly adjuncts) to staff such courses. Changes are made, and yet the unsettling norm of eggshells to be walked upon and topics to be avoided reasserts itself. In 2020, we must ask, is this past prologue to the future?

Eggshell avoidance. If ever there was a measure of White fragility, that might be it! The "individual and collective psyche" within a school remains unchanged, no more able to respond to the next racial crisis than it did before. And occur they do, at some of our highest ranked schools. For example, in 2019, New York University Silver School of Social Work admitted to "institutional racism here at Silver, especially in classrooms," when an international student openly stated he'd prefer to have discussions of racism without the one African American in the classroom (Smith, 2019). The school's leadership committed that "in the wake of this painful incident, it is our hope that we will find an opportunity for self-reflection, learning, and professional and institutional growth" (Smith, 2019). A year later, in direct conversations with the affected student, such opportunities have yet to occur. Despite the wringing of hands, the old equilibrium had been reestablished.

A similar outcry occurred in 2019 at the University of Maryland, Baltimore's, School of Social Work, including formal charges brought by students and alumni to the CSWE (University of Maryland School of Social Work, 2020). However, unlike at New York University, what is both tragic and telling about these charges is one finds on their present web page a genuine, in-depth review (unlike at New York University Silver School of Social Work) where for years the school has challenged itself to create a "climate of openness" to diversity, equity, and inclusion in systematic and new ways. Laced throughout their reports is a tone of disillusionment, hurt, and anger among African Americans, as well as pain and an almost desperate desire to get things right on the part of others. The sound of so many eggs cracking hurts.

Maryland's story is a cautionary tale for every agency and social work program responding to the post–George Floyd era of race relations on which to end this chapter, for the school is a well-regarded institution with a history of actions, events, and expressed commitments to diversity and racial inclusion dating to at least 1997, when the school hired faculty with the expressed mandate to develop courses on cultural competency. All that work, year after year, and yet in the wake of the Freddie Gray murder by Baltimore police, the school's flat-footed leadership response began a spiral of resentment and eventual hostility throughout the school community. Its mission, centered on social justice, couldn't stop the angry pushback. The hard work of the few faculty members (both people of color and White) who had championed anti-oppression work couldn't stop it. The established committees on diversity couldn't stop it. The lesson is clear: If a program and its people aren't grounded in the humble challenge to be forever adaptive to the lived experiences of everyone who walks through its doors before a crisis, such stoppage isn't possible. Lacking grounding, the seeds for the next disruption are already being sewn.

The racialized eggs in any institution break apart when achievements of the "othered" few are lauded and then made invisible; when the primary framework for practice excellence is implicitly individualized and abstracted from the gritty, racial realness of everyday work life; when the tragedy of America's racial story is always about *understanding parts of them* and not the *painful universality of knowing all of us.* The awkwardness of response, the fragility emanating from that cauldron of fear, guilt, and defensive anger and the resultant hostility and exasperation among those asked to shoulder that boulder once again cannot be overcome by well-crafted pronouncements or hastily formed committees. We each, instead, must embrace and live the words that the Aboriginal activist Lila Watson credits to her Aboriginal collective: "If you have come here to help me you are wasting your time, but if you have come because your liberation is bound up with mine, then let us work together" (Watson, 2020).

Isn't it about time to begin that work?

THE CONCLUDING POLEMIC: WE CAN'T REACH THE MOUNTAINTOP IF WE DON'T WALK TOGETHER

In many ways, the concluding polemic of this chapter has been written already in its preceding pages. It explains a seeming anomaly within our schools and agencies that must be dealt with if true work on systemic racism is to be successful: How can a school or agency with a growing, diverse staff, endless projects to combat racism, and weekly web page blurbs triumphing the success of otherwise marginalized clients still be perceived as overwhelmingly White?

The fight against racism and toward genuine restoration of our mutual human prospect requires a commitment to a woven tapestry of daily lived commitments by everyone, not wordy pronouncements by the few. It means that Barbara Solomon and Elaine Pinderhughes deserve to be in the pantheon of practice theorists, alongside the likes of Helen Harris Perlman and Grace Coyle, for their contributions to the entire field. To locate them elsewhere is to "other" their work, which diminishes their enduring brilliance and thus our entire profession.

It means that seeking "cultural competency" or any other variation of that term rather than adaptive grounding in one's racial awareness and racial healing is a fool's errand. Such an outcome-based and Eurocentric focus sets up everyone—leader, professor, practitioner, and student—for the individual and collective psychic wounds of fear and frustration, anger, and remorse that have forever affected America's soul. It, therefore, lingers just below the surface, ready to tear us apart all over again at the next minor utterance or major act of violence.

Finally, to believe that one can work to resolve racial tensions (or any other social difference) and create the prospect of community restoration through committees, curricular revisions, and program initiatives alone is to put that boulder of responsibility again on the backs of those who have forever lifted it. Such well-intentioned yet fractured efforts thus foreshadow the future slippage that awaits us, complete with eggshells to be avoided and racial fears to be normalized once again. As a seasoned, dedicated, and wounded academic and social justice advocate stated, "There can't be one answer. It takes a lot of people, all pulling in the same direction. It takes many people with various talents leading the way *before* a crisis happens. *No one gets to opt out.*" (Because of tenure and promotion considerations, this speaker requested anonymity.) Her hard-won wisdom has a powerful message: Either everyone who professes commitment to social justice joins this project as part of their own process of self-discovery and an end to their own dehumanization alongside those who forever have been standing alongside us or we perpetuate the delegitimizing failure to address social justice that corrodes our profession.

CHAPTER 7

HOW MANY CASES DOES IT TAKE TO MAKE A CAUSE?

"Don't Fret, Organize" ... for Years to Come!

INTRODUCTION

As I began this chapter, our entire world is gripped by the most serious health crisis in over 100 years, one whose death spiral is yet to be counted. Likewise, no one yet knows the extent of social and economic devastation to the communities in which we work. More people have been thrown out of work, businesses shuttered, millions upon millions quarantined, a 1930s aura of Depression hovering, minus overcrowding on the bread lines. Social disparities abound; add social distancing to the litany of privilege: New York subways to Wall Street at 9 a.m. are deserted, while 7 a.m. bus lines carrying porters, grocery clerks, and pharmacy techs remain crammed. Families living doubled up no longer have the minimal convenience of schooling and work to avoid 24/7 overcrowding. Homeschooling assumes the economic advantage of multiple laptops and high-speed internet service that millions can ill afford as their part-time jobs in the gig economy dry up. No wonder it's no surprise that data at the time of this writing reveals that African Americans are dying at rates exponentially worse than their White counterparts (Oppel, Searcey, & Eligon, 2020).

And then George Floyd was murdered in front of America's eyes; we were unable to turn away in horror for 8 minutes and 46 seconds. The social disparity already exposed through the pandemic took on the racial hue there all along, revealing to White Americans that such police brutality was not an occasional judgment error of the few but a profound and brutal symptom of systemic racism that lays beneath so much of American history. In the summer of 2020, the cries of anguish from the coronavirus (COVID-19) pandemic and anger over so much brutal racial history can hardly be distinguished. America has entered a racial and social reckoning not seen since the 1930s.

And yet, as history shows, crises create unforeseen opportunities too. First, the vice-like grip of the neoliberal shibboleth that the state cannot create massive expenditures because of a need for tax cuts has been blown to bits by the initial $2.2 trillion bailout rolling out across America, with a future job creation/infrastructure project in the works of an equally mammoth sum. There is no natural law of economics precluding state expenditures (Krugman, 2020). As 2020 pandemic-based legislation revealed, if the political will is there, money can be found.

There's been an interesting cultural shift underway as well. The twin horrors of the pandemic and wanton racial violence at the hands of police make clear who and what matters as never before. In July 2020, was anyone paying much attention to celebrity culture? Did anyone notice what the Kardashians are doing? The monetarization of relationships through celebrity, gossip, reality show–fueled drama, and social media stardom from one's bedroom has been exposed for the emptiness that was there all along. In its place has been the recalibration of old friendships, family ties, respected work colleagues, and neighbors that has placed a premium less on its exchange value—*what can I get for this?*—with use value—*what can I do for you*? (Even Karl Marx would have been pleasantly surprised!)

Finally, two remarkable phenomena have sidestepped the individuated isolation of postmodern life. First, there has been a resurgence of 19th-century community support and 20th-century mutual aid—not just by professionals in health care or schools but also by everyday folk reaching out to neighbors and strangers, lending a hand to the isolated elders, poor children without internet access, exhausted parents needing a break from their needy children, teens bored with online games, and boomers tired of talking about the '60s. While disparities cannot be ignored, the commonality of mutual fear and illness across every economic class and social group has created an opening of common connection that can be built upon. The number of book clubs, shared service programs, gift-buying services to aid local restaurants and shops, and food co-ops have grown exponentially across the land, begun by concerned neighbors, creative artists, and regular folk tired of waiting for government relief and seeking connection as well. Mutual aid has resurfaced not as a historic relic to gloss over but a modern-day resource to embrace. Options for meaning, purpose, and connection are no longer sought just through the market but from within the community itself.

Second, the specter of racial violence by the police has led to an unprecedented level of sustained mobilization in the streets not seen since the militant activism of the LGBTQ movement's response to government inactivity on AIDS. Importantly, the multiracial movement, led by BLM activists as young as 15, has continued to happen in large urban centers, as well as, surprisingly, small towns, such as Marion, Ohio; Simi Valley, California; Richmond, Kentucky; Washington, Pennsylvania; Athens, Georgia; and Groton, Connecticut (Buchanan, et al, June 6, 2020). Instead of dissipating into sporadic looting or dispirited rallying, the movement continues to grow in focus, urgency, and resolve. It's as if the Progressive Era of mutual aid and the militant humanism of the civil rights' 1950s and '60s have come together at the same time!

Of course, who am I kidding? All these shifts in the state, culture, and community could be blown away by some unanticipated yet ever-possible directive that marshals a return to old, deeply entrenched policies and norms that continue the march toward greater social inequality and economic austerity. An opposing American impulse is at play in 2020 as well—individualistic, territorial, even potentially violent. Champions of "liberty" in some of our western and southern states see their government officials' calls for social distancing as dangerous government intrusion into their private lives, as well as trampling on their constitutional rights. On the flip side, some governors, such as Rhode Island's Gina Raimondo, have imposed a form of martial law by license plate, mobilizing state police to stop every out-of-state car, requiring the unenforceable but restrictive requirement that anyone arriving and then staying within state borders to quarantine for 14 days (Mooney, 2018). Finally, as awareness of the pandemic's reach became apparent nationwide, 2.2 million new guns were purchased in the month of March, greater than at any time since 9/11 (Becket, 2020). As COVID-19 germs cannot be seen let alone shot at, it's frightening to consider who people were setting their sights on.

There is so much social, economic, and political possibility—in either direction. A crisis as widespread, long-lasting, and intense as this has been will have unforeseen results and unintended consequences that no one can glibly forecast. But disaster specialists agree that the stronger and more tight-knit a community is before a crisis, the greater the likelihood of a resilient and flexible response of benefit to all (Henry, 2018). As has been evident since 2016, if not before, that kind of unity in America no longer exists across the land. This pandemic has exposed those social fissures even more clearly. Yet, fortuitously, we can find bridges being built and people reaching toward each other in unprecedented ways not seen in generations. Hope—that emotional mix of past fear or frustration coupled with the possibility of a better future—is present. How long that hope remains depends in a modest yet significant part on what social workers find themselves capable of doing, both in response to the pandemic and to systemic racism and, interconnectedly, to the conditions and concerns of social workers themselves.

What follows is an immodest program designed to bring that significance of social work into being while engaging in the broader social movements these times require. That said, just as this book began with the stunning recognition of how far behind in income and status our field is from the former "sister professions" of nursing and education, this chapter begins with the sad awareness of how the efforts of social workers (and, by extension, the profession itself) were ignored throughout this crisis. Yes, this pandemic has been a health crisis of historic proportions, and doctors, nurses, and all medical staff deserve the adulation and thanks they have received. Likewise, we now give thanks to the often-overlooked grocery and drug-store clerks, mail carriers, and delivery staff (disproportionately non-White) who worked under difficult conditions and yet showed up to work every day. Finally, the depth of historic racism that permeates everyday life, as well as the institutional order, is at last getting necessary attention. In combination, these crises have revealed the level of racial and social inequality that permeate our society.

And throughout these upheavals, countless social workers—large numbers of whom are people of color—have also continued as the first responders they always have been: child protection workers are still entering homes filled with fear and poverty and a complete absence of Clorox wipes; homeless shelter staff members are helping stressed families cope under the same difficult conditions that made social distancing impossible; the geriatric social worker is still seeking out isolated elder folks who are lacking internet service; community workers are creating support groups for clients struggling with mental illness or drug use; the countless facilitators of mutual aid projects who just happened to have a BSW or MSW are also still offering services. That others during the pandemic have received so much gratitude is all to the good. That social workers have been ignored is not others' fault. As the previous six chapters made clear, it's been 50 years in the making, and we've done it mostly to ourselves.

Specht and Courtney (1995) analyzed this trend of broad public irrelevance presciently more than 25 years ago; their work remains a searing indictment of the profession's moves into psychotherapy since the 1960s. Where they fell short was not in their analysis of the problem but in their academic prescription for how to resolve it. They developed a detailed blueprint in the latter chapters on a "community-based system of social care" while focusing their academic emphasis on "community education." Both their programmatic focus and educational ideas were sound—indeed, they are worthy of adoption today. They again documented the by now well-known research finding related to clinical treatment: that all psychodynamic models of intervention (cognitive behavioral therapy, dialectical behavioral therapy, Gestalt, etc.) have the same degree of success. Given the relative similarity of outcomes, as well as cost efficiencies (most people can ill afford long-term treatment and most insurance plans won't cover it anyway), emphasizing longer term therapeutic models benefits few, save the professors teaching them and their students who live with the momentary illusion of someday having a sustainable private practice. Furthermore, they point out, most of what poor people, as well as others living on the economic and/or social margins (a far larger group than many realized before COVID-19), "need" is less about individualized talk therapy and more about economic assistance, housing, social isolation, and social stigma.[1]

---

1   For example, the U.S. Federal Reserve's research has found that more than 40% of all households do not have savings to cover an unexpected emergency expense—a figure obviously far greater in 2020 following our economic slowdown (Board of Governors of the U.S. Federal

As their research suggested, the vast majority of people in need are far more likely to benefit from a mixed method of individual, group, and community interventions that harken to the rich historical traditions of our profession than clinical therapy alone. If social work wants to reclaim its legitimacy as a profession, Specht and Courtney suggest we need to embrace the approaches of the past as models to emulate in action, not just read about.

Their programmatic recommendations are also sound, emphasizing a mix of social care connected to social services, voluntarism expanding mutual aid, and support through groups, as well as using a variety of localized settings, such as schools and other community facilities. Reading Specht and Courtney's words, one could start looking around for Jane Addams and Bertha Reynolds to head their efforts up, with Mary Richmond in charge of quality assurance. Making clear that such services should be provided through federal and state financing and not private charity, they posed their programs with less a nostalgic eye to the past than a harkening to a time when the field received at least some of the recognition it deserved. They saw their mix of multimethod practice and layered service interventions as a way to recapture a deservedly respectful status for the profession's work with the poor, oppressed, and marginalized.

Curiously, however, they end their educational and programmatic emphases with the final chapter's return to lamenting the inevitable resistance that their ideas would generate from neoliberal politicians, professional leaders, and psychoanalytic clinical social workers. Rather than detail how one would confront and overcome this institutional resistance, they end with a mix of exhortation for the value of community services over individualized ones, as well as a poignant observation: "Generally we are of the view that professions are incapable of reforming themselves … . Most of them have been practicing with some degree of success for a number of years; they find satisfaction, status, and financial benefits in what they do, and they have little reason to be re-educated" (Specht & Courtney, 1995, p. 172).

To end a searing critique of the profession without casting a way forward is where the rest of this chapter will differ. The institutional responses to Specht and Courtney's brilliant work reminds one of the responses to the SC to Advance Macro Practice noted in Chapter 1: lots of handclapping, verbal air kisses, and …

Reserve, 2019). Likewise, despite the advances in marriage equality and against job discrimination in some communities, hate crimes against LGBTQ folks have grown, not diminished (Huack, 2019). That Black, Latinx, and Native Americans have suffered at twice the mortality rates as their White counterparts from COVID-19 will not be addressed through clinical treatment, except for the residual trauma wrought by such racialized economic and social conditions (Henry, 2020). Likewise, the developmentally disabled living in group homes are 5 times as likely to get the virus and die than their nondisabled counterparts (Hakim, 2020). If such underlying systemic issues are addressed, then longer-term treatment models could be of benefit. But first things first.

you're on your own. A quick perusal of reviews of their work found it lauded as "important" and "must be read," followed by not much. They, too, were nicely thanked for sharing; now, back to exactly the same social order!

Twenty-five years later, as this book has detailed, such status, satisfaction, and financial reward have all but disappeared for far too many social workers. Specht, who began his career as a community organizer, and Courtney, whose early career focused on programmatic advocacy for disadvantaged youth, both well knew that institutionalized power does not give way on the basis of a program's soundness or even moral righteousness. As BLM learned in the wake of the murders of Trayvon Martin and Michael Brown, institutionalized power is challenged only through some other countervailing power that has organized and sustained itself over years of effort. What follows is an organizing strategy, complete with a few concrete demands and one inspiring case example, to do just that.

IT TAKES YEARS TO BUILD A NEW VILLAGE: AN ORGANIZING STRATEGY FOR THE LONG-HAUL TRANSFORMATION OF THE SOCIAL WORK PROFESSION

You do not overcome 40 years of neoliberalism, the codification and institution-alization of private practice as the core of the profession's interests, a professional and academic leadership aligned to sustain that interest, and systemic racism inside and outside the profession through a year- or even 2-year-long campaign of exhortation.

Recent research on successful organizing that altered power relations reinforces that awareness:

> These groups (that succeeded in altering institutionalized power relations) had leaders who were strategists. They acted like generals, corporate executives or football coaches navigating complex and uncertain environments to win. These leaders built organizations designed to strengthen relationships with and among members. At the center of the organizations were people with real-world problems that the leaders were committed to solving, instead of meeting donors' arbitrary "metrics for success.
>
> These strategists knew that *people* were the source of their power. So at house parties, church meetings or membership assemblies, leaders made space for members to develop the skills they needed to take risks, develop political strategies, work with others, hold their peers and people in power accountable, build coalitions and, through all of this, put their

hands on the levers of change. None of this can be done by sitting behind a computer or with a couple of one-off rallies. (Han, 2019)

A Framework for Strategic Possibility

Using Han's findings as a guide, the following strategic approach begins with an understanding that this is a 5- to 10-year battle, not a calendar-year skirmish. As a further reminder, students and young social work professionals have for generations been inspired by the bravery, risk taking, tactical brilliance, and eloquence of the civil rights movement in the American south, initiated by the courage of Rosa Parks refusing to move to the back of a Montgomery, Alabama, bus in 1955. Glossed over all too often is the all-but hidden historical fact that the leader of the Montgomery NAACP, E. D. Nixon, had worked with others for the previous 5 years to end segregated seating on the buses and had chosen the Highlander (Organizing) Center–trained Parks to be the symbol of that resistance (Branch, 1989). As Han discovered and Nixon and Parks lived, if you are going to struggle to alter power, prepare for years of organizing, not months.

Second, as Nixon knew, the seamstress Parks confirmed, and Han analyzed, successful strategies emphasized accountability from below, not above. As Han (2019) wrote, "These leaders were successful strategists because they were not working to move up the party establishment hierarchy, make a donor happy or satisfy someone else's vision. Such people are often unwilling to take risks or reject their party orthodoxy. Being accountable to real people with real problems not only created urgency but also sparked creativity" (Han, 2019). This 5-year strategy requires organizers to focus on themselves and the people with whom they work—frontline social workers and supervisors, students, community members, clients, and activists from other social movements—for inspiration and guidance, not from above.

This, too, can prove difficult, as the soothing language of established social work leaders, as seen in their responses to the SC, can create a social justice glove that hides the iron fist of indifference beneath it. Sure, there will be some older, established leaders and professors who meet the test of genuine commitment by what they *do*, but looking upwards for guidance and direction as a default position over the coming years would be a mistake. As any seasoned organizer knows all too well, *be open to everyone—and trust only what people do, not what they say.*

Third, carry with you the recognition that institutional leadership depends on the illusion of their established authority to command deference—the bestowing of awards, official gatherings, newsletter proclamations. Their actual power in terms of mobilized membership numbers may be far less. If you've ever attended the annual membership meeting of CSWE at its yearly conference, you'll have noticed that CSWE staff outnumber actual members in attendance. A "business meeting" with less than 40 or so people to vote out of a membership numbering in the thousands suggests a hollowness of participation at its core that can be overcome with sustained effort. Likewise, while many local NASW chapters have long been populated by a mix of eager young professionals hoping to make a difference and mid- to late-career academics and midlevel executives committed to the profession's advancement, a telling number at the national level, working with already overstretched staff supporting them, show little interest beyond the licensed-based status quo. Not unlike states during the pandemic, local chapters across the country engage in innovative work without seeking national approval. Unfortunately, the moves toward "modernization" at the national level that occurred in the early 21st century have stripped locals of much of their autonomy. The push-pull between activism at the local level and resistance at the national level can sap the morale of committed young and seasoned professionals alike. Only through a concerted and unified, long-term campaign that connects chapters in common purpose and drive can a new national direction be developed and acted upon.

The silver lining here connecting both NASW and CSWE reform efforts is that neither is meeting the actual needs of the majority of its rank-and-file members. Given the substantive hollowness within both organizations (which should not be confused with a lack of power), each has the potential to be transformed, especially as young activists meet up with that small but real group of seasoned professionals who are well versed in each organizations' policies and procedures. (Darlyne Bailey and Terry Mizrahi, cochairs of the SC, are examples of such committed, experienced professionals.) Five hundred social work professionals, drawn from agency and academic life, working together across the country over the next 5 years in chapters and other groups, such as Radical Social Workers and the Social Welfare Action Alliance, could make a powerful impact on the profession. Found across the nation, activists would, of course, use social media tools for connection and support, ranging from mutual aid, celebration of local victories, and enhancement of strategic leverage nationally. In this manner, these committed social workers could further develop a program for transformation centered as much on the well-being of their fellow workers as their clients, creating a great possibility of exponentially expanding your numbers and thus democratically attaining real power within these moribund organizations.

Fourth, while such systemic transformation is possible, such radical reform is only viable *after* the members of a bottom-up, grassroots effort have had the opportunity to grow and develop in their own resilient capacities for debate, problem solving, and decision making. As Han's research found, "Leaders made space for members to develop the skills they needed to take risks, develop political strategies, work with others, hold their peers and people in power accountable, build coalitions and, through all of this, put their hands on the levers of change" (Han, 2019). This is no small matter: democracy in civil society is not just at the polls but in meetings, caucuses, and affinity groups where we learn that *give-and-take is about both and not one or the other*. For that give-and-take to occur, leaders need to want to share power and not replicate what those they seek to replace have always done. The works of Freire, Gramsci, Brown, and Rowbotham matter here as people relearn that democracy is not a zero-sum game of domination or loss but of genuine trust that difference makes us stronger, not weaker (Brown, 2017; Freire, 2000; Gramsci 1971; Rowbotham, 2014).

Fifth, that give-and-take must be built around discussions of a program that combines attainable, concrete demands, as well as aspirational possibilities. Concrete, relatively "small," and winnable demands are created within a context where one side has almost all the power and the other side next to none. Aspirational demands imagine a context where those power relations are reversed and what seemed completely infeasible before is now attainable. Before COVID-19, the power dynamics embedded in our political context made "Medicare for All" seem to many a Bernie Sanders's led pie-in-the-sky possibility; in the midst of the pandemic, it is now a plausible outcome. Likewise, BLM calls for dismantling militarized police forces seemed romantic at best, and yet in 2020, it is being acted on in cities across the country. (That said, whether such programmatic shifts can be *sustained* will depend in great part on the consistent, adaptable organizing that takes place in the months and years ahead.)

Developing a program with initially winnable demands without power and then scaling up as shifts in power and authority between groups occur is not an academic exercise. It is through this process of *transitional demands* that organizers connect to people's immediate self-interest while framing other possibilities as attainable as members' consciousness about who deserves decision-making authority begins to shift. We are not going to change the leadership of CSWE and NASW and with it the decades-long accommodation to neoliberal policies 2 years from the publication of this book. Its membership would rightly view such a takeover as a coup, not a democratic transition. One instead develops a program that begins with a demand based on "where the people are at" and goes on to include a series of "where they are at-plus one" demands that can be attained over time.

As this book makes clear, where to start is straightforward, concrete, and winnable: *The code of ethics needs to be thoroughly rewritten to include the self-interest, well-being, and dignity of the social worker.* Deleting any mention of pro bono work among already underpaid social workers is long overdue. As the code of ethics of far-better-paid nurses' associations and their unions have stipulated for years, it is not possible to maintain the well-being of patients or clients without attending to the well-being of the professionals themselves. To start with such a demand is to open up a conversation among members that is equally overdue: *Who benefits from frontline worker sacrifice? Why is self-interest all too often equated with selfishness in our field? Why is individualized self-care the primary remedy for exhaustion and burnout rather than collective action?*

These conversations are the fertile breeding ground for consciousness raising as debates among colleagues and others ensue. "Consciousness raising" in this context returns the term to its original meaning developed within the 1970s women's movement. It's what Paulo Freire described as *"conscientizao"* or critical reflection, where a person reflects on their own sense of power and agency in relationship to other more dominant actors (in the 1970s and again today, women and men; in the 1930s, workers and managers; for centuries, racialized "others" and Whites). As one tries to win that opening demand, the give-and-take of difference and opposition hopefully leads to a dawning awareness that as such a demand is won, other demands become more attainable because one's own sense of "agency" or "subjectness" (Freire, 2000) has grown as well. *If a group wins on changing the code of ethics, its members not only feel empowered to want more; their relationship to dominant authority has changed as well.* The Montgomery bus boycott took a year to win and with it came a sense of possibility on ending the stranglehold of White supremacy. That it took another 10 years to win the federal right to vote and put an end to racial segregation is, of course, an awfully long time. That institutionalized White supremacists couldn't stop it from happening is because the mindset—the consciousness—of southern Black people of their deserved place in the democratic sun could not be extinguished. While obviously on a more minor scale, the strategic dynamic of *demand-discussion/debate-reform—repeat* is the same here. It is through such a process that new social worker numbers are won to your side, authority shifts, and what seemed impossible in the past becomes a real possibility tomorrow.

AN OUTLINE FOR A TRANSFORMED SOCIAL WORK PROFESSION

To lay out a detailed organizing program beyond the opening demand regarding the code of ethics would be both meaninglessly abstract and elitist. To see the value of people's give-and-take means just that—a belief that only as others, perhaps moved by some of the ideas and issues raised in this book, come together in some as-yet unknown future context can such a program be created. How many of us imagined the outcome of the 2016 election? Of the 2020 pandemic? Of the upsurge in the fight against systemic racism? Not me. Such a "social work transformation program" would occur, perhaps in 2021 or 2022 and beyond, where its details would be shaped by political contexts (and thus shifts in authority and power) yet to be created and responded to.

What can be offered is an outline of issues that form the contours in which to fit those future transitional demands:

- Crafting a distinctive social work response to neoliberal policies as they affect the welfare state, the individuals, and communities impacted by those policies and the people who work within the welfare state itself
- Reimagining the workers and working conditions within the nonprofit and public sectors
- Creating models of practice that distinguish and legitimate the distinctive work of social work
- Carving out a research agenda and blended academic approach to professional training that equally elevates worker, client, and community

Crafting a Distinctive Social Work Response to Neoliberal Policies as They Affect the Welfare State, the Individual, and the Communities Impacted by Those Policies—and the People Who Work Within the Welfare State Itself

Let's be clear: There can be no substantial systemic reform within social work and in the work lives of social workers if there is not an equally substantial alteration of the relationship between the state, its political actors, and the primary beneficiaries of the present-day global economy. The intensification of social and racial inequality detailed in the second and sixth chapters includes social workers (disproportionately people of color) who are living under greater and greater financial strain. Such inequality cannot be substantially altered for social workers and millions of others without sufficient political will demanding a profound shift in taxation and revenue creation that benefits the majority of American citizens—including social workers.

Such political will comes from social movements large enough and sustained by working people from all sectors—from the poor to the professional, BLM activists and suburban liberals, students and elders, grocery clerks and nurses' aides, factory workers and frontline child welfare staff. As each group recognizes that their own self-interest is connected to the interests of others, the *collective interest* such awareness inspires has the potential power to withstand the neoliberal blowback such a movement will enflame. (*Corporations will leave! The rich will move! China will benefit!*)

Maintaining collective interests will be hard. It's here where the strength of research-rich arguments will matter to counter the 40 years of "truth" fabricated through supply-side economics thinking (i.e., only if businesses are freed from tax burdens can jobs be created). It would be helpful if our profession's thought leaders, as represented by the American Academy of Social Work and Social Welfare, were to focus far more of its "challenges for the 21st century" on the failures of neoliberalism and its effect on the working conditions inside agencies, on the diminished work life of too many social workers, on workers' eroding income, and on the dilution of the professional standards needed to provide quality service and care. The Academy's curious emphasis on micro- and mezzo-level interventions connected to pilot program–type innovations is of little benefit to the agency worker or the agency struggling to survive in the 21st century—the very target of the academy's "12 Challenges." Such a shift would be of real benefit in what promises to be a long-term battle to move away from supply-side economics policy and its stranglehold on the welfare state to a set of equity-based, redistributive policies that tax the rich, end offshore shell companies and tax havens, and provide funding for a robust welfare state. Medicare for All and the Green New Deal can't come in existence without such profound changes. While no one should wait for established social work academics to take up this challenge, it would be a powerful support were some of the academy's members to do so. (This includes greater inclusion of economics as part of basic professional training in BSW and MSW programs, which will be discussed in a separate section next.)

The present pandemic crisis has created an opportunity through the common connection we now see among health workers, grocery clerks, porters, and professionals where "collective interest" has real meaning. (This may even extend to awareness about systemic racism for the first time since Reconstruction in the 1870s.) How long that collective meaning lasts is an open question, for eventually a bill will come due as to who pays for the trillion-dollar expenditures taking place in early 2020. Will it lead to deeper cuts to Medicaid and Medicare, harming millions and laying off thousands of social workers? Or will it be "Medicare for All"? Getting a positive answer will require social workers in unprecedented numbers to join with countless others in this common connection that will bring "collective interest" and "collective strength" into alignment.

To make this kind of connection to a larger set of workers and professionals will create another challenge within the profession for its members, one partly internal and one partly external. The internal is tied to the social psychology of social workers themselves: guilt over admitting to self-interest and the ensuing passivity such guilt creates. Only by directly confronting this head-on with other like-minded professionals, perhaps as people campaign for changes to the code of ethics, can social workers overcome an internal struggle not shared by most nurses or teachers. *Wanting to be paid well with good benefits is not selfishness.* That it might require those on the other side of the inequality divide to pay more is not a fretful problem to avoid but a powerful solution to embrace.

The external challenge is the paradoxical other side of the professional coin from guilt. It's the face of some social workers' elitist fears of aligning too closely with unions and the working-class aura that unionization implies. Such fears are nurtured not by supreme confidence in one's domain but by the gnawing uncertainty that social work isn't truly a profession. If we're aligned organizationally with unions and, say, clerical workers on an economic inequality campaign, maybe we're not "professionals" after all! As Chapters 4 and 5 suggest, the real causes of this uncertainty is the widespread overuse of a plethora of clinical interventions and watered-down standards using truncated evidence throughout the field. Were the field to distinguish itself in its work with the poor, marginalized, and oppressed through a distinctive set of practice approaches and programmatic interventions, as suggested by Specht and Courtney, there would be much less cause for defensive evasion in aligning with other groups of working people who are also suffering from economic inequality.

Overcoming these forms of resistance to join collective social movements centered on social and economic inequality is crucial, for social workers have a vital role to play in these campaigns. Who better knows the rise of case after case of increasing domestic violence during the pandemic than social workers? Who better knows how many young people are going hungry because of their lost part-time jobs? Who better knows the number of elders forced to choose between prescription drugs and their next meal? Social workers' voices, strengthened by awareness that their own self-interest is tied to the same things as their clients, can have a powerful impact affect others will come to recognize. As campaigns for ending social and economic inequality *integrate multiple cases of individual need into a collective cause* that can join millions in common purpose, social workers can legitimate their roles as actors in one of the most important political and economic social movements of the 21st century.

Reimagining the Workers and Working Conditions Within the Nonprofit and Public Sectors: The Executive Challenge

As Chapter 3 detailed, the explosion of nonprofit social service agencies occurred as neoliberal federal and state policies cut back on welfare state functions through public agencies. As neither poverty and its dislocations ended nor the activism of marginalized groups abated, nonprofit-sector agencies became the Dollar General option for service innovation: lowered overhead, cheaper salaries, longer hours. Substituting genuine commitments of staff for the issues at play for healthy working conditions, this sector, perhaps, has reached its limit on what can be tolerated as acceptable professional work.

Many nonprofit executives understand this and in the last few years have worked in tandem to advocate with their staff for pay increases. For example, the New York State 3-for-5 Campaign consists of agencies across the state in a first-time legislative advocacy push for a 3% increase for each of the next 5 years as their workers and agencies are "in crisis" (3for5Campaign, 2020). Drawn from every social service sector—mental health, developmental disabilities, homelessness, aging, etc.—their efforts are a good foundation to draw upon—both for their data on the severity of the need and on their hard-earned wisdom as to why this seemingly blue state political leadership has failed to act on their demands. As both the pandemic and the racial fault line of 2020 make clear, future campaigns for economic equity will have to be bolder and more confrontational as the choice over the costs of "who pays" become even starker—all of which is multiplied tenfold if systemic racism is to be addressed as well. It is one thing, in terms of strategic risk, to ask to be funded at higher levels—whether hat in hand or raised fist, such demands admirably do challenge present funding streams; they do not challenge the economic relationships between the state and those corporate interests who at present benefit disproportionately from those arrangements. (If anyone doubts the unfairness of these present arrangements, consider some of the provisions in $485 billion small business loans passed in early April 2020. Dozens of publicly traded firms gained $300,000,000, while millions of service workers—still otherwise "essential"—have received nothing from any aid package to date [Manskar & Kosman, 2020]). When social work leaders at all levels of the profession join with others to push for a more equitable redistributive tax system, that challenge will increase as entrenched economic and social interests long comfortable with supply-side economics policy are tested for the first time since the 1960s.

There is more that executives can do without waiting for politicians to act. First, there has to be an end to their staff's individualized self-care as an agency response to secondary and vicarious trauma. I was an executive coach to a public-sector child welfare leader who in the span of 2 weeks had two staff members die (one of whom was only 40 yet had the "immune system of an elderly person brought on by stress" according to her attending physician), three went on medical administrative leave because of hypertension, and her remaining staff members were left with increased workloads. A few months later at a nonprofit foster care agency, a supervisor had two accidental deaths of clients in the span of a month yet felt obligated to return to full-time work because she didn't want to be a burden to her staff. Similar stressors can be found in domestic violence shelters, among isolated elders, working with LGBTQ youth, and almost every other population with whom social workers are involved. It is executives' responsibility to break this normative cycle of secondary trauma, ill health, understaffing, and overwork by instituting agency policies that place a premium on staff wellness as an agency duty and not solely on the workers themselves.

One of the ways to do this is for agency leaders to develop contracts with a small percentage of their budget directed at "staff good health and welfare." A leading settlement house director, Jack Doyle, has done just that for 30 years—adding a modest 1%–3% to each contract, whether for $5,000 or $5,000,000 (Burghardt & Tolliver, 2009). Such numbers add up to allow for quality meals at monthly meetings, frontline staff attending professional conferences alongside their directors, caring birthday celebrations each month, and thoughtful gestures of bereavement. Doyle's actions stemmed from his awareness that client commitment and staff commitment are one and the same. If agency directors wish to lower the unending churning turnover among their own staff, Doyle's budgetary approach has a lot to offer.

While doing the aforementioned does require attention to staff as much as clients, it is without much financial risk and could easily be incorporated into future campaigns. What would be riskier is for the coalitions of agency leaders, trade association officials, and others to approach foundations for a reconfiguration of how they frame their funding options. Streamlining foundation approaches to be more collaborative among themselves so that there is more unity and complementarity in truly diminishing levels of, say, domestic violence, homelessness, and child mortality associated with abuse is long overdue. To its credit, the Bill & Melinda Gates Foundation has taken this approach *over the last 20 years* to focus on extreme poverty in the world. While the foundation would admit it has not achieved all it had once hoped, it has made significant progress through the systematic and long-term approach it applied to this problem (Gates Foundation, 2020). Were foundation leaderships able to overcome their own individualized loss of personal prestige in pursuit of the greater good of, say, truly diminishing the level of domestic violence or foster care deaths, substantial progress could occur in ways that would both improve the lives of these at-risk groups and the credibility of those working with them.[2]

Don't Fret, Organize![3]: Frontline Staff Confront Their Own Self-Interest

As has been discussed in Chapter 4 and referred to earlier in this chapter, social workers' *internal* challenge is to overcome personal guilt that self-interest is selfishness. It is far easier for a social worker to imagine rushing into a burning building to save a child than it is to ask for a 15% raise so that her income matches her spouse's teacher's salary! Perhaps the grueling demands of the pandemic and the ensuing use of mutual aid groups facilitated by social work professionals sharing information and providing support to each other can provide some of the resilience needed to overcome the inevitable pushback any such salary demands would provoke. Be prepared: Entreaties to see management and frontline staff as like-minded and equally

---

2   It's important to note that the number of children placed in foster care has dropped dramatically through the mostly distinct efforts of Casey Family Programs and Annie E. Casey Foundations. Were they to work together on the foster care issue, who knows what might be accomplished! Likewise, it must be noted that the Gates Foundation's top-down approach to education has floundered because of its overly centralized approach to oversight.

3   As many organizers know, Joe Hill, the famous Wobbly organizer who was hanged during labor unrest in 1915, coined the phrase "Don't Mourn, Organize!" as a rallying cry when genuine labor wars were at play 100 years ago. I've modified it here to fit today's context for social workers.

committed to the "agency's _____ clients" (in the previous space put in one or all of the following words or phrases: *poor, struggling, more desperate, alone and frightened, often hungry, marginalized, at risk, endangered and far worse off than you and I*) will soon follow.

Frontline salary demands will at last lay bare how sharp the horns of the nonprofit executive's dilemma has been all along: *Under the austerity wrought through the last 40 years of neoliberal welfare state policies, the only way to deliver more services to poor and other marginalized groups is to underpay frontline staff.* Under present financial constraints that agencies live under, pay them like a nurse, and serve far fewer clients and develop far fewer programs; pay them two thirds of what a nurse makes, and services can expand. As made clear in Chapter 2, until there is a more redistributive and equitable tax system and ensuing larger revenue stream, there really is not enough money to pay professional social workers as well as their medical peers and still deliver services.

Such a dilemma need not deter committed professionals. After all, over time, exhausted and financially stressed professionals, increasingly asked to spend more and more hours on time-consuming oversight measures, are less and less likely to deliver the quality of services both they and the agency's mission aspire to. There are other options for addressing these difficult conditions without waiting for a revamped set of federal and state tax policies. For starters, executives and staff can work together on a suitable wellness program that no longer places all self-care responsibilities on the individual worker. As agencies and schools have learned through the pandemic, allowing staff to work at home or to stagger their hours, while first applied to COVID-19 safety measures, could be adapted for other wellness initiatives.

Many agencies will say they are too small for responding to collective staff demands—after-school programs, preventive measures, smaller programs working with LGBTQ youth, or sheltered elders—all of them may have fewer than 20 staff members. They're too small to organize together! Well, if gig workers can begin to organize, so can social workers in small agencies.

As *The Progressive* wrote, "New entities are working to build on ... informal gig worker networks, sometimes in collaboration with nonprofit organizations like Coworker.org or labor unions. One sign of their success appeared in the nation's largest market for ride-hailing—New York City. The Independent Drivers Guild was initially founded to represent the black car industry, but now encompasses Uber, Lyft, Juno, and other app-based drivers, in partnership with the Machinists Union. They are actively lobbying for worker protections, including what they hope will be the first fair pay legislation for gig workers in the country" (Coca, 2018). The aspirations of the Freelancers Guild, as well as their approach to expanding benefits, suggest that even small agencies working together can creatively solve some of their staff's material concerns.

Of course, the proverbial line in the sand for executives already stretched by budget shortfalls is drawn when their workers demand unionization—wellness programs, creative approaches to benefit expansion, lobbying for higher across-the-board pay increases. All of that can be accomplished in partnerships, even uneasy ones. But unions? Oh my. However, it is here where what follows might surprise you. I well recognize that unionized workers have higher salaries and better benefits than their nonunion counterparts, although the vast number of those better contracts were structurally put in place between the late 1940s (industrial workers) through the 1960s (public-sector workers). As their labor history shows, working together collectively for raises, as well as job safety and job protection measures, is far more effective than individual workers going it alone. However, there is another, little-known history here at play with its own dilemmas (Wolff, 2013). After World War II, organized labor, when confronted with the combined forces of industrial leaders, both political parties, and a growing fear of Communism, agreed to limit its demands from a broader social agenda to strictly their labor-management contracts (Chesters, 2016). By removing itself from other social movements far broader in scope, organized labor's success at the bargaining table came at the expense of progressive social movements' resilience in the face of anti-Communism. While this is not the place for an extended (and discursive) discussion on such history, the narrower focus on the contract provisions over the years has led all too often to a reactive, resistance-to-change union culture that has limited much innovation inside public-sector unionized social service organizations when reform-minded executives attempted to improve services to children, older adults, and the homeless (Green, 2007; National Center for Youth Law, 2007).

Some of the resistance is more than understandable; the high turnover, exhausting hours, and low pay documented in Chapter 4 are genuine barriers to trust between frontline staff and executives. But the barriers created by "work to rule" within narrowly defined contractual limits when a child is at risk or a homeless family lacks shelter are problems that also discredit workers and their unions when they refuse to consider new approaches to long-term problems. It's as if executives and unionized employees are locked in a dance of discouragement and despair, with neither side able to trust the other enough to alter long-established moves on how better to serve the children, elders, and others in need of their services.

For significant change to occur, a different paradigm between social workers and agency executives needs to be created regarding working conditions and basic labor relations. It's obvious by now that neither mandates from above nor reactive opposition from below are going to significantly shift working relations between these two groups. Social service executives have to stop proclaiming that all agency interests are the same for everyone; they are not. Likewise, frontline staff members have to stop imagining that they are just like their auto and steel counterparts; holding up an assembly line of cars is more than a little different from refusing to visit children at risk of abuse because they have clocked out for the day.

An example of such a paradigm shift for North America would look to Germany and their far more successful approach to worker-employer relations. As William

Greider wrote in *The Nation*, "The German system is more democratic and far more respectful of worker rights. Instead of the relentless unionbusting and virulent anti-labor propaganda common in US industry, German labor law requires consultation and collaboration with workers in the *Betriebsrat* or works council—people directly elected by the employees, blue-collar and white-collar alike" (Greider, 2014). Such an approach doesn't do away with executive power, but it significantly alters how decisions are made. As Greider (2014) went on to say, "A works council usually doesn't have veto power over corporate decisions, but its objections can discourage policy ideas that workers think are wrongheaded. That sets the stage for ongoing consultations." Ongoing consultation is perhaps what's needed between nonprofit agency leaders and frontline staff—the latter knows the actual service experience with clients and the former the budget constraints that have to be confronted. Such consultation is hardly a panacea—let's not forget neoliberal economic policies' 40-year impact on human services!—and if it fails, then traditional unionism is an obvious answer. However, attempting to build up a reservoir of trust through respectful debate and discussion on pressing service *and* labor issues may create new rhythms in agency relationships that also foster alignment in other larger political arenas for the longer term political campaigns that await them both.

Creating Models of Practice That Legitimate the Distinctive Work of Social Work

As Specht and Courtney made clear more than 25 years ago, part of social work's decline in professional status is that it can make little claim on either distinguishing itself from other clinical modalities or serving as a reliable intervention that actually improves the social problems of a community. "The evidence to support the efficacy of individual psychotherapy in dealing with social problems is extremely weak" (Specht & Courtney, 1995, p. 133). They go on to quote an influential meta-research study: "Despite the plethora of purportedly distinct psychotherapeutic treatments, influential reviews of comparative outcome research ... appear to support the conclusion that outcomes of diverse therapies are generally similar in efficacy ... . The verdict of the Dodo bird in *Alice's Adventures in Wonderland* ... . Everybody has won and all must have prizes' captures this situation most vividly" (Stiles, Shapiro, & Elliot, 1986).

If a profession's central treatment modality of clinical practice has neither distinctiveness nor an identified effect on the problems the people its mission purports to serve, there is little wonder that popular opinion hardly elevates social work's status and legitimacy. If that downward spiral caused by an overexpansion of its membership and a watered-down academic product is to be reversed, there needs to be at least two legs on which our profession stands: first, its dominant clinical modality must be framed in ways that rebuild the profession's earlier historic claims that focused directly on the poor, the marginalized, and oppressed; second, it must be an intervention that distinctively addresses the history, social problems, and individual interpersonal stressors of those populations. Perhaps if we had built upon Solomon's and Pinderhughes's works, such a task might not be necessary, but it is. Luckily, there are two recent works that go a long way in meeting these requirements.

Janet Finn's *Just Practice: A Social Justice Approach to Social Work* (2016) has a framework that powerfully integrates client *history, context, and meaning* in ways that capture how to use the social problems of clients without ignoring either their individual stressors or the historical background that shapes their present-day impact. Because of her social justice framework, Finn argued that the *meaning* of a client's problem can only be fully understood if *context and history* of the client are integrated into the clinical intervention. For example, the meaning of today's pandemic, in its mix of concrete suffering for hundreds and hundreds of thousands of people while remaining ever present yet invisible, is unsettling for everyone. Yet its *meaning* becomes even more traumatizing for immigrants who as young children escaped dangers that their families faced from military regimes in Peru, the Ukraine, Somalia, and Slovenia. These immigrants (all students of mine in the Spring of 2020) had even more intense (albeit unanticipated) reactions than their counterparts. The meaning of the pandemic was altered by history in profound ways for them as it activated buried traumas of the past. Likewise, two of them have lived in a present-day context of poor medical treatment in clinics and hospitals that made them even more frightened that they might be forced to seek medical attention during the pandemic. Such responses were much more intense, prolonged, and conflicted than their fellow classmates.

This example underscored Finn's insight that a practitioner must factor in the varied social history and context of each client to correctly interpret the meaning to a client's behavior, emotions, and attitudes. Of course, this sounds as obvious as any other differential diagnosis on the face of it, but Finn's social justice perspective adds a crucial element: *power.* By power, Finn underscored that whether one validates and uses a person's history and context, *especially if attached to meanings distinct from dominant narratives*, constructs either a social justice, empowering intervention—or its opposite. In many ways, expanding on Solomon's insights from 40 years ago, a client's perceived "resistance" or "overly fearful" behavior in the time of the pandemic (or child removal or domestic violence, etc., at any time), Finn argued, can be socially constructed to create *possibilities* to further empower them—if the client's history and context, which will include race, class, religion, and other social constructs, are acknowledged and valued in the work.

As Solomon also wrote, Finn underscored that this approach centers the lived experience of the people with less power—the client's—as of tremendous value. Finn further stressed that "history" and "context" are not left at the door of the family itself but extend into the present community for context and past generations for history. Furthermore, like Solomon, Finn's framework shapes context in a dynamic social construct—culture must be understood, races named, and resource inequities acknowledged before any interpretation of client capacity is undertaken. Likewise, attention to generational experience, whether related to educational access, economic opportunity, or the seemingly casual task of walking down the street must be raised and integrated into any assessment of a client's perceived motivation, capacity, and opportunity (Finn, 2017).

To be able to do so where dynamics of race, culture, gender, and sexuality are at play means that the practitioner doesn't shy away from raising such issues concretely. "Disparity" is not an abstraction to a client when her child's classroom has ceilings that leak while White and other middle-class children's schools a few miles away are dry and warm. "Generational trauma" is not an academic term to empathically sympathize about but a possibly very real experience where jobs have been denied, ideas stolen, physical danger is a daily reality, and racial or ethnic violence is a family's legacy-based teachable moment that most White, middle-class people don't know exists as it does for that person sitting across from you. Finn's *Just Practice* requires the same level of discomfort as Solomon's and Pinderhughes's did years ago. *If you want to form a working, trusting relationship with clients, growing comfortable with the discomfort of centering attention to social issues in their concrete, real expression in a person's life is not an add-on.*

The type of social awareness embedded in *Just Practice* makes obvious what dominant clinical social work paradigms give lip service to while avoiding its underlying meaning for the clinicians themselves: If you seek a meaningful, trusting clinical experience for and with the client, your growing comfort with race and racism, sexuality and homophobia, gender and misogyny is the only way that therapeutic alliance is possible. Researchers discovered years ago that such an alliance is the most powerful indicator for future success (Lambert & Barley, 2001). Social work programs need to center anti-oppression work throughout their curricula if they seek to elevate their students' performance. What good is it for a student to understand ego defenses if the defensiveness in the room emanates from the way somebody looks or how the professional fails to truly see the client for who they actually are?

Finn's *Just Practice* is a powerful framework, especially in helping professionals assess the ways in which they understand, engage, and work with clients. Its approach serves as a 21st-century alternative capable of examining power and privilege in the client-worker relationship in ways that expand and deepen the traditional biopsychsocial tools that have been used with little change over the last 40 years (Borrell-Carrió et al., 2004). As with Solomon and Pinderhughes, Finn demanded that social workers claim their historic responsibility to the poor and marginalized by embracing an anti-racist approach to relationship building—humbly, uncomfortably, and, in the end, far more freely as power is shared and lessons learned flow from everyone. The challenge will be whether social work educators embrace the same approach in our classrooms and in the requisite continuing education programs. Can the guideposts of the *Just Practice* framework be integrated throughout social work education or remain that popular elective offered once a year for the lucky few?

There is at least one other practice approach that can elevate social work as a profession grounded in effective interventions with the poor, marginalized, and oppressed: The Liberation Health Model pioneered by Dawn Belkin Martinez and Ann Fleck-Henderson. Their exciting work, germinating for many years as they and other like-minded practitioners struggled to craft a way forward with work genuinely empowering with those whom others would objectify, marginalize, and oppress, especially during the long epoch of neoliberalism (Belkin-Martinez & Fleck-Henderson, 2014). What elevates their work is that they provide concrete tools for young (as well as all) practitioners to immediately begin using and framing these tools within a powerful, liberating paradigm. As they wrote,

> Embedded in these practical tools, however, are visions of what social work should be. Liberation health envisions a practice of social work that is:
>
> - Holistic: situating individuals' problems in their full matrix of personal, structural, and ideological determinants;
> - Critical: refusing to accept neo-liberalism and refusing to accept the notion that social ought to subordinate itself to its social agenda;
> - Empowering: seeking to liberate clients and social workers from the confining belief that current conditions are inevitable and beyond the power to change; seeking to support their becoming active allies of individuals and movements working for social change;
> - Hopeful: rescuing the memory of a valuing "the collective human capacity to create change." (Belkin Martinez & Fleck-Henderson, 2014, p. 4)

Thus, their tools are openly embedded within a theoretical framework that requires a practitioner to reflect consistently and critically on how the tool is being used. Such critical reflection is at the heart of Paulo Freire's approach to co-creation with the oppressed. The worker is challenged to examine with learners the actual sources of presenting problems together rather than distantly interrogating the client (Freire, 2000). In the LHM, this process occurs through the use of a triangle for assessment consisting of three legs: (1) the personal, (2) the cultural, and (3) the institutional. These factors are designed to help the social worker and the client to think more broadly about the problem at hand. They readily admit that distressed clients hardly walk in the door and identify their presenting problem as the patriarchal nature of capitalist relations. It will be about depression and anxiety, harmful family dynamics, distracted children, and failing grades. By posing questions from all three legs of the triangle, "in talking about their problems in a broader context of individual, biological and social factors, cultural practices and messages, and institutions, clients begin to see their problems in a radically new light, to critically reflect on the language and assumptions they previously used to describe it, and to understand and narrate the problem in a new 'thicker' and empowering way" (Belkin-Martinez & Fleck-Henderson, 2014, p. 24).

To engage in this triangulated problem, one must harken back to Pinderhughes's powerful insights of the worker's inevitable discomfort when raising cultural issues where differences of privilege regarding race, gender, sexuality, etc., are at play. A White social worker posing a cultural question to a Latinx immigrant woman suffering from domestic violence needs to have interrogated their own lived experience and comfort with racial and social difference if that question is to be perceived as purposely helpful rather than invasive. There is no better way to develop cultural humility than through this kind of reflection.

An insightful clinical student, who asked to remain anonymous, beautifully captured both the discomfort and the possibility such effort creates in her work with an underemployed, married Latinx man we will call B.

> Within all of the work that B. and I have done together, the most difficult of all has been living in the discomfort and the struggle that I needed to feel to create real change within our counseling room, within B., and on a larger level, within the contexts that we live in. Whether it was during discussions of citizenship, race, class, or otherwise, I found myself uncomfortable with the power and position that I hold within all of the systems of stratification that promote people like me and demote people like B.
>
> The most difficult conversation I had with B., but one that I believe led to the biggest amount of change for both of us, was about his marriage. His marriage causes him enormous amounts of stress as he vacillates between feelings of inadequacy ... . At one point during a discussion, B. turned to me and asked me, as a woman, do I expect my future husband to provide for me, and how do I know when I am in love? I was immediately overcome with feelings of embarrassment, shame, and anger at him for putting me on the spot with such personal and uncomfortable questions. I felt myself get defensive and wanted to remind him that such personal questions will not be accepted. Despite my countertransference reaction, I instead used the discomfort to tap into skills, like asking "why" questions, which helps clients problem pose and discover for themselves the roots of their anxiety, and the liberation

health model, which helps set clients free from the cultural and institutional systems holding them back.

[I had learned that] key to using the liberation health model is understanding that a person's views are affected by the views held by the institutions with which they interface … . Therefore, I asked B. questions like, 'what does it mean to be a husband and to be a wife, why do you want to be the breadwinner in your marriage … ?' Through answering these questions, B. and I were able to tap into the roots of where his feelings of obligation come from, many of which were based in cultural and institutional beliefs about gender roles and perfect, idealized marriages that he had internalized throughout the course of his life … and gender role expectations across cultures. B. explained that he was raised surrounded by a society in Colombia that emphasizes the man's duty as the breadwinner, and that his father always reminded him of his duty to make money for his future wife and family. (Anonymous, April, 2020)

True to the LHM, this student understood that the purpose of such questions was not just to arrive at answers but to alter their relationship to address the problem. "Together, we deconstructed the dominant messaging that B. had been told about how men and women are supposed to act and hypothesized about what would happen if B. actually did not abide by the cultural and social sets of rules for manhood. These discussions led B. to develop an understanding of the ways in which gender roles and conceptions about marriage and love are socially constructed. By breaking free of these messages, B. was able to gain a sense of control about his own life. Although this practice was extremely trying and required me to address a topic that made me uncomfortable, it was through the feelings of discomfort that allowed me to trust myself and trust B. to problem solve together" (unpublished manuscript, 2020).

The use of this discomforting yet liberating triangulation leads a person to feel empowered to act differently as well—the essence of Freire's *praxis.* Belkin-Martinez and Fleck-Henderson pose other tools as well. By seeing "a problem in its totality," this allows social workers and clients to work on a comprehensive action plan that provides a client a variety of options for action—some personal, some group, some institutional. Work is broken into columns: "one for the various aspects of the problem; what needs to change in relation to each; the long range vision or goal related to each; and specific activities and initiatives for the work (in each)" (Belkin-Martinez & Fleck-Henderson, 2014). Because all three triangle factors are considered, actions can range from micro, individual work (a domestic violence client works with the worker on job readiness for economic independence); mezzo, or group work (she joins a mutual aid group of other domestic violence survivors); and macro or collective (worker and client attend a rally supporting improved legislation regarding domestic violence survivors and their families). Such an action framework accomplishes two things. First, it situates responsibility and support at various levels of society, thus lessening client interpretations of personal blame and shame and fostering empowerment. Second, it relocates the social worker within the rich and vibrant tradition of social work service and social action as joint professional hallmarks no longer found within the dusty archives of 100 years ago but in the 21st century. What better way for a profession to reclaim its credibility?

CARVING OUT A RESEARCH AGENDA AND BLENDED ACADEMIC APPROACH TO PROFESSIONAL EDUCATION THAT EQUALLY ELEVATES WORKER, CLIENT, AND COMMUNITY

A Way Forward Through Participatory Action Research. An area that social work academics and other professionals can rightly be proud of is in their expansive use of participatory action research (PAR). McDonald's brief synthesis nicely exemplifies what can be found in countless articles, dissertations, and books on PAR. "Participatory Action Research (PAR) is a qualitative research methodology option that ... is considered (a) democratic, equitable, liberating, and life-enhancing qualitative inquiry that remains distinct from other qualitative methodologies" (McDonald, 2012). Using PAR, qualitative features of an individual's feelings, views, and patterns are revealed without control or manipulation from the researcher. The participant is active in making informed decisions throughout all aspects of the research process for the primary purpose of imparting social change; a specific action (or actions) is the ultimate goal (McDonald, 2012).

That the PAR framework commits to an engaged, respectful, and reciprocal relationship with the clients and community members one is studying is the essence of what progressive social work is all about, seeking to democratize service, as well as research encounters. While the limitations of time—including the complexities of creating reliable research designs, validating research instruments, and participating in the peer-review process—can slow down the process of building trusting relationships with participants otherwise marginalized in their lives, the aspirations and efforts on the part of social workers engaged in PAR seems genuine (Silva et al., 2018). PAR researchers seek to use their work to impact the world, not only study it.

While some limitations will be discussed next, some of the criticisms of PAR seem unfair and others not fully contextualized. Researchers and community members who understandably may seek their work to be of use to the broader public may disseminate their findings through popular means (from podcasts to popular journals) and thus be perceived by some with the academy as not meeting standard measures of credibility in the dissemination of their findings (Silva et al., 2018).

That PAR researchers would rather put their findings to immediate use and not wait for peer-reviewed journal articles to appear 3 years later always seemed admirable; in these pandemic-ridden days of unrelieved uncertainty and ambiguity, even more so.

Alternatively, Silva and her colleagues pointed out that measuring "public impact" of PAR has been difficult and often inconclusive. Their definition is a worthy one: "Public impact scholarship in social work is characterized by intentional efforts to create social change through the translation and dissemination of research to nonacademic audiences" (Silva et al., 2018). While rightly pointing to the work of Sherraden and his colleagues that there have been some positive results through asset building, a special issue of the *Journal of the Society for Social Work and Research* (volume 10, number 4, 2019) underscored that there is less impact to measure than many have desired. In many ways, expecting significant PAR public impact in communities living under the lash of a neoliberally reduced welfare state is less about putting the cart before the horse than not recognizing that there's an underfed horse still inside the barn.

It's thus no accident that most PAR focuses on populations and practices at the micro and mezzo levels. The *Journal of the Society for Social Work and Research's* most recent articles make that clear: parenting and substance abuse, sex offenders, young adult tutors, WTC program participants (volumes 9 & 10, 2019); such work is laudatory, for it has the potential to impact *practice*. Of course, for that to occur in ways consistent with other expressed values of PAR for client engagement, mutual dialogue, and partnership, the practice models themselves must embrace the same values. Preaching the value of partnership and dialogue in research while teaching practice from boundary-laden models of professional intervention undercuts the effect of the former and the legitimacy of the latter.

Part of the way forward through this impasse is to move away from the academician's risk-free world of exploring client issues and instead examine at least two others: first, the work experience and working conditions of social workers. Such PAR work might include, for example, the demographic differences between social work executives, managers, and frontline staff; comparisons of leadership styles between executives with MSWs and MBAs; the long-term effect of untreated secondary trauma for social work first responders; the financial struggles of social workers, from new workers living with student debt to retirees; and comparisons in working condition under unionized and nonunionized work places. The risk here is that these topics would release the profession from the 40-year stranglehold that the field's overarching story is one of the romanticized, readily suffering social worker as a paragon of quiet strength and forbearance more committed to the downtrodden than their own well-being. In its place might emerge a picture of hard-working and dedicated professional workers whose commitment to the poor and marginalized can only be achieved as both receive their "just due" in working conditions, financial security, and respect.

The other important topic to explore is closer to academics' home: a systematic study of what exactly is "competent" in "competency-based education." As laudatory as the desire to measure performance in terms of measurable outcomes may be, "competency" is more often given the flaccid scrutiny of at best short-term behaviors in a classroom and at worst (and far more often) perceived self-reporting. Developing internally valid indicators of competency and reliably measured outcomes that actually sustain new practice behaviors is the moonshot the profession needs if our stance in the larger word is to stand alongside the credibility and legitimacy found in the medical professions. Apollo 11's landing on the moon took 8 years from John F. Kennedy's speech until Neil Armstrong's walk. With commitment, PAR researchers could do the same in half that time.

Curricular Additions for the 21st Century

With excoriating clarity, the combination of the pandemic; obvious racial violence directed at African Americans and Latinx; the ensuing economic and social fallout across every public, nonprofit, and private institution; and the awareness of structural racism—all occurring in the first 5 months of 2020—has laid bare shortcomings in our own training and preparation for what awaits us (and every other profession) over the coming decades. There is much to be proud of: social workers have remained first responders in child welfare, adult services, work with the homeless, and many others in need throughout the pandemic. Almost always ignored in the popular press, social workers have continued to work directly with clients, even without personal protective equipment (Oliwashui, 2020) or adequate testing.[4]

We can assume that social workers will remain deeply engaged in responding to ongoing crises associated with the pandemic and entrenched racial inequality—the social and economic fallout of previous systemic inequality now laid bare, the reality that globalization is far more than former American goods being produced in China or services offered from India, and the many forces in nature, often warped by human intervention, letting us know how fragile our existence as a species might be.

To be change agents more than reactive keepers of a patched-up status quo, social workers need at least two significant additions to our standard curricula, alongside the anti-racism and anti-oppression recommendations in the previous chapter: (1) political economy and (2) environmental and climate change. At

---

4   It's been striking to see how little attention has been given to social work first responders, as well as seemingly no pushback within the field for staff to be given the same protections that nurses and doctors receive when social workers enter the home of at-risk children, veterans, and older folks. The combination of leadership inattention and frontline staff socialization to deference to "niceness" at the expense of their well-being covered in Chapter 4 can have dire consequences during a pandemic.

first blush, each seems outside social work's purview: most social workers don't study business cycles and are terrified of math; climate change is about science and, relatedly, public health.

While these popular definitions are accurate, they are also incomplete. The social and economic fallout from the pandemic now affecting millions of Americans—many of them at long last recognized "essential" and more likely to be Black, Brown, and/or an immigrant than White—has the potential to wreak permanent destruction on urban and rural communities in ways not seen since the Great Depression. This damaging potential is possible only if Americans continue to accept arguments that austerity, balanced budgets, and regressive taxation (taxes that burden the poor and middle class more than upper classes) are needed for economic prosperity (Lent, 2020). Social workers, by couching their argument only in moral terms of unfairness, have not been able to withstand the seemingly empirical truth of graphs, expenditures, and lost revenues that have been thrown around since the halcyon days of Ronald Reagan and his financial guru, Milton Friedman (Denning, 2013). Social workers need to be educated to interpret economic data and their implications for either growth and greater equality or recession and intensified inequality offered by popular economic writers, such as Paul Krugman and Joseph Stiglitz (Krugman, 2020; Stiglitz, 2019). In this way social workers will join their awareness of personal and community suffering with the analytical resilience these authors offer, thus gaining the standing that the profession deserves as the social and economic arguments intensify in the years ahead.

As for more systematic attention to climate change and environmentalism, the pandemic has made even more clear that the dramatic—and terrifying—"natural" disruptions of "100 year" hurricanes, tsunamis, tornadoes, floods, heat waves, fires, and—yes—viruses are a permanent part of our lives and not once-a-century events. The results are not simply geological and atmospheric; they are also primary causes of social inequality, massive migrations, life expectancy, health disparities, and even war (World Health Organization, 2011). All of these issues that cascade outward from environmental degradation are core issues in our field. To not understand the causes of these endemic social problems not only doesn't help future social workers learn how to teach others how to fish—there won't be any fish at all.

Both these additions, combined with other identified curricular needs discussed in this book on racism and other forms of oppression, including the exploitation of social workers themselves, have one other implicit curricular criticism: the failure of systems theory to account for the inherent systemic conflict embedded in social and economic relationships. Systems theory, long popular throughout social work, whether "general," "ecological," or "multi-theoried," they all pose the inevitable return to "homeostasis" or smooth functioning between the complex weave of interconnected subsystems—family, neighborhood, institutions, communities, states, the world!—that is substantively not only wrong but also misguided. If you accept the long-term struggle underway in our global world, both socially and environmentally, then systems theory's framework that suggests systems seek "equilibrium" is harmful, not helpful. That people in the short-run may develop effective coping mechanisms to adapt and live comfortably in their day-to-day world—who other than a few teenagers want to feel crisis and change *all* the time?—is not a justification for seeing entrenched, conflictual, and inequitable systems as seeking the same stability—unless one means the stability of authoritarianism. Social work academics need to develop a deeper structural analysis based on the mix of conflict and release and struggle that is a primary feature of 21st-century life if we seek to prepare professionals for the world they are to work and live in.

A Profession's Case Study of Courage and Commitment to Racial Justice—With a Cautionary Coda

The previous set of campaign issues and call for transformative change is obviously daunting. How can so much change be wrought in the years ahead? As stated before, some campaigns, such as on revenue creation, Medicare for All, and reinvestment in higher education, require the marshaling of social forces far beyond any one profession's numbers. Social work needs to embrace such campaigns actively. However, connected to these broader campaigns must be progressive social worker's own sustained efforts to shift its priorities toward an authentic commitment to the poor, marginalized, and oppressed. Luckily, there is a recent exemplar of how just a small number of committed activists—in the very beginning, just three—can make a lasting contribution to our field despite initial indifference, more than occasional official resistance, and only modest financial resources at best. That its 13-year campaign ends with a reassertion of national leaders' and staff's prerogatives to control local dissent cannot diminish the lasting legacy of their effort to make racial justice central to the profession's mission.

The organizing work of Sandy Bernabei, a White clinical social worker from Westchester County, a suburb just north of New York City; Mary Pender Greene, an African American chief of social work and assistant executive director of a prestigious New York City social service agency; and Bob Schachter, the White executive director of the New York City chapter of NASW didn't start with the three of them sitting in a room to map out a strategy for racial justice. It perhaps began when Sandy, in the mid-1990s was speaking with Phyllis Frank, the executive director of VCS Inc., a county-wide counseling program. Bernabei was invited by the director to an anti-racism workshop sponsored by a group in New Orleans that went by the intriguingly long name of the People's Institute for Survival and Beyond. A few years later, over in New York City, Schachter, impressed with her smarts and organizational acumen, spoke with Pender Greene about becoming president of the local chapter. Pender Greene, wary at again being one of the few people of color in a roomful of leaders, demurred at the time. Schachter, who had an organizer's genome pattern of persistence in his DNA, again made the request a few years later. Pender Greene, respecting Schachter's obvious sincerity and concerned about the country's drift toward conservatism, agreed this time.

It was a few months later that serendipity played its own part in their story. (Serendipity is an overlooked element of successful organizing: Does anyone remember that Martin Luther King Jr. was initially the compromise choice to head the SCLC?) Bernabei's previous attendance at the People's Institute's workshop had, as she said, caused her head to feel like "Beam Me Up, Scottie" as she had entered a whole new, previously unobserved world. Now understanding the depth of historical, institutional, and professional racism in our society, as well as the unearned privilege of Whites such as herself, she had felt compelled to act since the workshop. As a social worker, she felt the profession, with its talk of social justice, was the place to start, but she had been unsuccessful in leveraging exactly where to and how to make a significant difference.

Meanwhile, Pender Greene was excited to begin chapter presidential work with Schachter, although her action program was still unformed. Her career as a clinical social worker had had a paradoxical mix of both great support and intense resentment and outright racism from White social workers throughout her career. Such a history had made her understandably cautious about when and with whom issues of race and racism were discussed. "When you're the only person of color in every room you enter, it gets exhausting. Early in my career, I was told that race was not to be brought up. Navigating that reality on the job was part of my everyday existence."

And yet there were Pender Greene and Bernabei one day in early 2000 at Columbia Teacher's College, getting a chance to chat during a workshop break. Sandy talked about this amazing anti-racism workshop and her hopes to get NASW involved. Mary mentioned she had just become president of the New York City chapter—the largest in the country. Sandy, while she didn't express this in her interview, must have felt that she had died and gone to heaven. As Mary drolly recounted years later, "From then on, Sandy kept asking me to go this workshop. I wasn't sure at first, but I gave in. And it blew my mind apart! That People's Institute workshop changed the trajectory of my work and my life."

Few workshops cause people to have Star Trek out-of-body experiences or blow the minds of seasoned professionals, but the People's Institute's had done just that. The institute's program, facilitated with a group of at least half people of color and the rest Whites, began with a finely honed synthesis of the centrality of race in American history and the ensuing violence on African Americans and other people of color. It went on to detail how race itself was a social construction, ideologically normalizing the value of Whiteness by simultaneously degrading all others with even a drop of another racial color in their blood. Such constructions thus gave justification for the variety of laws, practices, and norms permeating every American institution—schools, the courts, families, policing, elections—thus ensuring the enduring subjugation of an entire people. While centuries of organizing had chipped away at many of the more egregious practices of racism, every American institution—and the people within it—was still riven with it, privileging Whites over all others. Such racism extended to its professions—social work included. It would thus be the responsibility of its members to actively root out a profession's own racist practices as its contribution to "survival and beyond" in the United States.

Meeting up soon after with the strategically savvy Schachter, who at the urging of Pender Greene had attended and been greatly affected by the workshop as well, the three did what all good organizers do first: *They planned.* Their long-term goal was for the profession to confront its own racist history and to alter its focus to one that put the struggle against racism at the forefront of its work. Its primary tactical objective would be for the People's Institute workshops to be sponsored by chapters across the country, which in turn would inspire social work professionals to engage in anti-racist work within their chapters and agencies. However, they realized that while their aspirations were noble, how they began their first foray into the profession in New York City would concretely determine their future efforts. While such workshops ideally would later be open to everyone—students, new professionals, other agency staff—they had the tactical foresight that their first chapter-sponsored workshop had to include social service and educational leaders. It would be these leaders' social capital that could serve as a legitimating springboard for widespread acceptance of this work.

Make no mistake: Bernabei, Pender Greene, and Schachter were challenging their own professional careers in this undertaking. Since the mid-1990s, social welfare was operating under President Bill Clinton's Personal Responsibility and Work Opportunity Act, an all-but-openly racist piece of legislation that instituted work requirements for welfare, reduced food stamp allocation to families in need, and put in place anti-immigrant policies that laid the foundation for today's immigration nightmare under the Trump administration (Lind, 2019). Furthermore, George W. Bush took office in an even more conservative time. Given agency reliance on so many federal grants, there was as much likelihood of executive blowback as there was interest. And yet they were willing to take that risk: leaders of major public and nonprofit social service agencies, the United Way and Human Services Council, as well as well-known academics, were invited, cajoled, and enticed to attend this 2-day event. (As discussed in Chapter 3, given their workload demands, getting executives to commit to that amount of time took great powers of persuasion and a dollop or two of *chutzpah.*)

After months of effort—remember, Bernabei and Greene had full-time jobs and Schachter widespread membership services and programs to oversee—the People's Institute leaders Ron Chisom, David Billings, and Maria Reinat-Pumarejo arrived in New York to begin what would turn out to be one of their most pivotal workshops—for it was an outstanding success. Executives of major social service agencies and leaders of large-scale umbrella groups, such as United Way and Black Agency Executives, were inspired by the institute's work and gave critical legitimacy to the organizers' efforts moving forward.

And move forward they did! Over the next 3 years, working with Bernabei and Pender Greene's wide New York City networks and Schachter's chapter contacts across the nation, promoting the work at schools and convincing agencies to hold workshops for their staff, the three exemplified the organizers' backbone of patience and persistence to push the work forward. Today's BLM activists inside the social work field and future organizers would be wise to seek out their hard-won counsel on building a movement inside the profession. Using Schachter's contacts, they began recruiting other chapter leaders to attend the workshops, as well as continuing to recruit in the New York metropolitan area. The workshops, while time-consuming to organize themselves, were actually tactics toward a larger end of recentering the profession itself as an anti-racist institution, with its membership mobilized to confront racist practices in their organizations and communities.

Fortunately, Pender Greene's replacement as chapter president, Paul Kurzman, a social work professor of social work well regarded in the profession, doubled down on their commitments by helping establish chapter field placements for students committed to anti-racist work, thus increasing the cadre of people who could spread the word on the workshops, as well as, in some cases, developing into workshop leaders themselves. Kurzman also used chapter resources and won the board's approval that anyone to serve on the board had to attend a People's Institute workshop. Such chapter involvement served as a model that could be used elsewhere in other chapters as Bernabei and Pender Greene expanded the work to other state chapters across the country.

This slow and steady progress at the local level was combined with attention to the national level as well. Schachter saw an opportunity in 2005 at the planned NASW National Congress, where leaders from across the country, including CSWE and deans and directors of social work programs, would be in attendance. Invited to create the priorities for the next decade through an open-ended, 2-day dialogue, Schachter saw the event as the ideal opening for a more systematic intervention. After interested leaders attended a breakfast meeting, a group of 40 attendees agreed on pushing NASW national to adopt an anti-racism platform as one of its two primary calls for action over the next 10 years. Spread out across the large hall, they triumphed: the national Congress voted overwhelmingly to support their anti-racist plank.

Such consistent, steady work began enrolling new members from across the country in their campaign. Besides the local work of putting on People's Institute workshops and enrolling student leaders as activist interns, a number of well-regarded professionals and academics began drafting a powerful white paper that could serve to contextualize the history and meaning of their focus for future generations. The result was an extraordinary document endorsed in 2007 by the national leadership called "Institutional Racism and Social Work: A Call to Action" (de Silva et al., 2007).

It had to be an exciting time: local organizing at the grassroots, an expansion of local activists and leaders committed to the work, growing national influence and legitimacy, and a narrative recentering social work's stated commitment to social justice to an active anti-racist stance. Ten years of effort, begun with only three people, had created a national social movement inside the social work profession. Like New York, local state chapters in Seattle, Boston, Austin, and Atlanta created their own transmission belts from education to organizing, as professionals and students attended the People's Institute workshop, became inspired to act, and brought their commitment to racial justice into their agencies and schools. Remarkably, some agencies' leadership took the unprecedented step of enrolling their employees in the workshop, leading them to be certified as anti-racist agencies. When you consider the traditional board-leadership relationships, where mostly volunteer and often wealthy board members hold agency executives accountable for long-term strategic direction, such open commitment was indeed extraordinary.

Over the years, the leaders also recognized that other social issues within the profession couldn't be ignored. Bernabei, now NASW New York City chapter president, and Schachter, working closely with their chapter board, developed an economic platform that centered itself on the financial hardship endured by all social workers without diminishing the centrality of racial equity as well. Introduced as "Thrive New York: Race, Equity and Intersectionality," the proposed bill would address the growing gap in social work salaries discussed in Chapter 4. Meanwhile, on the national front, a think tank paper that was to serve as an organizing model for addressing racial equity inside the profession, as well as the communities in which social workers lived and worked, started to be developed in 2012. Working with the Social Work Policy Institute based in Washington, DC, the report *Achieving Racial Equity: Calling the Social Work Profession to Action* (Social Policy Institute, 2014) was designed to help every chapter in the United States have a basic road map for organizing their racial equity work.

A Cautionary Coda Arises

More than 12 years of effort, begun after two women and one man attended what they each initially thought would be an informative educational workshop run by a veteran group of anti-racist organizers working out of New Orleans, was now a national social work movement impacting NASW chapters, social work agencies, and academic institutions across the country. A National Conference called for 2013 seemed to be the ideal time to further solidify its standing and purpose throughout the profession. With an African American, Angelo McClain, about to be appointed as national executive director and the president of the NASW board, Darrell Wheeler, also an African American, it would have seemed a propitious moment for even more widespread reform.

However, the outgoing executive director, Betsy Clark, supported by then president Jean Anastas, initiated a reorganizational effort titled "Modernization through Centralization." On paper a call for greater financial efficiencies where all dues would be collected through the national office, the plan had the draconian impact of diminishing the financial and organizational autonomy of each local chapter. In fact, modernization resulted in a flip of this membership organization from a membership-driven model to one replaced by a corporate model that was able to consolidate power and authority to the paid administration at NASW headquarters in DC. Recognizing how devastating this centralization would be, Bernabei, Pender Greene, and Schachter, joined by other local leaders, fought to block the initiative emanating from the national office, but their efforts were too late. Lacking enough support from other formal leaders who passively supported outgoing executive director Clark's initiative as her final signature act, the national "modernization" carried the day—and with it, carried off the 13-year momentum toward racial justice as central to the profession itself.

Not that their work stopped. Nor did many other professionals across the nation curtail their own efforts. Anti-racist workshops offered by people trained by the People's Institute were offered as continuing education units for interested social workers. Some schools, led by Smith College School of Social Work, began to adopt a more assertive commitment to anti-racism and anti-oppression materials in their curricula. But the social movement mix of concrete local actions, developing consciousness, and national campaigns could not help but be dissipated over time as financial resources dried up. Bernabei now works as an organizer, clinician, and consultant, and Pender Greene is president and CEO of MPG Consulting, an organization with a focus on agencies seeking to undo racism and enhance racial equity and inclusion; Schachter, a long time practitioner of *qigong*, now offers workshops on this healing art, often for people dealing with either the trauma of racism directly or the secondary trauma wrought by institutional practices that expose the lacerating impact of racism on clients and community members. Proud of all they accomplished, they, nevertheless, carry the quiet regret of knowing how so much more their beloved profession could have accomplished. Given all that is now unfolding in the Spring of 2020, they, too, hope for another movement, perhaps BLM, that will use their legacy not simply as a historic memory but also as a foundation for social work's recommitment that centers its practice on racial and social justice.

THE NEXT LONG WALK TOWARDS THE PUBLIC GREATNESS OF SOCIAL WORK

This chapter is ending at a time when a terrifying pandemic has taken the lives of more than 200,000, with numbers rising, 30 million people are unemployed and hoping for a return to work in businesses that may never reopen, state spending for education and services has been severely cut, and, tragically, racial violence has again captured on video, including the murder of George Floyd by Minneapolis police and the fictional profiling by a White woman of an African American birdwatcher, Christian Cooper who, if he had not used his phone, might have been the Emmitt Till of 2020. As a friend noted, the United States is going through the pandemic of 1918, the economic catastrophe of the 1930s, and the racial unrest of 1968, all at the same time. No one alive who is reading this book, other than immigrants who have escaped genocide and state murder in their home countries, has lived through a more harsh and desperate time.

Such a time would be cause for despair if we did not have history to point us forward with hope. For there was a time, for example, in 1990, when a majority people lived in a nation under legally sanctioned segregation known as apartheid and their leader was in prison for more than 25 years. Against them was a codified set of laws affirming the need for racial discrimination and a massive military and police presence well-practiced in violently suppressing dissent for generations. How could anyone imagine a way forward then? And yet someone did—Nelson Mandela. In 1992, he and his people left their respective prisons to chart their own history together.

That Mandela could do so much while imprisoned is a testimony to his unique fortitude and resilience—and a quality anyone seeking transformational change must have—as well as the internal strategic vision that serves as one's North Star, guiding one forward no matter the unforeseen roadblocks and struggles that lie ahead. Such a vision tests its core values, day in and day out, by maintaining:

- a belief that those without power have the capacity to change the world for the better;
- a belief in the moral goodness and organizational effectiveness embedded in the collective struggle for equality as well as freedom;
- a belief in the economic and social good that comes from economic redistribution that impacts social workers and community members alike; and
- a belief in the quiet joy of hearing the voices of those who once had been invisible and ignored resonating with a sense of shared power and democratic purpose.

Such values have formed the vision of this book. May some of them guide you as you build the socially just and liberational social work profession you deserve and that our world needs now more than ever.

REFERENCES

3for5campaign. (2020, January 30). *Join the 3-for-5 campaign to hike funding for human service non-profits by 3% for each of the next 5 years!* https://www.nyaprs.org/e-news-bulletins/2020/1/30/join-the-3-for-5-campaign-to-hike-funding-for-human-service-nonprofits-by-3-for-each-of-the-next-5-years

Abramovitz, M. (1998). Social work and social reform: An arena of struggle. *Social Work, 43*(6), 512–526.

Abramovitz, M. & Zelnick, J. (2018, October). *Business as usual? A wake-up call for the human services.* Touro College/Silberman School of Social Work. https://s27588.pcdn.co/wp-content/uploads/2018/10/report_human_services_workforce.pdf

Acemoglu, D. & Robinson, J. (2015). The rise and decline of general laws of capitalism. *Journal of Economic Perspectives, 29*(1), 3–28.

Addams, J. (2002). Moral and legal protection of children. In J. B. Elshtain (Ed.), *The Jane Addams reader* (p. 192). Basic Books.

Alexander, L. & Lichtenberg, P. (1978). The "casework notebook": An analysis of its content. *Journal of Sociology and Social Welfare, 5*(1), 55–65.

All About America. (2018, January 11). What are the most respected professions in the US? *VOA News.* https://blogs.voanews.com/all-about-america/2018/01/11/what-are-the-most-respected-professions-in-the-us/

American Academy of Social Work and Social Welfare. (2016). *The 12 grand challenges.* http://grand-challengesforsocialwork.org/grand-challenges-initiative/about/

American Academy of Social Work and Social Welfare. (2020). https://grandchallengesforsocialwork.org

American Bar Association (ABA). (n.d.). *Standing committee on pro bono and public service.* https://www.americanbar.org/groups/probono_public_service/

American Nurses Association (ANA). (2015). *Code of ethics for nurses with interpretive statements.* https://www.nursingworld.org/practice-policy/nursing-excellence/ethics/code-of-ethics-for-nurses/coe-view-only/

American Psychiatric Association. (n.d.). *Ethics.* https://www.psychiatry.org/psychiatrists/practice/ethics

Annie E. Casey Foundation. (2016, November 1). *Responsible demolition: A Baltimore case study with national implications.* https://www.aecf.org/resources/responsible-demolition-a-baltimore-case-study-with-national-implications/

Anonymous. (2019). *I suspect it is hard to be a social worker. We get up early and don't have time to drink* [Status Update]. Facebook.

Anonymous. (2020). *Reflections on using the liberation health model.* Unpublished paper.

Argyris, C., & Schön, D. (1978) *Organizational learning: A theory of action perspective.* Addison-Wesley.

Argylis, C., & Schön, D. (1995). *Organizational learning II: Theory, method, and practice.* Addison-Wesley.

Arnstein, S. R. (1969). A ladder of citizen participation. *Journal of the American Institute of Planners, 35*(4), 216–224.

Ashwin, P., Boud, D., & Coate, K. (2015). *Reflective teaching in higher education.* Bloomsbury.

Auerbach, D., Buerhaus, P., Staiger, D., & Skinner, L. (2017). *2017 data brief update: Current trends of men in nursing.* Montana State University Center for Interdisciplinary Health Workforce Studies. http://healthworkforcestudies.com/publications-data/data_brief_update_current_trends_of_men_in_nursing.html

Ayala, J., Drolet, J., Hewson, J., Letkemann, L., Baynton, M., Elliott, G., Judge-Stasiak, A., Blaug, C., Tétreault, A. G., & Schweizer, E. (2018). Field education in crisis: Experiences of field education coordinators in Canada. *Social Work Education: The International Journal, 37*(3), 281–293. https://doi.org/10.1080/02615479.2017.1397109

Baines, D., Davis, J., & Saini, M. (2009). Wages, working conditions, and restructuring in Ontario's social work profession. *Canadian Social Work Review, 26*(1), 59–72.

Banks, S. (2011). Ethics in an age of austerity: Social and the evolving new public management. *Journal of Intervention, 20*(2). https://www.journalsi.org/articles/abstract/10.18352/jsi.260/

Barnett, R. (1997). *Higher education: A critical business.* Open University Press.

Barrit, D. (2012, October 24). Today's faculty. *Chronicle of Higher Education.* http://chronicle.com/article/Todays-Faculty-Stressed-and/135276/

Bateson, G. (1972). *Steps to an Ecology of Mind: Collected Essays in Anthropology, Psychiatry, Evolution, and Epistemology.* University of Chicago Press.

Baum, S. (2013, October). *The evolution of student debt in the U.S.: An overview.* The Urban Institute. http://www.upjohn.org/stuloanconf/Baum.pdf

Baxter, E., & Hopper, K. (1981). *Private Lives/Public Spaces: Homeless Adults on the Streets of New York City.* Community Services Society.

Becket, L. (2020, April 1). Americans purchasing record-breaking numbers of guns amid coronavirus. *The Guardian.* https://www.theguardian.com/world/2020/apr/01/us-gun-purchases-coronavirus-record

Belkin-Martinez, D., & Fleck-Henderson, A. (2014). *Social justice in clinical practice: a liberation health framework for social work.* Routledge.

Berger, P., & Luckmann, T. (1967). *The social construction of reality.* Anchor Books.

Bernstein, S. (1991). *Managing contract services in the nonprofit agency.* Temple University Press.

Bill & Melinda Gates Foundation. (2014). *Annual letter 2014.* https://www.gatesfoundation.org/who-we-are/resources-and-media/annual-letters-list/annual-letter-2014

Birdsell, D. S., & Mazzio, D. (2003). *The next leaders: UNBYC grantee leadership development and succession management needs.* United Way.

Black, P. N., Jeffreys, D., & Hartley, E. K. (1993). Personal history of psychosocial trauma in the early life of social work and business students. *Journal of Social Work Education, 29*(2), 171–180. https://doi.org/10.1080/10437797.1993.10778812

Blair, C. (2010). Stress and the development of self-regulation in context. *Child Development Perspectives, 4*(3), 181–188. https://doi.org/10.1111/j.1750-8606.2010.00145.x

Bo, A., Qin, G., & Lluang. (2018). Understanding social worker turnover: Intentionally using the unified theory of behavior [Paper presentation]. Society of Social Work and Research Twenty-Second Annual Conference, Miami, FL, United States.

Bogo, M. (2015). Field education for clinical social work practice: Best practices and contemporary challenges. *Clinical Social Work Journal, 43*(3), 317–324.

Bok, D. (2012). *Our underachieving colleges: A candid look at how much students learn and why they should be learning more.* William G. Bowen.

Boris, E., de Leon, E., Roeger, K., & Nikolova, M. (2010, October 7). *Human service nonprofits and government collaboration*. Urban Institute. https://www.urban.org/research/publication/human-service-nonprofits-and-government-collaboration-findings-2010-national-survey-non-profit-government-contracting-and-grants

Bornstein, R. (2001). The impending death of psychoanalysis. *Psychoanalytic Psychology, 18*(1), 3–20. https://doi.org/10.1037/0736-9735.18.1.2

Borrell-Carrió, F., Suchman, A. L., & Epstein, R. M. (2004). The biopsychosocial model 25 years later: principles, practice, and scientific inquiry. *Annals of family medicine, 2*(6), 576–582. https://doi.org/10.1370/afm.245

Borrell-Carrió, F., Suchman, A. L., & Epstein, R. M. (2014). The biopsychosocial model 25 years later: Principles, practice, and scientific inquiry. *Canadian Journal of Action Research, 13*(2), 34–50.

Bouie, J. (2020, June 29). Beyond white fragility. *New York Times*, A-20.

Boyatzis, R. E. (1982). *The competent manager: A mode for effective performance*. John Wiley and Son.

Brager, G., & Purcell, F. (1967). *Community action against poverty: readings from the mobilization experience*. New College & University Press.

Branch, T. (1989). *Parting the waters; America in the King years 1954–63*. Simon & Schuster.

Brauner, T. (2015). Contemporary clinical practice: A private practitioner's perspective. *Journal of Clinical Social Work, 43*(3), 294–303.

Braverman, H. (1975). *Labor and monopoly capital*. Monthly Review Press.

Brenan, M. (2018, December 20). *Nurses again outpace other professions for honesty, ethics*. Gallup. https://news.gallup.com/poll/245597/nurses-again-outpace-professions-honesty-ethics.aspx

Brockbank, E., & McGill, C. (1998). *Facilitating reflective learning in higher education*. Open University Press.

Brown, A.M. (2017). *Emergent Strategy: Shaping change, changing worlds*. AK Press.

Brown, B. (2012). *Daring greatly: How the courage to be vulnerable transforms the way we live, love, parent, and lead*. Avery Publishing Group.

Brown-Manning, R. (2013). We don't give birth to thugs, we give birth to children: The emotional journey of African-American mothers raising sons American racism [Unpublished doctoral dissertation]. CUNY Graduate Center, Silberman School of Social Work.

Bureau of Labor Statistics. (2019). *Occupational outlook handbook*. U.S. Department of Labor. https://www.bls.gov/ooh/community-and-social-service-workers.htm

Buchanan, L., Bui, Q., & Patel, J. (2020, July 3). *Black Lives Matter May Be the Largest Movement in U.S. History*. The New York Times. https://www.nytimes.com/interactive/2020/07/03/us/george-floyd-protests-crowd-size.html

Burghardt, S., & Tolliver, W. (2009). *Stories of transformative leadership in the human services: why the glass is always full*. SAGE.

Burton, J. (2006). *Gender trouble: feminism and the subversion of identity*. Routledge.

Butler, J. (2006). *Gender trouble: Feminism and the subversion of identity*. Routledge.

Butler, P. (2011, May 10). *Munro report: child protection workers need freedom to do jobs*. The Guardian. https://www.theguardian.com/society/2011/may/10/munro-report-child-protection-workers-freedom.

Carroll, B., Levy, L., & Richmond, D. (2008). Leadership as Practice: Challenging the Competency Paradigm. *Leadership, 4*(4), 363–379. https://doi.org/10.1177/1742715008095186

Cazenave, N. (2007). *Impossible democracy: The unlikely success of the war on poverty action program*. SUNY Press.

Cherry, K. (2018). *Teaching political economy in macro theory: The case of pay for success* [Paper presentation]. Council on Social Work Education Annual Program Meeting, Orlando, FL, United States.

Cherry, K. (2020, March 4). *APA ethics code principles and standards*. Verywell Mind. https://www.verywellmind.com/apa-ethical-code-guidelines-4687465

Chesters, G. (2016). Social unionism and the framing of "fairness" in the Wisconsin uprising. *Local Economy, 31*(4). https://doi.org/10.1177/0269094216646995

Child Welfare League of America. (2019, March). *The nation's children.* https://www.cwla.org/wp-content/uploads/2019/04/National-2019.pdf

Coca, N. (2016, August 7). The gig economy workers are organizing. *The Progressive.* https://progressive.org/dispatches/the-gig-economy-workers-are-organizing-180807/

Collins, P. H. (2008). *Black feminist thought: Knowledge, consciousness, and the politics of empowerment.* Routledge.

Corley, Y., & Young, S. (2018). Is social work still racist? A content review of recent literature. *Social Work, 63*(4), 317–326.

Council on Social Work Annual Public Meeting. (2018). *Expanding interprofessional education to achieve social justice.* https://www.cswe.org/Events-Meetings/2018-APM/APM-Information/Preliminary-Program/2018APM_PrelimProgram.aspx

Council on Social Work Education (CSEW). (2020). CSWE accreditation standards. https://www.cswe.org/getattachment/Accreditation/Standards-and-Policies/2015-EPAS/2015EPASandG-lossary.pdf.aspx)1234

Council on Social Work Education (CSWE) & CSWE Commission on Accreditation. (2015). *Education standards for baccalaureate and master's social work programs.* https://www.cswe.org/getattachment/Accreditation/Accreditation-Process/2015-EPAS/2015EPAS_Web_FINAL.pdf.aspx

Council on Social Work Education (CSWE). (2019). *2019 APM information.* https://cswe.org/Events-Meetings/2019-APM.aspx

Council on Social Work Education (CSWE). (2020, June 2). *CSWE statement on social justice.* https://www.cswe.org/News/Press-Room/CSWE-Statement-on-Social-Justice

Courtney, M. (1992). Psychiatric social workers and the early days of private practice. *Social Service Review, 66*(2), 199–214. https://www.jstor.org/stable/30012162?seq=1

Craig, R. A. (2008). *Empowerment and social work research—participatory action research and the relationship between the extent of recipients' involvement in research and its capacity to serve an empowering function.* Semantic Scholar. https://www.semanticscholar.org/paper/Empowerment-and-social-work-research-participatory-Craig/15fa37337cb499febaa2a785b9a509169b95fdd0.

Curtis, J., & Thornton, S. (2013). Here's the news: The annual report on the economic state of the profession, 2012–13. *Academe.* https://www.aaup.org/report/heres-news-annual-report-economic-status-profession-2012-13

Davis, M. (1999). *Prisoners of the American dream: Politics and economy in the history of the U.S. working class.* Verso.

de Silva, E. C., President, J. V., Wong, J., Oldman, V., Lopez, L., & Schachter, R. (2007). Institutional racism and the social work profession: A call to action. NSSW Press.

Denning, S. (2013). The origin of "the world's dumbest idea": Milton Friedman. *Forbes.* https://www.forbes.com/sites/stevedenning/2013/06/26/the-origin-of-the-worlds-dumbest-idea-milton-friedman/#19633c27870e

Dewey, J. (1916). *Democracy and education.* Echo Library.

DiAngelo, R. (2018). *White fragility: Why white people find it so hard to talk about racism.* Beacon Press.

Dominelli, L. (2010). Globalization, contemporary challenges and social work practice. *International Social Work, 53*(5), 599–612. https://doi.org/10.1177/0020872810371201

Donaldson, S. I., Christie, C. A., & Mark, M. M. (2015). *What counts as credible evidence in evaluation and applied research.* SAGE Publications.

Dowd, A., & Bensimon, M. E. (2015). Engaging the race question. Columbia Teachers College Press.

Dubb, S. (2018, December 20). The economy is changing-and so must we: A new charge for nonprofits. *Nonprofit Quarterly.* https://nonprofitquarterly.org/2018/12/20/the-economy-is-changing-and-so-must-we-a-new-charge-for-nonprofits/

Du Bois, W.E.B. (1897, August). Strivings of the Negro people. *The Atlantic Magazine*. https://www.theatlantic.com/magazine/archive/1897/08/strivings-of-the-negro-people/305446/

Edwards, T., & Lerner, J. (2019, October 25). CSWE Annual Program Meeting, Denver, Colorado.

Egan, B. (2019, May 6). *The male nurse: Benefits and percentages of men in nursing*. Southern New Hampshire University. https://www.snhu.edu/about-us/newsroom/2019/05/male-nurse.

Elliott, W., III, Henly, J. R., Lambert, S. J., Lein, L., Romich, J. L., Shanks, T. R., & Sherraden, M. (2016). *Policy recommendations for meeting the grand challenge to reduce extreme economic inequality*. American Academy of Social Work & Social Welfare. http://grandchallengesforsocialwork.org/grand-challenges-initiative/12-challenges/reduce-extreme-economic-inequality/

Emberline, K. (2013). *What happens after a police officer uses deadly force?* Police 1. https://www.policeone.com/health-fitness/articles/what-happens-after-a-police-officer-uses-deadly-force-Pko1xmTB2dbHXDOu/

Engeström, Y. (2008, September 8–13). *The future of activity theory* [Paper presentation]. ISCAR Conference, San Diego, CA, United States. http://lchc.ucsd.edu/mca/Paper/ISCARkeyEngestrom.pdf

Ennis, R. H. (1962). A concept of critical thinking: A proposed basis of research in the teaching and evaluation of critical thinking. *Harvard Educational Review, 32*, 81–111.

Etzioni. A. (1970). The semi professions. Free Press. https://doi.org/10.1111/j.1744-6198.1970.tb00436.x

Fabricant, M. (1985). The industrialization of social work practice. *Social Work, 30*(5), 389–395.

Fabricant, M, & Brier, S. (2016). *Austerity blues: fighting for the soul of higher education*. Johns Hopkins Press.

Fabricant, M., & Burghardt, S. (1992). *The welfare state crisis and the transformation of social service work*. M.E. Sharpe.

Fabricant, M., & Fine, M. (2012). *Charter schools and the corporate makeover of public education: What's at stake?* Teachers College Press.

Facione, P. A. (2011a). *Critical thinking: What it is and why it counts*. Insight Assessment.

Facione, P. A. (2011b). *THINK critically*. Prentice Hall.

Finn, J. (2016). *Just practice: A social justice approach to social work* (3rd ed.). Oxford University Press.

Fisher, A. (2001). *Critical thinking: An introduction*. Cambridge University Press.

Fisher, J. (1936). *The rank and file movement in social work 1931–36*. New York School of Social Work.

Fisher, R. (1994). *Let the people decide*. Twayne Publishers.

Fisher, R. F. (1981). *Christian coalition organizing manual* [Unpublished manuscript].

Fisher, R., & Schragge, E. (2013). We are radical: The right to the city alliance and the future of community organizing. *Journal of Sociology and Social Welfare, 60*(1), 157–182.

Freire, P. (2000). *Pedagogy of the oppressed (30th anniversary ed.)*. Continuum.

Freire, P. (2018). *Pedagogy of the oppressed (50th anniversary ed.)*. Bloomsbury Academic.

Gambrill, E. (2014). Evidence-based practice: Sea change or the emperor's new clothes? *Journal of Social Work Education, 39*(1), 3–23.

Gamer, M. (1970). Semi-professions and their organization; Teachers, Nurses, Social Workers. *Nursing Forum, 9*(1), 9–11.

Geyman, J. (2017). *Crisis in US health care: Corporate power vs the common good*. Copernicus Healthcare.

Gibson, M. (2016). Social worker shame: A scoping review. *British Journal of Social Work, 46*, 549–565.

Giovannoni, O. (2014). *What do we know about the labor share and the profit share? Part III: Measures and structural factors*. Levy Economics Institute of Bard College.

Glassdoor. (2020, August 10). *Corporate lawyer salaries*. https://www.glassdoor.com/Salaries/corporate-lawyer-salary-SRCH_KO0,16.htm

Goldbach, J., Amaro, H., Vega, & Walter, M. (2016). The grand challenge of promoting equality by addressing social stigma. American Academy of Social Work and Social Welfare. http://grandchallengesforsocialwork.org/wp-content/uploads/2016/01/W16-The-Grand-Challenge-of-Promoting-Equality-by-Addressing-Social-Stigma1-1-2.pdf

Goleman, D. (1985, April 30). Social workers vault into a leading role in psychotherapy. *New York Times*, 1.

Gonzalez, M., & Gelman, C. R. (2015). Clinical social work practice in the 21st century. *Clinical Social Work Journal, 43*(2), 257–262.

Gough, I. (1979). *The political economy of the welfare state*. Macmillan.

Gramsci, A. (1971). *Prison notebooks*. International Publishers.

Green, J. (2007). Improving workforce conditions in private human service agencies: A partnership between a union and human service providers. *New England Journal of Public Policy, 13*(1). https://www.socialworkers.org/LinkClick.aspx?fileticket=SWK1aR53FAk%3D&portalid=0

Greenwood, B. (n.d.). How Have Salaries Changed for Nurses. *Chron.com*. https://work.chron.com/salaries-changed-nurses-23316.html

Greider, W. (2014, March 24). Can Germany reform American labor relations? *The Nation*. https://www.thenation.com/article/archive/can-germany-reform-american-labor-relations/

Gronberg, K. (2001). U. S. nonprofit human service sector: A creeping revolution. *Nonprofit and Voluntary Sector Quarterly, 30*(2), 276–297. https://doi.org/10.1177/0899764001302006

Hall, C., & Spencer, R. (2019, October 25). Developing culturally responsive practitioners through cross cultural supervision [Paper presentation]. CSWE Annual Program Meeting, Denver, Colorado, United States.

Hakim, D. (2020, April 8). *'It's Hit Our Front Door': Homes for the Disabled See a Surge of Covid-19*. The New York Times. https://www.nytimes.com/2020/04/08/nyregion/coronavirus-disabilities-group-homes.html.

Halpern, D. F. (2003). *Thought & knowledge: An introduction to critical thinking* (4th ed.). Lawrence Erlbaum & Associates.

Han, H. (2019, December 16). When does activism become powerful? *New York Times*. https://www.nytimes.com/2019/12/16/opinion/activism-power-victories.html

Harrington, M. (1997). *The other America: Poverty in the United States* (anniversary ed.). Scribner. (Original work published in 1962)

Hauck, G. (2019, June 28). Anti-LGBT hate crimes are rising, the FBI says. *USA TODAY*. https://www.usatoday.com/story/news/2019/06/28/anti-gay-hate-crimes-rise-fbi-says-and-they-likely-undercount/1582614001/

Haynes, L. (2018). *Majority of social workers looking to leave their job within the next 16 months, says new research*. Community Care. https://www.communitycare.co.uk/2018/10/30/majority-social-workers-looking-leave-job-within-next-16-months-says-new-research/

Heilbroner, R. (1974, January 24). The human prospect. *New York Review of Book*. https://www.nybooks.com/articles/1974/01/24/the-human-prospect/

Henry, A. (2018). How to prepare your community for a disaster. *New York Times*. https://www.nytimes.com/2018/02/15/smarter-living/prepare-your-community-for-a-disaster.html

Heron, G. (2007). Critical thinking in social care and social work: Searching student assignments for the evidence. *Social Work Education, 25*(3), 209–224.

Holliman, D., Dziegielewski, S. F., & Teare, R. (2003, August 1). Differences and similarities between social work and nurse discharge planners. *The Free Library*. https://www.thefreelibrary.com/Differences and similarities between social work and nurse discharge...-a0107491386.

hooks, b. (1994). *Teaching to transgress*. Routledge.

Hulmes, A. (2020, April 8). *How are social workers coping during the pandemic?* Sefydlian Bevan Foundation. https://www.bevanfoundation.org/commentary/how-are-social-workers-coping-during-the-pandemic/

Hunter, R. W. (1999). *Voices of our past: The rank and file movement in social work*. Portland State PDX Scholar.

Ife, J. (2000). Localized needs and a globalized economy: Bridging the gap with social work practice. *Canadian Social Work, 2*(1), 50–64.

Institute on Taxation and Economic Policy. (2019). *Who pays taxes in America?* https://itep.org/who-pays-taxes-in-america-in-2019/

Jackson, K. (2014). Social worker self-care—the overlooked core competency. *Social Work Today, 14*(3), 14. https://www.socialworktoday.com/archive/051214p14.shtml

Jaffe, S. (2019). Striking lessons: How solidarity and radical organizing paved the way to victory in the L.A. teachers' strike. *The Nation*, 22–25.

Jamrisko, M., & Kolet, I. (2012, August 15). Cost of college degree in U.S. soars 12 fold: Chart of the day. *Bloomberg*. http://www.bloomberg.com/news/articles/2012-08-15/cost-of-college-degree-in-u-s-soars-12-fold-chart-of-the-day

Jansson, B. (2019). *The reluctant welfare state* (9th ed.). Cengage.

Jeffery, D. (2007). Radical problems and liberal selves: Professional subjectivity in the anti-oppressive social work classroom. *Canadian Social Work Review, 24*(2), 125–139.

Karger, H. (1981). Burnout as alienation. *Social Service Review, 55*, 270–283. https://doi.org/10.1086/643917

Kelber, H. (2015). *How the New Deal created millions of jobs to lift the American people from Depression*. Labor Educator. http://www.laboreducator.org/newdeal2.htm

Kim Foundation. (2019, July 28). *Understanding the importance of self-care*. https://www.thekim-foundation.org/blog/understanding-the-importance-of-self-care/

Kim, H., & Stoner, M. (2008). Burnout and turnover intention among social workers: Effects of role stress, job autonomy and social support. *Administration in Social Work, 32*(3), 5–25. https://doi.org/10.1080/03643100801922357

Kirst-Ashman, K. K., & Hull, G. H. (2018). *Generalist practice with organizations and communities* (7th ed.). Cengage Learning.

Kivel, P. (2000). *Social service or social change? Who benefits from your work?* http://paulkivel.com/wp-content/uploads/2015/07/socialserviceorsocialchange.pdf

Kivel, P. (2018). *Social service or social change? Who benefits from our work?* Racial Equity Tools. https://www.racialequitytools.org/resourcefiles/SocialServicesorSocialChange.pdf

Kivel, P. (2016). Navigating neoliberalism in the academy, nonprofits, and beyond; social service or social change? *Scholar and Feminist Online, 13*(2). http://sfonline.barnard.edu/navigating-neoliberalism-in-the-academy-nonprofits-and-beyond/

Kramer, J. (2016, September 16). *Social work's gender problem. Governing*. http://www.governing.com/gov-institute/voices/col-social-work-gender-diversity-problem.html

Kramer, M. (2016). *Attempts to get homeless into shelters fail 99 percent of time, data show*. CBS News. https://newyork.cbslocal.com/2016/08/29/homeless-shelter-failure/

Krugman, P. (2020). *Arguing with zombies: Economics, politics, and the fight for a better future*. W.W. Norton & Company.

Krugman, P. (2017, February 10). *When the fire comes. New York Times*. https://www.nytimes.com/2017/02/10/opinion/when-the-fire-comes.html

Kulys, R., & Davis, M. A. (1987). Nurses and social workers: Rivals in the provision of social services? *Health & Social Work, 12*, 101–112. https://doi.org/10.1093/hsw/12.2.101

Lambert, M. J., & Barley, D. E. (2001). Research summary on the therapeutic relationship and psychotherapy outcome. *Psychotherapy: Theory, Research, Practice, Training, 38*(4), 357–361. https://doi.org/10.1037/0033-3204.38.4.357

Le Dem, G. (2019, March 13). New York nurses threaten major strike over "understaffing." *Gotham Gazette*. http://www.gothamgazette.com/state/8351-new-york-nurses-threaten-major-strike-over-understaffing

LeBourveay, K., & Leslie-Johnson, M. (2014). The reemergence of environmental activism within social work. In S. Burghardt (Ed.), Macro practice in social work for the 21st century (pp.). SAGE Publications.

Lederman, D. (2020, August 26). 3 million and counting. *Inside Higher Ed*. https://www.insidehighered.com/news/2010/08/26enroll

Leighninger, L., & Knickmeyer, R. (1976). The rank and file movement: The relevance of the radical social work traditions to modern social work practice. *Journal of Sociology and Social Welfare*, 4(2). https://scholarworks.wmich.edu/cgi/viewcontent.cgi?article=1181&context=jssw

Lent, J. (2020). *Coronavirus spells the end of the neoliberal era. What's next?* Open Democracy. https://www.opendemocracy.net/en/transformation/coronavirus-spells-the-end-of-the-neoliberal-era-whats-next/

Lewis, T. (2013, April 8). Gap widens for faculty at colleges, report finds. *New York Times*.

Liebson, R. (2019, October 29). Housing works is cast in unusual role: Corporate overlord. *New York Times*. https://www.nytimes.com/2019/10/29/nyregion/union-housing-works-nyc.html

Lind, D. (2019, April 11). *The border is in crisis. Here's how it got this bad.* Vox. https://www.vox.com/2019/4/11/18290677/border-immigration-illegal-asylum-central-america-mexico-trump.

Lipksy, M. (2010). *Street-level bureaucracy: Dilemmas of the individual in public services* (30th anniversary, expanded ed.). Russell Sage Foundation.

Lipsky, M., & Smith, S. (1989). Non-profit organizations, government and the welfare state. *Political Science Quarterly*, 104(4), 625–648.

Littleton et al., (2007). Adult coping and defense strategies used by adults. https://www.blueknot.org.au/Workers-Practitioners/For-Health-Professionals/Resources-for-Health-Professionals/Coping-into-Adulthood.

Lloyd, M.F. (2008). *Origins of the functional school of social work*. University of Portland.

Lord, S. A., & Iudice, J. (2011). Social workers in private practice: A descriptive study of what they do. *Clinical Social Work Journal*, 40(1), 85–94. https://doi.org/10.1007/s10615-011-0316-7

Lucas, E. T. (1978). Review: Black Empowerment: Social Work in Oppressed Communities by Barbara Bryant Solomon. *Explorations in Ethnic Studies*, 1(2), 47–48. https://doi.org/10.1525/ees.1978.1.2.47

Manskar, N., & Kosman, J. (2020, April 21). Dozens of public companies got $300M in coronavirus small business loans. *New York Post*.

Marguerite Casey Foundation. (2016). *Who we are*. https://www.caseygrants.org/who-we-are/

Rosenman, M. (2013). *Progressive foundations need to unite*. file:///Users/owner/Desktop/Progressive%20Foundations%20Need%20to%20Unite%20to%20Build%20a%20Better%20Government%20-%20The%20Chronicle%20of%20Philanthropy.webarchive

Mayo Clinic Bulletin. (2019). *Stress management*. https://www.mayoclinic.org/healthy-lifestyle/stress-management/in-depth/stress/art-20046037

McCarty, N. (2018, January 4). America's most and least trusted professions [infographic]. *Forbes*. https://www.forbes.com/sites/niallmccarthy/2018/01/04/americas-most-and-least-trusted-professions-infographic/#510f64e165b5

McClain, A. (2019). *A culture of collaboration*. National Association of Social Workers. https://www.socialworkers.org/News/Social-Work-Advocates/2019-Feb-March/A-Culture-of-Collaboration

McDonald, C. (2012). Understanding participatory action research: A qualitative research methodology option. *Canadian Journal of Action Research*, 13(2). https://doi.org/10.33524/cjar.v13i2.37

McKenzie, L. (2019). A reckoning for 2U, and OPMS? *Inside Higher Ed*. https://www.insidehighered.com/digital-learning/article/2019/08/01/bad-day-2u-highlights-vulnerability-online-program-management

McMillen, J. C., Morris, L., & Sherraden, M. (2004). Ending social work's grudge match: Problems versus Strengths. *Families in Society*, 85(3), 317–325.

McMurty, L. (2016). *Effective teaching practices in online higher education* [Doctoral dissertation, Nova Southeastern University].

Merriam-Webster. (n.d.). Integrity. In *Merriam-Webster.com dictionary*. https://unabridged.merriam-webster.com/collegiate/integrity

Merriam-Webster. (n.d.). Profession. In *Merriam-Webster.com dictionary*. https://www.merriam-webster.com/dictionary/professions

Meyer, C., & Financial Finesse. (2018, July 1). Is taking student loans for graduate school worth it? *Forbes*. https://www.forbes.com/sites/financialfinesse/2018/07/01/is-taking-student-loans-for-graduate-school-worth-it/#104908d922bd

Middleman, R. R., & Wood, G. G. (1990). *Skills for direct practice in social work*. Columbia University Press.

Mishel, L., Gould, E., & Bivens, J. (2015, January 6). *Wage stagnation in nine charts*. Economic Policy Institute. https://www.epi.org/publication/charting-wage-stagnation/

Morgan, P. (1973). Changing analysis of domestic violence. *Kapitalstate*, *3*(1).

Morgan, P. (1983). The state response to social movement demands: the battered women's movement. *Kapitalstate*, *1*(3).

Morton, T. (2017). *The pernicious failure of child welfare reform*. The Imprint. https://chronicleofsocialchange.org/child-welfare-2/pernicious-failure-child-welfare-reform/28708

Munro, E. (2011). *The Munro review of child protection: Final report*. Secretary of Education.

National Association of Social Workers (NASW). (2017). *Code of ethics*. https://www.socialworkers.org/About/Ethics/Code-of-Ethics/Code-of-Ethics-English

National Association of Social Workers (NASW). (2018). *From social work education to social work practice: Results of the survey of 2018 social work graduates*. https://www.socialworkers.org/LinkClick.aspx?fileticket=eLsquD1s2qI%3d&portalid=0

National Association of Social Workers (NASW). (2020). *Social Work Salaries*. https://www.socialworkers.org/Careers/Career-Center/Kickstart-Your-Job-Hunt/Social-Work-Salaries.

National Association of Social Workers (NASW). (2020). *Why Choose the Social Work Profession?* https://www.socialworkers.org/Careers/Career-Center/Explore-Social-Work/Why-Choose-the-Social-Work-Profession.

National Association of Social Workers New York City Chapter. (2017, March 6). *Actions in the current social/political climate*. https://c.ymcdn.com/sites/naswnyc.site-ym.com/resource/resmgr/docs/What_NASW_is_Doing_3-6-17.pdf

National Center for Education Statistics. (2007). Estimated annual salary of teachers in public elementary and secondary schools: Selected years 1959–60 through 2005–06. *Digest of Education Statistics*. https://nces.ed.gov./programs/digest/d07/tables/dt07_075.asp

National Center for Youth Law. (2007). *Improving the child welfare workforce: Lessons from Class Action Litigation*. https://youthlaw.org/publication/improving-the-child-welfare-workforce/

National Institute for Mental health. (2019). *5 things you should know about stress*. https://www.nimh.nih.gov/health/publications/stress/index.shtml

National Nurses United (comprising affiliates National Nurses Organizing Committee, California Nurses Association, and Minnesota Nurses Association). https://www.nationalnursesunited.org/organizing

New York State Society of Clinical Social Work. (2020). https://www.nysscsw.org/.

O'Connor, J. (1973). *The fiscal crisis of the state*. St. Martin's Press.

O'Connor, J. (1984). *Accumulation crisis*. Basil Blackwell.

O'Connor, K. (2008). *The body and the brand: How Lycra shaped America. Producing Fashion*. University of Pennsylvania Press.

Offe, C. (1972). Political authority and class structure: an analysis of later capitalist societies. *International Journal of Sociology*, *2*(7).

Oluwasusi, K., Dreher, B., & Krstic, Z. (2020, May 14). *I'm a Social Worker, and I'm Facing the New Realities of My Job During the Coronavirus Pandemic*. Good Housekeeping. https://www.goodhousekeeping.com/life/inspirational-stories/a32419828/coronavirus-social-worker-hospital/.

Omi, M., & Winant, H. (2015). *Racial formation in the United States*. Routledge Publishers.

Oppel, R. A. Jr., Searcey, D., & Eligon, J. (2019). ACLU: Raimondo's order on stopping out-of-state cars "deeply troubling." *Providence Journal*. https://www.providencejournal.com/news/20200330/aclu-raimondorsquos-order-on-stopping-out-of-state-cars-rsquodeeply-troublingrsquo

Oxford Dictionary. (n.d.). Profession. In *Oxford Learner's Dictionaries*. https://www.oxfordlearners-dictionaries.com/us/definition/english/profession?q=profession

Ozawa, M. N., & Law, S. W. (1993). Earnings history of social workers: A comparison to other professional groups. *Social Work, 48*(3), 542–551. https://doi.org/10.1093/sw/38.5.542

Ozawa, M. N., Leon, J., Morrow-Howell, N., & Rice, C. (1988). Household income of retired social workers. *Social Work, 33*(3), 239–243. http://www.jstor.org/stable/23715557

Parrot, J. (2017). *Undervalued and underpaid: How New York State shortchanges nonprofit human services providers and their workers*. Restore Opportunity Now.

Pettijohn, S., Elizabeth, B., De Vita, C. J., & Fyffe, S. D. (2013, December 5). *Nonprofit-government contracts and grants: Findings form the 2013 survey*. Urban Institute. https://www.urban.org/research/publication/nonprofit-government-contracts-and-grants-findings-2013-national-survey

Pettijohn, S. L., & Boris, E. T. (2014, July 24). (rep.). *Contracts and Grants between Human service Nonprofits and Government: Comparative Analysis*. Urban Institute. Retrieved from https://www.urban.org/sites/default/files/publication/22806/413189-Contracts-and-Grants-between-Human-Service-Nonprofits-and-Government-Comparative-Analysis.PDF

Piketty, T. (2014). *Capital in the twenty-first century*. Belknap Press.

Piketty, T. (2017, December). We must rethink globalism or Trumpism will prevail. *The Guardian*. https://www.theguardian.com/commentisfree/2016/nov/16/globalization-trump-inequality-thomas-piketty

Pincus, A., & Minihan, A. (1973). *Social work practice: Model and method*. Peacock Press.

Pinderhughes, E. (1989). *Understanding race, ethnicity and power: The key to efficacy on clinical practice*. The Free Press.

Pinderhughes, E. (2004). *My struggle to understand racism and injustice: How I kept my sanity as a pioneer in multicultural practice, teaching, research, and consultation*. Reflections. https://reflectionsnarrativesofprofessionalhelping.org/index.php/Reflections/article/view/1179

Quinion, M. (2007). *On "Ivory Tower." World Wide Words.org*. Retrieved April 24, 2007, from https://www.worldwidewords.org/qa/qa-ivo1.htm

Ravalier, J. (2017). UK social workers: Working conditions and wellbeing [Unpublished report].

Ray, L. (2017, July 5). *Social work career benefits*. Career Trend. https://careertrend.com/social-work-career-benefits-25403.html

Registered Nurse (n.d.). *Is Becoming a Nurse Worth It?: Top RN Career Benefits*. https://www.topregisterednurse.com/registered-nurse-benefits/.

Reisch, M., & Andrews, J. (2001). *The road not taken: A history of radical social work in the United States*. Brunner-Routledge.

Reisch, M. (2013). Social work education and the neo-liberal challenge: The U.S. response to increasing global inequality. *Social Work Education, 32*(6), 715–733. https://doi.org/10.1080/02615479.2013.809200

Reynolds, B. (1975). *Social work and social living*. National Association of Social Workers.

Rossman, S. (2018, March 30). Teachers are striking all over. What is going on? *USA Today*. https://www.usatoday.com/story/news/nation-now/2018/03/30/teachers-striking-oklahoma-west-virginia-arizona-kentucky/472742002/

Rothman, J. (2008). *Strategies of community intervention* (7th ed.). Eddie Bower.

Rowbotham, S. (2014). *Women, resistance and revolution: a history of women and revolution in the modern world*. Verso.

Ryan, W. (1999). The new landscape for nonprofits. *Harvard Business Review*. https://hbr.org/1999/01/the-new-landscape-for-nonprofits

Saleebey, D. (2004). Response to "Ending Social Work's Grudge Match." *Families in Society, 85*(4), 588–590. https://doi.org/10.1177/104438940408500418

Saleebey, D. (2006). Introduction: Power in the people. In D. Saleebey (4th ed), *The strengths perspective in social work practice* (pp.1–24). Allyn and Bacon.

Saleebey, D. (2007). *The strengths perspective in social work* practice (6th ed.). Prason.

Sales, K. (1975). *Power shift: the rise of the southern rim and its challenge to the eastern establishment.* Random House.

Schechter, S. (1982). *Women and male violence: Visions and struggles of the battered women's movement.* South End Press.

Schon, D. (1992). *The reflective practitioner: How professionals think in action.* Basic Books.

Schon, D., & Argylis, C. (1978). *Organizational learning: A theory of action perspective.* Addison-Wesley.

Schorr, L. (2019). *Evidence: What it means and how we use it.* http://www.lisbethschorr.org/reconsidering-evidence-what-it-means-and-how-we-use-it/

Sherraden, M. W., & Gilbert, N. (1992). *Assets and the poor: A new American welfare policy.* Routledge.

Sherraden, M. W. (Ed.). (2005). *Inclusion in the American Dream: Assets, poverty, and public policy.* Oxford University Press.

Shersher, J. E. (2020). *Self Care Tips for Social Workers.* Social Work Licensure. https://socialworklicensure.org/articles/self-care-tips/.

Shulman, L. (2015). *Empowerment series skills of helping individuals, families, groups & communities* (8th ed.). Cengage.

Silva, S. M., Greenfield, J. C., Bender, K., & Freedanthal, S. (2018). Introduction to the special section on public impact scholarship in social work: A conceptual review and call to action university of Denver. Journal of the Society for *Social Work and Research, 10*(4), 529–544. https://www.journals.uchicago.edu/doi/pdfplus/10.1086/706112

Simon, B. (1994). *Social Work, Volume 53 # 3,* 2008

Simpson, G., & Murr, A. (2015). The dialectics of change in social work. *Journal of Practice, Teaching and Learning, 13*(2), 93–116.

Smith, M. (2019, February 24). NYU social work school acknowledges 'institutional racism' after classroom episode. *Washington Post.* https://www.washingtonpost.com/education/2019/02/22/nyu-social-work-school-acknowledges-institutional-racism-after-classroom-episode/

Social Work Policy Institute. (2014). *Achieving racial equity: Calling the social work profession to action.* National Association of Social Workers. http://www.antiracistalliance.com/SWPIRacialEquityReport.pdf

Solomon, B. (1977). *Black empowerment: Social work in oppressed communities.* Columbia University Press.

Sonoma County Fire Chief's Association. (2010, November 10). *Recommended standard for firefighter rehab.* http://sonomachiefs.org/home/sonomafirechiefs/Standard%20Operating%20Procedures/APPROVED%20SOPs/SOCO%20REHAB%20SOG_Final.pdf

Specht, H., & Courtney, M. (1995). *Unfaithful angels: How social work has abandoned its mission.* Simon & Schuster.

Sternberg, R. J., Halpern, D. F., & Roediger, H. L. (Eds.). (2006). *Critical thinking in psychology* (1st ed.). Cambridge University Press.

Stiles, W. B., Shapiro, D. A., & Elliott, R. (1986). "Are all psychotherapies equivalent?". *The American psychologist, 41*(2), 165–180. https://doi.org/10.1037//0003-066x.41.2.165

Stiglitz, J. (2019). *People, power, and profits: progressive capitalism for an age of discontent.* W. W. Norton & Company.

Stoesz, D., & Karger, H. J. (1992). *Reconstructing the American welfare state.* Rowman & Littlefield.

Taft, J. (1933). *The dynamics of therapy in a controlled relationship.* MacMillan & Co.

Tangney, J. P., & Dearing, R. (2004). *Shame and guilt.* Guilford.

The Bill & Melinda Gates Foundation. (2020). Financial Services for the Poor. https://www.gatesfoundation.org/What-We-Do/Global-Growth-and-Opportunity/Financial-Services-for-the-Poor.

Thomas, J. T. (2016). Adverse Childhood Experiences Among MSW Students. *Journal of Teaching in Social Work, 36*(3), 235–255. https://doi.org/10.1080/08841233.2016.1182609

Thyer, B., & Pignotti, M. G. (2015). *Science and pseudoscience in social work.* Springer.

University of Maryland School of Social Work. (2020). *Committed to diversity and anti-oppression excellence.* https://www.ssw.umaryland.edu/dao/

US News Best Education Jobs. (n.d.). High school teacher salary. https://money.usnews.com/careers/best-jobs/high-school-teacher/salary

USC Webpage. (2020). *Sample course sequences for the MSW@USC.* https://cdn1.msw.usc.edu/content/58af63c8fef24ad28e1280c5d8693831/USC-MSW_CourseSequence_update.pdf?_ga=2.167512318.1987275653.1578415439-2027494206.1578415439

Wadia, J. (2019). *Rising tuition costs and the history of student loans.* Student Debt Relief. https://www.studentdebtrelief.us/news/rising-tuition-costs-and-the-history-of-student-loans/

Wasek, J. (2018). Fake news: Why social security isn't going broke. *Forbes.* https://www.forbes.com/sites/johnwasik/2018/06/08/fake-news-why-social-security-isnt-going-broke/#2ebe94324e55

Watson, L. (2020). *Lilla Watson quote.* Good Reads. https://www.goodreads.com/quotes/844825-if-you-have-come-here-to-help-me-you-are

Weiser, S. (2019, June 3). Lawyers by day, Uber drivers and bar tenders by night. *New York Times.* https://www.nytimes.com/2019/06/03/nyregion/legal-aid-lawyers-salary-ny.html

Wenocur, S., & Reisch, R. (2001). *From charity to enterprise: Development of American social work in a market economy.* University of Illinois Press.

Westover, T. (2018). *Educated.* HarperCollins.

WIA Report. (2017, April 12). *The percentage of women teachers in the nation's schools continues to rise.* https://www.wiareport.com/2017/04/percentage-women-teachers-nations-schools-continues-rise/

Widbin, B. (2013). Impact of agency climate on burnout [Masters dissertation, St. Catherine University/University of St. Thomas School of Social Work]. https://sophia.stkate.edu/cgi/viewcontent.cgi?referer=https://duckduckgo.com/&httpsredir=1&article=1274&context=msw_papers

Wilson, R. (2012). Why are associate professors so unhappy? *The Chronicle of Higher Education.* http://chronicle.com/article/Why-Are-Associate-Professors/132071/

Winocur, S., & Reisch, M. (1989). *The road not taken.* SAGE Publishing.

Wolf, R. (2013, September 2). Organized labor's decline in the US is well-known. But what drove it? *The Guardian.* https://www.theguardian.com/commentisfree/2013/sep/02/labor-unions-decline-can-turnaround

Woods, A. (2013). *The ideas of Karl Marx.* In Defense of Marxism. https://www.marxist.com/karl-marx-130-years.htm

World Health Organization. (2011). *The social dimensions of climate change.* https://www.who.int/globalchange/mediacentre/events/2011/social-dimensions-of-climate-change.pdf

Wyman, O. (2018). *A national imperative: Joining forces to strengthen human services in America.* Oliver Wyman, Alliance for Strong Families and Communities, American Public Human Services Association. https://www.oliverwyman.com/content/dam/oliver-wyman/v2/campaign-assets/January2018/A%20National%20Imperative_Finalscreen.pdf

Wyman, O. (2018). *A national imperative: Joining forces to strengthen human services in America.* CBS News. https://newyork.cbslocal.com/2016/08/29/homeless-shelter-failure/

Xi, D., & Xi, Y. (2019). *The limits and opportunities of higher education.* American Enterprise Institute. https://tacc.org/sites/default/files/documents/2019-03/the-promises-and-limits-of-online-higher-education.pdf

Zhao, R. (2017, November). Are nonprofits more equitable than for-profits? An estimate of the gender pay gap in the U.S. human service industries [Paper presentation]. Association for Research on Nonprofit Organizations and Voluntary Action Annual Conference (ARNOVA), Grand Rapids, MI, United States.

INDEX

ABOUT THE EDITOR

Steve Burghardt, M.S.W., Ph.D. is a professor of social work at Silberman School of Social Work at Hunter College-CUNY. He is the author or co-author of numerous articles and over ten books, including *A Guide for Sustaining Conversations on Racism, Identity, and our Mutual Humanity*, co-written with Kalima Desuze, Linda Lausell Bryant, and Mohan Vinjamuri (Cognella 2018). He is an eight-time teaching award winner, including the co-winning of the CSWE-Sage national award for innovative teaching. His activism began as a student organizer in the sixties; decades later, he was deeply involved with Occupy Wall Street and more recently as a leader in the Age Justice movement. His work as a consultant, trainer, and executive coach in the public and nonprofit sectors led him to a deep appreciation and respect for the committed work of frontline, as well as executive, staff for their unyielding commitments to those with whom they work—especially the poor, marginalized, and oppressed.

CPSIA information can be obtained
at www.ICGtesting.com
Printed in the USA
BVHW012153080922
646638BV00015B/140